PRIVATE LAW SOURCES AND ANALOGIES OF INTERNATIONAL LAW

(WITH SPECIAL REFERENCE TO INTERNATIONAL ARBITRATION)

BY

H. LAUTERPACHT

Dr.Jur., Dr.Sc.Pol. (Vienna), LL.D. (Lond.)

THE LAWBOOK EXCHANGE, LTD.
Clark, New Jersey

ISBN 978-1-58477-184-5

Lawbook Exchange edition 2002, 2013

The quality of this reprint is equivalent to the quality of the original work.

THE LAWBOOK EXCHANGE, LTD.
33 Terminal Avenue
Clark, New Jersey 07066-1321

Please see our website for a selection of our other publications and fine facsimile reprints of classic works of legal history:
www.lawbookexchange.com

Library of Congress Cataloging-in-Publication Data

Lauterpacht, Hersch, Sir, 1897-1960.
Private law sources and analogies of international law: with special reference to international arbitration / by H. Lauterpacht.
p. cm.
Originally published: London: Longmans, Green and Co., 1927.
(Contributions to international law and diplomacy).
Includes bibliographical references and index.
ISBN 1-58477-184-4 (cloth: alk. paper)
1. International law—Interpretation and construction. I. Title.
II. Contributions to international law and diplomacy.

KZ1285 .L38 2001
341—dc2l 2001041399

Printed in the United States of America on acid-free paper

PRIVATE LAW SOURCES AND ANALOGIES OF INTERNATIONAL LAW

(WITH SPECIAL REFERENCE TO INTERNATIONAL ARBITRATION)

BY

H. LAUTERPACHT

Dr.Jur., Dr.Sc.Pol. (Vienna), LL.D. (Lond.)

LONGMANS, GREEN AND CO. LTD.

39 PATERNOSTER ROW, LONDON, E.C.4

NEW YORK, TORONTO

BOMBAY, CALCUTTA, AND MADRAS

1927

Made in Great Britain

FOREWORD

I GLADLY comply with Dr. Lauterpacht's request that I should add a few words by way of introduction to his book. It seems to me to do at least two things of real value. The first is a thorough exploration of the justification of that part of Article 38 of the Statute of the Permanent Court of International Justice which directs the Court to apply, amongst other rules, 'the general principles of law recognised by civilised nations.' The result of this investigation is to vindicate the practice of resort to rules and conceptions of private law for the purpose of the development of international law, and to give to it the dignity of a scientific basis. The modern detractors of this practice are apt to treat it as being at best an ingenious and empirical expedient for filling up a gap or getting out of an impasse; but I venture to think that the author makes good his claim to establish it on grounds of intrinsic merit and reasonableness. If the Permanent Court of International Justice, and the many other tribunals which will of necessity be influenced by its example, are to push forward with energy the frontiers of international law into territory not yet included in its domain, it is essential that the resources of private law should be exploited ungrudgingly and to the full. This book will, I think, help to remove any surviving reluctance to work this rich seam.

In the second place, the author has in the course of his investigation inevitably extracted (unearthed, I am tempted to say) a mass of legal material from the awards and proceedings of international tribunals. His classification and study of this material, without converting what he modestly describes as a monograph into a digest of international arbitration, will afford most useful guidance to those engaged in the preparation and pleading of cases before international tribunals. The fact is that there is more international law in existence than is generally believed ; so much of it is not widely known and not readily accessible.

It is difficult to be impartial in assessing the work of one who is a friend and was formerly a pupil ; but I am hopeful that the reception of this book will confirm my opinion that Dr. Lauterpacht is a valuable recruit in the field of international law, and may be expected to make further contributions of high quality to its literature.

ARNOLD D. McNAIR.

GONVILLE AND CAIUS COLLEGE,
CAMBRIDGE,
March 1927.

THE AUTHOR'S PREFACE

It has become a custom with publicists writing on certain disputed questions of international law to base their argument on the assertion that the opinion with which they happen to disagree is nothing else than a misleading analogy to a conception of private law. It is now generally accepted that the recourse to private law, which was, perhaps, justified in the formative period of international law owing to the then prevalent patrimonial conception of State, has subsequently impeded the growth of international law, and ought to be discouraged. The habit of falling back on private law is looked upon as betraying a regrettable tendency to imitation, as ignoring the special structure of international relations, and as threatening to thwart, by introducing technicalities and intricacies of municipal jurisprudence, every attempt at a fruitful and creative scientific activity in the domain of international law. And even in those rare cases in which an author is forced, by the sheer identity of the legal relations with which he has to deal, to adopt a solution suggested by a general principle of private law, the recourse to analogy is usually accompanied by embarrassed counsels of caution or by apologetic explanations.

Does this disparagement of private law receive confirmation from the practice of States and from the history of international law? This was the question which the author set himself to answer. The student who surveys in its entirety the whole field of application of private (and Roman) law must realise that the reliance upon it is not solely a characteristic feature of the formative period of international law, and that there is in the constant recourse to analogy something more than a peculiarity of one historical period. A critical examination shows that the use of private law exercised, in the great majority of cases, a beneficial influence upon the development of international law; that in other cases international law ultimately adopts solutions suggested by private law, without paying regard to the so-called special character of international relations; that it adopts, even now, notions of private law whenever exigencies of international life seem to demand such a solution; that in international arbitration the recourse to private law, on the part both of governments and of tribunals, is a frequent feature of the proceedings and of the decisions: especially is this so in view of the fact that general principles of law, recognised by civilised States and adopted by customary and conventional international law as a source of decision in international disputes, are for the most part identical with generally recognised principles of private law.

The adoption, in Article 38 (3) of the Statute of the Permanent Court of International Justice, of 'general principles of law recognised by civilised States' as a binding—although, it seems, only supplementary—source of decision in the judicial settlement of disputes signifies that that practice, hitherto unsupported by universal and authoritative international enactment, and regarded by many as derogating from the strictly judicial character of international arbitration, has now received formal approval on the part of practically the whole international community. There lies the outstanding and, to a certain extent, revolutionary contribution made by the Statute to international law as a whole. This book is, in a sense, a commentary on Article 38 (3) of the Statute and a respectful acknowledgment of the great service rendered to the cause of international law by the Committee of Jurists assembled in 1920 at the Hague. As a result of earnest and prolonged discussions, they arrived at a compromise which honours equally the representatives of both Continental and British-American jurisprudence, and places the judicial function of the Court upon a solid foundation.

For it is especially in modern arbitration that the inadequacy of the positivist treatment of the problem comes clearly to light. Arbitral tribunals resort to private law because international relations demand such recourse to analogy, and because international law is not always developed enough to supply a solution itself. But the science of international law gives here no guidance to judges and arbitrators, because it rejects, under the influence of the positivist teaching, any analogy whatsoever. The same happens when in a treaty the parties resort to a conception of private law. It is not surprising, therefore, that publicists fall back upon political explanations of doubtful value.

It is the modern positivist doctrine which is chiefly responsible for the acceptance of the prevalent iconoclastic view. A true offspring of the doctrine of sovereignty, it could not countenance the intrusion, into the field of binding rules of international law, of notions and principles not directly derived from the will of the States. The same doctrine of sovereignty, with its conception of eternal and inalienable interests protected by the State and of their public and absolute character, was bound to reject any recourse to private law as concerned with interests deemed to be of an economic and lower order. It would have been an easy task, therefore, to criticise the current repudiation of private law from the point of view of the now so popular rejection of the doctrine of sovereignty. The author, however, decided not to avail himself of this method of approach.

The international lawyer, if he wishes to assist in the searching investigation which is now taking place on the subject of external sovereignty, will be well employed if he confines himself to the examination of the question whether the doctrine of sovereignty is in accordance both with the practice of States as expressed in customary and conventional international law, and with a rational and consistent system of international law as developed by international publicists, positivist and non-positivist. If he succeeds in showing that certain widely spread notions, directly and demonstrably resulting from the doctrine of sovereignty, run counter to the practice of States and to the conception of international law as taught by the general body of writers, he has done his share. The doctrine of sovereignty as a legal conception cannot be shattered by well-meaning publicists and pacifists who denounce it as mischievous and as out of date. It will only disappear when notions usually associated with it are shown to be inconsistent both with the practice of States and with the science of international law in its individual branches.

It is necessary to point out at this stage that when referring here and elsewhere in this book to modern positivism, the author in no way alludes to that legitimate aspiration of the science of international law which regards custom and treaties as the primary sources, whose authority, so far as existing law is concerned, is higher than any conflicting rule of natural law or morality. What he has in mind is the uncompromising tendency which isolates international law from any outside influence, which obstructs the task of interpretation and the attempts at consciously developing international law, and which not infrequently goes the length of disregarding the practice of States if the latter happens to run counter to positivist formulas.

There was, however, quite apart from the positivist

teaching, another reason which tended to render difficult an unprejudiced treatment of the problem. When confronted with the question of application of private law, international lawyers are too apt to forget the maxim, *ab abusu ad usum non valet consequentia.* The recourse to private law has been so frequently abused by writers lacking in originality and falling back upon ready-made constructions, by unscrupulous lawyers and diplomats championing doubtful causes, and by skilful counsel at international arbitrations, that some prefer to dispense with it altogether. Such an impatient attitude can hardly be commended. For after all has been said on the dangers of analogy, and on the difference of interests protected by the two spheres of law, the fact remains that, with regard to some of the most essential and most urgent questions of international law, it is in the approximation to the analogous general rules of private law that we see embodied the principles of legal justice and of international progress. The author believes that, amongst others, it is also on the realisation of this fact that the success of future attempts at creative juristic activity in the domain of international law depends.

It will be observed that the subject of this book is in no way connected with questions of international private law or with the relation between international and municipal law. It deals with problems of international public law only and exclusively. And even here its scope is restricted in so far as it is concerned with those relations only in which States appear as political entities and as subjects of public rights and duties. It is not concerned either with the bearing of international public law on private rights, or with the interpretation of treaties in which terms of private law are used for the purpose of defining private rights and duties, or with questions of private law arising out of the fact that States engage in trade or enter into purely financial or economic relations with one another.

However, considering the wide range of subjects covered by the problem of application of private law in international public law proper, the scope of this monograph approaches in many respects that of a treatise. On the other hand, the undertaking to illustrate the subject and to verify the propositions put forward in the monograph by reference to cases of judicial settlement of international disputes nearly resulted in a digest of international arbitration. The author is nevertheless but too conscious of the incompleteness of this attempt to deal in a comprehensive manner with his subject, and he only hopes that the very deficiencies of this attempt will prove useful as showing the necessity of a further detailed and independent study of this question.

I desire to express my thanks to Dr. Arnold D. McNair, C.B.E., LL.D., Reader in Public International Law in the University of London and Fellow of Gonville and Caius College in the University of Cambridge, whose help and encouragement have accompanied my work over this book from the beginning to its publication. I am indebted to him for advice and criticism; he has read the book in proof, and I was thus enabled to avail myself, at that stage also, of his suggestions.

I also thank the publishers, Messrs. Longmans, Green & Co. Ltd., for their helpful co-operation; Messrs. T. & A. Constable, of the University Press, Edinburgh, and their compositors and reader, for unfailing courtesy and accuracy; the Librarian of the British Foreign Office for kind permission to inspect the records of many otherwise inaccessible cases of international arbitration; and last—but not least—the Librarian and the Staff of the Fry Library of International Law at the London School of Economics and Political Science.

This book has grown out of a dissertation for the doctorate approved in 1925 by the Faculty of Laws of the University of London, and I have to thank the Publications Fund of the University for a grant in aid of its publication.

H. LAUTERPACHT.

LONDON,
March 1927.

ABBREVIATIONS

OF TITLES OF BOOKS AND PERIODICALS QUOTED IN THE MONOGRAPH

A.J.	= The American Journal of International Law.
Annuaire	= Annuaire de l'Institut de droit international.
Anzilotti	= Anzilotti, Corso di diritto internazionale, 1923.
Bluntschli	= Bluntschli, Das moderne Völkerrecht der civilisierten Staaten als Rechtsbuch dargestellt, 3rd ed., 1878.
B.Y.	= British Year Book of International Law.
Calvo	= Calvo, Le Droit international théorique et pratique, 5th ed., 6 vols., 1888-1896.
Despagnet	= Despagnet, Cours de droit international public, 4th ed. by Boeck, 1910.
Fauchille	= Fauchille-Bonfils, Traité de droit international public, 8th ed., vol. ii., 1921 ; vol. i., pt. 1, 1922 ; vol. i., pt. 2, 1925 ; vol. i., pt. 3, 1926.
Fenwick	= Fenwick, International Law, 1924.
Gemma	= Gemma, Appunti di diritto internazionale, 1923.
Hall	= Hall, A Treatise on International Law, 8th ed. by Higgins, 1924.
Halleck	= Halleck, International Law, 4th English ed., 1908.
Hatschek	= Völkerrecht, als System rechtlich bedeutsamer Staatsakte, 1923.
Heffter	= Das europäische Völkerrecht der Gegenwart, 8th ed. by Geffcken, 1888.
Holtzendorff	= Holtzendorff, Handbuch des Völkerrechts, 1885-1889.
Hyde	= Hyde, International Law chiefly as interpreted and applied by the United States, 1922.
Klüber	= Klüber, Europäisches Völkerrecht, 2nd ed., 1851.
La Fontaine	= La Fontaine, Pasicrisie Internationale, 1902.

Lammasch, Die Rechtskraft	=	Lammasch, Die Rechtskraft internationaler Schiedssprüche, 1913.
Lammasch, Die Lehre	=	Lammasch, Die Lehre von der Schiedsgerichtsbarkeit in ihrem ganzen Umfange, 1914.
Lapradelle-Politis	=	Lapradelle et Politis, Recueil des arbitrages internationaux, vol. i., 1905; vol. ii., 1923.
Liszt	=	Liszt, Das Völkerrecht, 12th ed. by Fleischmann, 1925.
Maine	=	Maine, International Law, 2nd ed., 1894.
Moore, *Digest*	=	Moore, A Digest of International Law, 1906.
Moore	=	Moore, History and Digest of the Arbitrations to which the United States have been a Party, 1898.
Niemeyer	=	Niemeyer, Völkerrecht, 1923.
Nys	=	Nys, Le droit international, 2nd ed., 1912.
N.Z.	=	Niemeyer's Zeitschrift für Internationales Recht.
Oppenheim	=	Oppenheim, International Law, vol. i., 3rd ed. by Roxburgh, 1920; vol. ii., 4th ed. by M Nair, 1926.
Phillimore	=	Phillimore, Commentaries upon International Law, 3rd ed., 1879-1889.
Pradier-Fodéré	=	Pradier-Fodéré, Traité de droit international public, 1885-1906.
Ralston	=	Ralston, The Law and Procedure of International Tribunals, 1926.
R.G.	=	Revue générale de droit international public.
R.I.	=	Revue de droit international et de législation comparée.
R.I. (Geneva)	=	Revue de droit international, de sciences diplomatiques, politiques, et sociales.
Rivier	=	Rivier, Principes du droit des gens, 1896.
Rivista	=	Rivista di diritto internazionale.
Scott	=	The Hague Court Reports, ed. by Scott, 1916.
Schücking	=	Schücking, Das Werk von Haag, 1915-1917.

Strupp	=	Strupp, Grundzüge des positiven Völkerrechts, 2nd ed., 1922.
Strupp, Wörterbuch	=	Strupp, Wörterbuch des Völkerrechts und der Diplomatie, 1923-1926.
Taylor	=	Taylor, A Treatise on International Public Law, 1901.
Twiss	=	Twiss, The Law of Nations, 2nd ed., 1884.
Westlake	=	Westlake, International Law, 2nd ed., 1910-1913.
Wheaton	=	Wheaton, Elements of International Law, 8th American ed. by Dana, 1866.
Z.V.	=	Zeitschrift für Völkerrecht.

CONTENTS

PART I

HISTORICAL AND THEORETICAL CONSIDERATIONS

CHAPTER I

INTRODUCTORY

The Science of International Law and the Problem of Private Law Analogies

CHAPTER II

PUBLIC INTERNATIONAL LAW AND PRIVATE LAW

I. *The Dogma of Sovereignty, the Positivist Doctrine, and the Application of Private Law*

PART II

THE PRACTICE OF STATES AND THE SCIENCE OF INTERNATIONAL LAW

CHAPTER III

PRIVATE LAW ANALOGIES APART FROM TREATIES

I. *The Legal Nature of Territorial Sovereignty*

II. *Acquisition of Territorial Sovereignty. Private Law Rules of Property and Possession*

III. *Sovereignty over the Sea, the Territorial Waters, and the Air*

IV. *Prescription, Acquisitive and Extinctive*

V. *State Servitudes*

VI. *State Succession*

VII. *State Responsibility*

VIII. *Interest and the Measure of Damages*

IX. *Other Instances of Analogy*

CHAPTER IV

PRIVATE LAW ANALOGY IN APPLICATION TO TREATIES

I. *Treaties as Contracts*

II. *International Leases*

III. *International Mandates*

CHAPTER V

PRIVATE LAW RULES OF EVIDENCE AND PROCEDURE

PART III

INTERNATIONAL ARBITRATION

CHAPTER VI

RECOURSE TO PRIVATE LAW IN INTERNATIONAL ARBITRATION

(*The Five British-American Arbitrations*)

I. *The Alabama Arbitration*

II. *The Behring Sea Arbitration*

III. *The British Guiana Arbitration*

IV. *The Alaska Boundary Dispute*

V. *The North Atlantic Coast Fisheries Arbitration*

CHAPTER VII

RECOURSE TO PRIVATE LAW IN INTERNATIONAL ARBITRATION

(*The Permanent Court of Arbitration*)

I. *The Pious Fund of California Case*

II. *The Venezuelan Preferential Claim*

III. *The Russian Indemnity Case*

IV. *Other Hague Cases*

CHAPTER VIII

RECOURSE TO PRIVATE LAW IN INTERNATIONAL ARBITRATION

(Miscellaneous Cases)

CHAPTER IX

'. . . *populi respectu totius generis humani privatorum locum obtinent.*'

Grotius, *Mare Liberum*, Cap. V.

'The Law of Nations is but private law "writ large." It is an application to political communities of those legal ideas which were originally applied to relations of individuals.'

Holland, *Studies in International Law*, p. 152.

PART I

HISTORICAL AND THEORETICAL CONSIDERATIONS

CHAPTER I

INTRODUCTORY

THE SCIENCE OF INTERNATIONAL LAW AND THE PROBLEM OF PRIVATE LAW ANALOGIES

§ 1. *The Points of Contact between International and Private Law.*—The various points of contact between international public law and private law can conveniently be grouped in three classes. The first relates to rights and obligations of States as political entities endowed with attributes of government, and comprises accordingly all cases in which legal relations normally forming the subject-matter of international public law proper are being shaped in accordance with or after the analogy of a conception of private law. When, for example, the question of sovereignty over a portion of territory is decided by application of the rules of prescription; when certain restrictions of territorial sovereignty are construed after the analogy of easements or servitudes in private law; when recourse is had to private law rules of inheritance and succession for the purpose of determining certain rights and duties of States in cases of changes of sovereignty; when the responsibility of States for international delinquencies is measured according to principles of private law; when before an international tribunal the conduct of a State is judged in accordance with a private law rule of evidence; when the question of payment of moratory interest for delay in the settlement of a war indemnity is decided by application of analogous rules of private law—in all these cases the legal relations to which analogy is applied have their roots in the ordinary political and public functions of the State's *imperium.* It is only and exclusively with them that this book is concerned.

To the second group belong cases in which States, in their capacity as *fisci* or through their administrative organs, contract business with one another without any direct relation to rights and duties of *imperium.* Thus, for example, when States grant to one another a loan or a purely economic lease,[1] or when they enter into a joint arrangement for the purpose of constructing and maintaining a bridge on a river dividing their territories,[2] there arises an occasion to apply private law.

The third class embraces all those instances in which international law determines or influences private rights such as those resulting indirectly from the internationally recognised position of aliens, or from the rules relating to private enemy property in time of war, or from the exercise of the right of angary or embargo, etc. Of special importance are, however, those cases within this group in which parties to a treaty avail themselves of a conception of private law in order to determine private rights, and the question subsequently arises as to the meaning of the particular term thus used.[3]

In the second and third group, States enter into

[1] See below, § 81.

[2] See, *e.g.*, the Exchange of Notes between Colombia and Venezuela concerning the construction of an international bridge on the river Tachira, of July 20, 1925, *League of Nations Treaty Series*, xxxix. pp. 15-24.—The above classification is necessarily a rough and provisional one. That the public and private law elements are frequently united in one transaction may be seen, for instance, from the Treaty of 1865 between Chile and Peru, in which a political alliance and the unification of naval forces for the purpose of conducting the war against Spain were combined with what may be called an agreement for a limited partnership with regard to the expenses connected with the common operations (see Moore, vol. ii. pp. 2085-2105).

[3] See, for instance, the Treaty of Commerce and Navigation, of April 1896, between Japan and Germany: Martens, *N.R.G.*, 2nd ser., xxiii. p. 269, and § 124, *infra.*

relations which but for the fact that the parties are States would belong to the domain of private law. The only question which here confronts the lawyer is: What private law is to be applied in such cases? The problem is here obviously not a question of recourse to analogy, but rather one of choice between the adoption of, on the one hand, the rules of one or another system of private law,[1] or, on the other, of a universal private law, a kind of a modern *ius gentium* based on comparative jurisprudence. However, interesting or important as it may be, it does not enter within the scope of this monograph, which, being exclusively concerned with the relation between private law and international law proper, is devoted to the investigation of the first-mentioned aspect of the problem.

§ 2. *Private Law in International Public Law proper.* —In the whole field of international law there is hardly a question of equal practical and theoretical importance to which less systematic attention has been paid than the problem of private law sources and analogies in international public law. We say 'systematic attention.' For, given the close relation, historical and juridical, between the two branches of law, it was impossible for international lawyers not to define occasionally their views on the admissibility of some particular concept of private law. There is no single monograph on this question, notwithstanding the fact that it occurs repeatedly in the framing of international law as a science, in the interpretation and the construction of treaties, and in the judicial settlement of controversies between States. The problem includes not only the vast subject of treaties and their analogy to contracts of private law with regard to rules governing their

[1] For a scholarly exposition of the relevant principles, see Ruegger in *N.Z.*, xxviii. (1919-1920) pp. 426-502.

formation, validity, and termination (the juridical nature of treaties, the influence of fraud, error and duress, the *pacta in favorem tertii*, the *clausula rebus sic stantibus*, rules of interpretation), and the part of international law relating to acquisition and loss of territory. It affects almost every branch of the international law of peace. The international law of tort and the problems of State responsibility; the measure of damages; the question of interest, moratory and compensatory; the theory of State succession; prescription; quasi-contracts; international servitudes; leases; international mandates under Article 22 of the Covenant of the League of Nations; private law rules of evidence and procedure, especially those of estoppel and *res iudicata*—they all come within its scope. To those instances cases may fairly be added in which doctrines originally created in close contact with Roman and private law developed subsequently without leaving visible traces of their private law origin. The historical influence of the institution of property on the formation of the theory of sovereignty, and the influence of the Roman law rules of possession and property on the conception of the freedom of the sea and on that of territorial waters, may be mentioned in this connection. How far has international law drawn, in these and similar cases, from the rich source of private law? Is this application of analogy a matter of form and metaphor, or of legal substance? If it is the latter, who is responsible for it? Is it the practice of States and the nature of international relations, or a regrettable lack of originality on the part of international lawyers who, unable to grasp the special and quite peculiar character of international relations, proceed to mould them after the private law pattern? Does the recourse to private law strengthen the scientific character of international law *qua* law, or does it result in transforming it into mere speculation or philosophy of law? And, finally, does the application of private law conduce to the realisation of ideals of legal justice in the domain of international public law?

§ 3. *The Science of International Law and the Application of Private Law.*—The fact that the treatment of and the answer to these questions are, on the whole, casual and unsatisfactory so far as the general body of international publicists is concerned can, no doubt, be attributed to the circumstance that the problem has become intimately connected with the controversy between the positivist and the natural law tendencies and with the ultimate victory of the positivist school. The reign of the latter at the end of the nineteenth century is undisputed; it is still predominant to-day. The reaction against the purely positivist way of thinking is, in international law, only of recent date; and although there are most clear indications to the effect that a vigorous movement for a more creative activity in the field of international law is setting in, it cannot be maintained that it has so far left the preliminary stages of general criticism. It certainly has not yet had time to come into closer grips with specific questions of international law.[1]

Now, the chief postulate of the positivist school can be expressed in one word: self-sufficiency. It rejects the taking over of rules and precepts from sources other than international custom or treaties. Such borrowing, it is alleged, destroys the independence of international law and hampers its free development. That this independence has in fact been threatened by the gigantic edifice of human thought and experience embodied in private law, is obvious. Here lies the

[1] On the modern revival of the 'naturalist' tendencies in international law, see following chapter, § 25.

explanation of the uncompromising attitude adopted by those writers who reject the idea of any organic connection between the two branches of law. The same forces which were fighting the influence of the law of nature advocated with vigour the purification of international law from its private law ingredients. The positivist disapproval of recourse to private law found, on the other hand, an ally in the current doctrine of sovereignty which brought about, *inter alia*, a conception of international law regulating interests of a higher value and adjusting public rights of an 'eternal and inalienable'[1] character; it seemed quite natural that such rights and interests should not be amenable to ordinary standards of private law, which are concerned chiefly with the evaluation of economic interests.[2] This attitude of dogmatic iconoclasm is made less conspicuous only by the fact of the majority of writers ignoring the problem altogether.

There are only two groups of writers who have faced the problem in a more general and comprehensive manner. The question has been dealt with in some detail by several representative publicists of the continental positivist school of international law. It has been answered, from a different angle, by English writers of the authority of Manning, Maine, Phillimore, and Westlake, who discussed with great thoroughness the relation between Roman law and the law of nations.

§ 4. *The Founders of International Law and the Problem of Analogies.*—The modern repudiation of private law as a source of international law seems, at the first sight, to have received some support both from Grotius and his forerunners and successors. This support shows that the controversy is not of recent date, and that the

[1] See H. B. Oppenheim, quoted below, § 11. [2] See §§ 20, 31, *infra*.

writers of the classical period who notoriously were relying to a large extent upon Roman and other private law were not doing so merely owing to their inability to perceive the essential differences between the two spheres of law—private and international. They had recourse to analogy after having faced the question as to the admissibility of such a procedure. Of course, it must not be assumed that the problem was clearly understood and dealt with by the general body of the writers of that period. The great majority do not mention it at all. The utterances of others, contradictory and confusing as they are, are, rather inconsistently, quoted by modern positivists both as showing that the danger of indiscriminate recourse to analogy was already fully appreciated by the founders of international law, and as a sad instance of the mischievous and hampering effects of indiscriminate recourse to analogy on the part of classical writers. Naturally enough, both the first and the second inferences are too general not to be misleading. For the problem which confronted those publicists was not, on the whole, identical with that which modern international law has to solve, namely, how far analogy is admissible between the rules of two fundamentally different systems of law (for so they are described) with different subjects and objects. The question before them was how far the law of one ancient Empire may, by reason of its comprehensiveness and its universally recognised conformity with right and justice, be resorted to as a source of international law. However, as that part of Roman law which was most developed and which was, accordingly, most used for the purpose of extracting analogies was private law proper, an examination of the part played by Roman law in the writings of some representative publicists of that period will be of more than passing interest for the subject under discussion.

§ 5. *Gentilis.*—Thus we find Gentilis urging gravely that civil law must not be cited rashly, and that 'what applies to a State must not be extended beyond the State absurdly.'[1] This attitude he explains by pointing out that while the ancient world constituted a single State the world is now divided into 'separate jurisdictions or principalities.' It seems that it is under the influence of these and similar passages that writers express the opinion that Gentilis 'broke away from his predecessors . . . in giving up largely the attempt to cast the law of nations in the mould of Roman civil law,'[2] or that even when resorting to Roman law he did not refer to it as implying an authoritative solution, but rather as illustrative of certain universal principles.[3]

However, it would be a mistake to regard such statements as a correct appreciation of Gentilis' method. The very opposite is the case. Gentilis himself, to whom the application of Roman law was not a matter of mere imitation, but a question of principle and scientific conviction, would have protested against such an imputation. He had no desire to be classed among the positivists of the day who were issuing warnings against the application of Roman law.[4] To the positivists of his time Gentilis replied that '*sana ratio exemplis anteponitur*,'[5] and that '*nuda historiarum recitatio*' is fruitless. '*Facta nos non quaerimus*,' he says, '*aut ex factis ius constituimus, sed ex iure examinamus facta.*'[6] Reliance on Roman law is accordingly a characteristic feature of his writings. Apart from numerous references

[1] *Hispanicae advocationis libri duo*, 1613, newly edited in Scott's *Classics of International Law*, with an English translation by F. F. Abbott, 1921, p. 110.

[2] Abbott, *op. cit.*, *Introduction*, p. 19*a*.

[3] Phillipson, in the *Journal of Comparative Legislation and International Law*, New Series, vol. xii. (1912), p. 58. See also Nézard, in *Les Fondateurs du Droit International*, 1904, p. 83.

[4] See, for instance, Bodin (to whom he refers), *De la République*, 1577, l. v. c. vi.

[5] *De Jure Belli*, 1598, b. ii. ch. 18.

[6] *Op. cit.*, b. i. ch. 20.

to it on particular questions,[1] he frequently expresses his opinion in a more general form. 'All Sovereign Princes,' he says, 'are obliged to be governed by the Civil Law in the disputes between them'; [2] 'Every one submits to the Civil Law as to a sort of law of nations.' [3] He expresses the same view when dealing with the instructive incident to which civilians and lawyers of his time devoted much discussion. Philip II., when confronted with the question of succession to the throne of Portugal, rejected the learned opinion of the civilians from the Academy of Coimbra, who, basing themselves on Roman law, decided in favour of the Duke of Bragance. But the Emperor would not rely even upon the opinion of his own jurists, who urged that disputes between princes should be decided by application of the law of nations, and not of the fictions of the law of Justinian. He preferred his own view, namely, that 'Empires are not given or taken away in accordance with the opinions of jurisconsults, but it is necessary to acquire and retain them by recourse to arms.' And he acted upon this view—with complete success. Gentilis, however, when dealing with the question, had no hesitation in affirming that the law of Justinian is not a particular law, but the law of nations.[4] In fact, it is as a staunch civilian in matters of international law that he is regarded by publicists, frequently not without reproach. From Selden, who emphatically

[1] See, for instance, his treatment of military pacts from the point of view whether they are *bonae fidei* or *stricti iuris* (b. i. ch. 22), or of the question of exterritoriality of ambassadors (*De Legationibus*, 1585, b. ii. ch. 16, 17; newly edited in Scott's *Classics of International Law*, with an English translation by Laing, 1924).

[2] *De Jure Belli*, b. i. ch. 5. See especially the much-quoted passage in *De Jure Belli*, b. i. ch. 3: "*ius etiam, illis perscriptum libris Iustiniani, non civitatis est tantum, sed et gentium, et naturae et aptatum sic est ad naturam universum, ut imperio extincto, et ipsum ius diu sepultum surrexerit tamen, et in omnes se effuderit gentes humanas.*"

[3] *Advocatio Hispanica*, b. i. ch. 21.

[4] *De Jure Belli*, b. i. ch. 3. For an account of this case, see Sir Arthur Duck, *De Usu et Authoritate Juris Civilis Romanorum in Dominiis Principum Christianorum*, 1653, vol. ii. ch. vii. s. 15, 16.

rejected his opinion on the universally binding force of Roman law,[1] and De Ferrière, the historian of Roman law, whose enthusiasm for the subject did not prevent him from pointing, not without some surprise, to the fact that Gentilis has gone so far as to identify Roman law and the law of nations,[2] through Ward, who thought that 'Gentilis cramps himself by supposing the Roman law to be the law of nations,'[3] to modern publicists, there is almost complete agreement on this point.[4] Some try to absolve him from a portion of the guilt by referring to passages, mentioned above, in which he exhibits a certain reluctance to adopt a rule of civil law. These passages, however, relate, as may be seen on closer investigation, to such rules of Roman law, mainly public law, as are peculiar to the Roman State and to its time, and which, to use Sir Robert Wiseman's expression, 'look homewards.'[5]

§ 6. *Grotius.*—Grotius himself has become, with regard to the question under discussion, a source of grave misunderstandings. There is scarcely a chapter in the three books of the *De Jure Belli ac Pacis* in which he does not reject a rule, because, as he says, it belongs to the civil law only and not to the law of nations.[6] Text-books quote eagerly his refusal to acknowledge that 'the contracts of kings and peoples are to be interpreted according to Roman law; except when Roman law has been accepted as belonging to the law of nations;

[1] *Mare Clausum seu de Dominio Maris Libri duo*, 1635, b. i. ch. xxiv. (Nedham's translation, 1652, pp. 152-156).

[2] *Histoire du Droit Romain*, 1718 (English translation, 1724, p. 136).

[3] *An Enquiry into the Foundation and History of the Law of Nations*, 1795, vol. ii. p. 613. See also Reddie, *Inquiries into International Law*, 2nd ed., 1851, p. 26.

[4] See, for instance, Kaltenborn, *Die Vorläufer des Hugo Grotius*, 1848, p. 231; Holland, *Studies in International Law*, 1898, p. 22; Vinogradoff, *Historical Types of International Law, Bibliotheca Visseriana*, vol. i. (1923) p. 56; and also Phillipson, *op. cit.*

[5] *The Excellency of the Civil Law*, 1656, p. 62.

[6] See, for instance, l. ii. c. iv. s. 10, 12, 13; c. v. s. 7, 10, 15, 29; c. vi. s. 1, 2; c. vii. s. 1, 2.

which is not lightly to be presumed.'[1] His view on prescription is cited as another example. But there is, on the other hand, no doubt that his work 'bristles with analogies,'[2] and Gessner's statement to the effect that Grotius' chapters on treaties read like a Roman private law treatise mixed with natural law ideas[3] is quoted with approval by many authors.

This contradictory attitude, however, is amazing only when we forget that some of the difficulties in the writings of Grotius which puzzle the student or the commentator are due to the fact that exactitude of terminology cannot be regarded as one of the achievements of the great lawyer. What confusion has, for instance, been caused as a result of his having chosen to attribute so many different meanings to his conception of *ius gentium*! Similarly, what he understood by civil law is not private law in general or Roman law, but rather positive municipal law, both private and public, in contradistinction to the law prevailing between nations. We see this at the very beginning of his work when he speaks of 'civil law both that of Rome and that of each nation in particular';[4] or of ambassadors who are not bound 'by the civil law of the people among whom they live';[5] or of the 'representatives of provinces, towns and others who are not governed by the law of nations but by civil law';[6] or of crimes which, by 'civil law,' may justly

[1] L. ii. c. xvi. s. 31.

[2] Dickinson, *The Equality of States in International Law*, 1920, p. 50.

[3] Holtzendorff, vol. iii. p. 11. Cf. also Walker, *A History of the Law of Nations*, 1899, p. 334.

[4] *Proleg.* 1.—'*Jus civile,*' says Cocceius commenting upon this passage, '*i.e. jus statutarium cujusque populi.*' He says again, when commenting upon l. ii. c. xvi. s. 31: '. . . *sane si plures gentes idem forte ius suis subditis statuunt, id non est jus gentium, sed jus civile, quod non inter civitates obtinet, sed in singulis saltem civitatibus.*' The following passage from L. 9, *Dig.*, *de iustit. et iure*, I. i. (taken from Gaius) will illustrate this conception of *ius civile*: '*Nam quod quisque populus ipse sibi constituit, id ipsius proprium civitatis, vocaturque civile.*' It is also in this meaning that the term is used by Gentilis; see, *e.g.*, *De Legationibus*, b. ii. ch. xvii. Cf. here also Fiore, *International Law Codified* (American translation, 1913), p. 83.

[5] L. ii. c. xviii. s. 4 (Whewell's translation).

[6] L. ii. c. xviii. s. 2.

be punished by death.[1] It is obvious, therefore, that the numerous statements in which he repudiates the use of civil law cannot have the meaning attributed to them now, namely, that of rejection of private law as such. He used the term 'civil law' as connoting rules of municipal law aiming at the 'tranquillity of *one* community.' And for this civil law he could have no use in a law of nations by which he understood rules applicable to the intercourse *between* States and sovereigns.[2]

Secondly, although he did not identify the law of nature with the law of nations, he certainly regarded the first as the obvious source from which we may fill the gaps of the 'instituted' law of nations. And the gaps were undoubtedly bigger than the actual rules. In this light, the blunder of those publicists who imputed to Grotius the identification noted above is, after all, not so misleading. And what were the sources or the evidence of this natural law? They, in turn, were in most cases identical with those rules of private and especially of Roman law which appeared to him as of sufficient generality and as suitable for the purposes of international law. *Rationes saepe optimas suppeditant ad demonstrandum id, quod iuris est naturae; et eidem iuri neque minus gentium iuri testimonium saepe praebent.*[3] He did not accept private law (or Roman law) as having *per se* obligatory force in international law, but he certainly was taking over, under a different name, its rules and principles whenever he deemed it to be evidence of the law of nature applicable to a given

[1] L. ii. c. i. s. 14. Cf. also l. ii. c. xi. s. 5, where he deals with the requirements of the validity of promises.

[2] This conception of civil law as understood by Grotius is discussed with much lucidity by Textor in his *Synopsis Juris Gentium*, 1680 (newly edited in Scott's *Classics of International Law*, with an English translation by Bate, 1916). He points out that the law of nations embraces law common to all or many nations, both public and private (see ch. viii. 41; ch. ii. 14, 15), and that it is not exclusively public law, although it is akin to public law and politics, 'some of its special topics being matters of the prerogative, like war, peace, treaties,' etc. (ch. i., 12).

[3] *Proleg.* 53.

case. What the right hand of the builder of a more positivist system formally rejected (if rejection it was in view of his conception of civil law), the left hand of the great expounder of natural law, of justice, and convenience was adopting with far-reaching thoroughness.[1]

§ 7. *Bynkershoek.*—Bynkershoek too, the positivist, is praised by some writers as a publicist who recognised in time the dangers of recourse to Roman law.[2] There is, no doubt, some evidence in his writings to support such an assertion. Thus he states, in one place, that the Roman law 'will not decide questions which belong to the law of nations.'[3] In another, he quotes approvingly Wicquefort to the effect that rules of public law cannot be derived from civil or canon law, because the two systems deal with different objects, and different principles must therefore apply to them.[4] But the same Bynkershoek is, on the other hand, extolled as a great admirer of Roman law, and as one whose recourse to it was by no means infrequent.[5] He does not fail to

[1] That it was his constant recourse to Roman law, and not his rejection of it, which was of decisive influence may be seen from the testimony of that great enthusiast of Roman law, Sir Robert Wiseman (*op. cit.*, p. 61). About a hundred years later, J. J. Moser, the positivist, observes dryly that the constant invoking of Grotius for the purpose of proving the admissibility of recourse to Roman law is quite irrelevant, because Grotius' book is a private work which cannot dictate laws to free nations (see p. 214, *op. cit.* below). That, on the other hand, some expressions of Grotius were taken in their literal sense may be seen, for instance, from the vigorous attack delivered upon Roman law by Johann Gottfried Heineccius, the influential expounder of the law of nature in its application to states and the commentator of Grotius. He opens his *Elementa Juris Naturae et Gentium* (1737) with a preface solely devoted to the refutation of Roman law as a source of authority in international law: '*Ea tamen [jurisprudentia Romana] nihil auctoritatis habitura sit in definiendis integrarum gentium litibus et controversiis, quippe, quae inter se non alio iure, quam quod ipsa natura inter homines peraeque constituit, reguntur; iure inquam, illo universali quod in foederibus, pactionibus, conditionibus populorum . . . versatur.*' (The English translation of the work appeared in 1789, without the preface.)

[2] Phillipson in the *Journal of Comparative Legislation and International Law*, New Series, ix. (1908) p. 33; Delpech in *Les Fondateurs, etc.*, 1904, pp. 390, 391.

[3] *De Dominio Maris*, 1702, ch. ix. (p. 95 of Magoffin's translation in Scott's *Classics of International Law*, 1923).

[4] *De Foro Legatorum*, 1721, ch. vii.; see also *ibid.*, ch. ii. and viii. *in fine.*

[5] See Phillimore, vol. i. p. 31.

supply an explanation of this apparent inconsistency. He says: '*Non quod in iis quae sola ratio commendat a iure Romano ad ius gentium non tuta sit collectio.*' For him 'the reason of the thing' thus becomes the form in which the reception of Roman law takes place. '*Quamvis non de Populi Romani sed de Gentium jurisprudentia agamus,*' he says in another work, '*non abs re tamen erit de Jure Romano quaedam praemonuisse, cum qui id audit, vocem fere omnium Gentium videatur audire.*'[1]

§ 8. *Moser.*—J. J. Moser is perhaps the only leading positivist of that time who is consistent to the very end in his rejection of Roman law. He regards it as a ridiculous *petitio principii* that disputes between free nations should be decided in accordance with the law of Justinian, and mentions, not without sarcasm, a civilian who advised the King of France to bring an action based on the *Lex Aquilia* against a German prince who invaded his territory. To those who point to the lead given by Grotius in this regard, he gives the curt reply that Grotius' book is a private work with no binding authority attached to it.[2] The reason why Moser could afford to take up such a consistent attitude — whereas the publicists mentioned above could not—is easily explained by the fact that the numerous and bulky volumes written by this learned positivist in no way go beyond a systematic collection of provisions of treaties. It may be said, without disrespect to Moser's great industry, that he obviously neither claims nor attempts a juristic discussion of the principles of international law.[3]

[1] *De Foro Legatorum*, ch. vi.

[2] See *supra*, p. 5, n. 1.

[3] His opinion, mentioned in the text, on the authority of Roman law is expressed in an obscure passage of *Teutsches Staatsrecht*, 1738, pt. ii., b. i., p. 214. For a melancholy, but true and accurate, account of the results of the uncompromisingly positivist method adopted by Moser, see Verdross in *Zeitschrift für öffentliches Recht*, vol. iii. (1923) pp. 16-102.

§ 9. *Neyron.*—Finally, Neyron, a writer less known but ably representing the prolific number of authors of monographs written in the seventeenth and eighteenth centuries, may be mentioned as an example of the characteristic attitude of alternately rejecting and adopting Roman law.[1] He complains, on one hand, of the great insecurity and confusion occasioned by exaggerated recourse to civil law, especially with regard to treaties. He shows how frequently Roman law had been used as an instrument in the hands of skilled civilians in order to defeat or to explain away provisions of a binding treaty. At one moment, he says, they discovered a flaw in the form of the treaty ; at another, they put forward the plea of lesion, or of restitution on account of minor age, or of duress or fraud, and so on.[2] This went so far that in many treaties a mutual renunciation clause had to be inserted to the effect that both parties renounce the benefits of civil law. Nevertheless, although he is fully alive to the dangers, practical and theoretical—he speaks of the 'difference of relations between individuals subject to authority and equal nations'—of recourse to analogy, he devotes a whole chapter to the 'Advantages brought by Roman Law to Public Treaties,' and impresses upon the reader the fact that 'many principles of Roman law, salutary in themselves and independent of Roman constitutions, have been adopted by the European Powers and retained by reason of their intrinsic value until to-day.'[3]

§ 10. *Modern International Law. The Positivist School in Germany.*—When we turn to modern international law, we are confronted once more with the same picture of alternate rejection and adoption of the

[1] He is the author of an excellent monograph entitled *Essai historique et politique sur les Garanties*, 1777.

[2] *Op. cit.*, p. 70.

[3] *Op. cit.*, p. 76.

recourse to private law, its repudiation in form going hand in hand with its adoption in substance, although under a name more general and apparently less objectionable. However, it is on a much wider plane that the modern positivist science of international law deals with the problem. For the object of the attack changes in the nineteenth century in so far as Roman law is replaced by private law in general. This may be seen specially in the German positivist jurisprudence. Although Heffter, who adopts the private law division into persons, things, and obligations, and who omits no opportunity of moulding international law relationships into institutions of private law, remains without doubt the most influential German international lawyer of his time, one is struck by the increasing tendency to eliminate altogether private law as a source of international law. The movement begins with warnings against exaggerated use of analogy; it does not yet exclude it as a matter of principle. Moreover, some writers expressly urge the admissibility, within limits, of recourse to analogy. Meier admits, in his *Abschluss der Staatsverträge*, that rules of international law are often only deductions from private law, and he adds: 'Arguments drawn from private law are *per se* permitted, although they ought to be used with caution.' [1] Bergbohm still adheres to the same opinion, although, as an avowed positivist, he allows only for a partial identification of international treaties—not, however, of law-making treaties—with private law contracts.[2]

But the rejection of private law on the ground of general juridical principle is already by this time receiving the support of writers of the authority of Holtzendorff and Bulmerincq. The first rejects not only Roman law, 'the analogies to which are more

[1] 1874, p. 38.
[2] *Staatsverträge und Gesetze als Quellen des Völkerrechts*, 1877, p. 79.

misleading than enlightening,'[1] but also the recourse to private law in general. He says: 'It can hardly be maintained that international law may, in deciding disputes between States (which are independent), follow the analogy of private relations between individuals (who are permanently subject to authoritative legislation).'[2] Bulmerincq, who follows the same line of argument, is even more emphatic. He asserts that frequent recourse to analogy has impeded the growth of international law, and that it should never have been undertaken.[3] However, although we see here already the beginnings of a more systematic treatment of the problem, there is hardly an attempt to explain what appears to be its crux: How, after all, do conceptions of private law enter into the corpus of international public law and remain embedded there while even the most sweeping positivism is unable to eliminate them?

§ 11. *Jellinek, H. B. Oppenheim, Nippold, Triepel. 'Conceptions of universal jurisprudence.'*—Here, as in many other directions, the important step has been taken by Jellinek. This great lawyer made only casual excursions into the domain of international law, but where he did so his influence was by no means negligible. He rejects, in principle, any analogy whatever. There is, to his mind, no justification for applying conceptions of a self-contained system of law as a *ius cogens* in a quite different sphere of law.[4] Analogy, he says, can only be permitted when it is expressly recognised as a source of law by a given system of law. But how are we to explain the actual similarity of rules which exists, for instance, between the law of private contracts

[1] *Handbuch des Völkerrechts*, 1885, i. p. 72.

[2] *Op. cit.*, p. 126.

[3] *Praxis, Theorie und Codification des Völkerrechts*, 1874, p. 130.

[4] *Die rechtliche Natur der Staatenverträge*, 1880, p. 51.

and of international treaties? The explanation, he points out, consists in the fact that both private and international law contracts are 'universal conceptions of law,' conceptions of general jurisprudence to which by the very nature of things similar rules must apply. Accordingly, these rules are not taken from private law, 'although private law has raised the universal element of contract into scientific legal consciousness.'[1]

This view was not an original one. It had been expressed as far back as 1845 by H. B. Oppenheim, who in his *System des Völkerrechts* voiced the opinion that analogy to private law is to be rejected, or, when used, to be applied *cum grano salis.*[2] To approach problems of public international law from the angle of private law is, to his mind, as disruptive in the field of international law as the idea of State contract was in the sphere of political theory.[3] But, he adds, this does not apply to the relation between international law and the philosophy and logic of law. Thus the notion of property cannot be altered, no matter who is the subject of that right; neither can the nature of contract be different in international law, for instance, with regard to the rule that only a free declaration of will constitutes a binding obligation. This is also true of the rule '*pacta tertiis nec nocent nec prosunt*' or '*nemo plus iuris in alterum transferre potest quam ipse habet.*' However, it needed Jellinek's authority to establish this theory of the legal universality of some notions common to different branches of law.

Nippold follows closely this line of argument, and, adopting Jellinek's view on the question, concludes the chapter on the relation between international and private law with the following strong appeal: 'It is an obvious task of the theory of international law to cease looking towards other branches of law, to constitutional or

[1] *Loc. cit.* [2] *Op. cit.*, 2nd ed., 1866, p. 8. [3] *Op. cit*, p. 80.

private law, for this is as unjustifiable as the artificial filling of the unfortunately small building of international law with natural law ideas or political maxims.'[1] As a precaution and a remedy against this mischievous borrowing, he advises the creation and an adequate development of a general science of law which should include conceptions common to all branches of jurisprudence. From this source international law could draw the necessary reinforcements without having recourse to private law.

It was left to Triepel not only to discredit even further the recourse to private law, but also to banish it almost completely as a problem of the international law of to-day. His attitude, actuated by the desire to establish the formal dualism of international and municipal law, may be shortly stated. He does not deny that international law has, in the past, taken over large parts of private and especially of Roman law; in common with other writers he explains this as being due to the domination of the natural law tendency in the formative period of international law, and to the fact that the Roman law, the *ratio scripta*, was regarded as approximating very closely to the law of nature. But he denies that international law of to-day has accepted those principles. This was undoubtedly the case in the international practice of the time, in which the patrimonial conception was predominant; this conception is, however, not only, as Bluntschli says, unworthy of our time, but it is simply no longer existent.[2] There remain only the cases in which States stand in economic relations to one another, as, for instance, when they lend money to one another, when they take over a collective guarantee for a loan, when they enter into actual economic partner-

[1] *Der völkerrechtliche Vertrag, seine Stellung im Rechtssystem und seine Bedeutung für das internationale Recht*, 1894, p. 91.

[2] *Völkerrecht und Landesrecht*, 1899 (translated into French in 1920); see especially the chapter dealing with private law, pp. 211-225.

ship, and so on.[1] What rules are to be applied here if treaties are silent and if there is no custom forthcoming to fill the gap? Triepel denies that there is, even here, any need to apply a particular rule of private law, or that Roman law forms an exception to the general rule.[2] He points out that the damage resulting from this attitude is negligible, considering that there remains that eternal source of all law which we call morality or the reason of the thing, and on which we may fall back whenever necessary. Thus when, *e.g.*, private law rules of contract and international law rules regarding treaties happen to be identical, they are not so as a result of analogy or deliberate adoption, but in consequence of the very nature of things.

There is no doubt that the general body of authors of text-books and monographs, especially in Germany, have adopted this positivist view on the application of private law. 'International law,' says Liszt, 'is an independent branch of law . . . ; that does not mean that the rich spiritual output of private law cannot be used for the purposes of international law. What really takes place is a developing of general notions and principles common to all law (general jurisprudence).'[3] Recent publicists do not fail to support their views on certain controversial subjects by referring to the devastating influence of private law. With them it is a commonplace to speak with regret of the damage

[1] For instances see *op. cit.*, pp. 222-223.

[2] See, however, Triepel in *Recueil des Cours, Academie de Droit International*, 1923, p. 101, where he admits that to certain treaties with private law contents rules of private law of one of the contracting parties may be applied.

[3] *Völkerrecht*, 1925, p. 79; cf. also Ullmann, *Völkerrecht*, 1908, p. 248. It is of interest to note the similar opposition in Germany to the application of conceptions of private law in the field of administrative public law, as well as the reluctant acquiescence in the use of some of them as universal conceptions of law. See, for instance, Jellinek, *System der subjektiven öffentlichen Rechte*, 1892, p. 62 (as such conceptions he regards those of negligence, error, condition, set-off, prescription), Tezner in *Archiv für öffentliches Recht*, ix. p. 563, and recently Meier-Branecke, *ibid.*, New Series, xi. pt. 2 (1926), pp. 230-285.

done to international law by obsolete private law analogies.[1] In fact, such is the current attitude in this respect, that authors attach almost decisive importance to being able to show that their opponents' standpoint is nothing more than an obsolete private law analogy.[2] The warning 'Beware of private law' has become a catchword uncritically accepted, eagerly copied, and widely disseminated; and its prestige is undimmed by the fact that the banished phantom reappears with unfailing regularity under the garb of 'general jurisprudence.'

§ 12. *English Publicists on the Application of Roman Law. Zouche, Sir Robert Wiseman.*—Although this negative attitude of German positivist writers gained much prominence in international jurisprudence both in and outside Germany, it would nevertheless be a mistake to assume that it alone holds the field. In fact, it seems that British and American international jurists have adopted an attitude which, it is believed, is more in keeping with the history and the organic growth of international law. It is true that English publicists writing in the nineteenth century

[1] See, for instance, Strupp, *Das völkerrechtliche Delikt*, 1920, p. 57, n. 1; the same in Schücking, *Das Werk von Haag*, 1914, vol. ii. p. 128. See also Ruegger in *N.Z.*, xxviii. (1919-1920) p. 427; Schönborn, *Staatensukzessionen*, 1913, throughout; Hofer, *Der Schadenersatz im Landkriegsrecht*, 1913, who devotes a whole chapter to the question of the influence of private law (pp. 16-22); the author, however, marches the well-trodden path adopted by the writers mentioned in the text.

[2] This method of approach is not limited to the orthodox school of positivist publicists. Even recent writers of unimpeached independence of thought, who discuss questions of international law on the basis of 'the pure discipline of law' (*reine Rechtslehre*), exhibit here a deplorable lack of original judgment. See, *e.g.*, Henrich, *Theorie des Staatsgebietes*, 1922, *passim*, and Kunz in Strupp's *Wörterbuch*, i. 627, and ii. 340. See also Spiropulos in *N.Z.*, xxxv. (1925 - 1926) p. 129, who merely repeats H. B. Oppenheim's phrase (*op. cit.*, p. 7) on the 'eternal and inalienable rights' protected by international law; he is, however, a strong believer in 'general principles of law.' See, on the other hand, Prof. Fleischmann's note 2 at p. 79 of his new edition of Liszt (1925) as an indication of a more critical attitude, and Schön, quoted at p. 142, *infra*.

confined themselves to one part of the investigation only, namely, to that of the authority of Roman law as a source of international law. Within these limits, however, their answer to the question is, with scanty exceptions, in the affirmative. They adopt Roman private law not only as a source of international law in the historical sense, *i.e.* as evidence of the part played by Roman law in the formation of the law of nations, but also as a living source from which its numerous gaps may be filled. Unlike the continental writers, they never discarded the idea that Roman law is the source most likely to contain the 'reason of the thing' on many a question of international law. Indeed, it may be said that the great respect for Roman law and the acknowledgment of its importance as a subsidiary source of international law have become one of the characteristic features of British international jurisprudence. We have seen how strongly Gentilis, Grotius' most scientific predecessor and Professor of Civil Law at Oxford, adhered to this view. Similar was the attitude of one of his successors at Oxford, the distinguished civilian and 'second founder of international law,' the positivist Richard Zouche. His classification of both the law of peace and that of war into *status, dominium, debitum,* and *delictum* is based on Roman law, and he refers to the laws of Rome on many controversial subjects.[1] Dr. Arthur Duck, the learned civilian and Zouche's colleague at Oxford, was at the same time extolling the virtues of Roman law as a source of the law of nations.[2] Three years later appeared that enthusiastic book of Sir Robert Wiseman, an

[1] *Juris et Judicii fecialis, etc.*, 1650. See Holland's Introduction to the Classics edition, 1911, p. xiv; Phillipson in *Journal of Comparative Legislation and International Law*, New Series, ix. (1908) pp. 285, 286; Scelle in *Les Fondateurs, etc.*, pp. 276-277.

[2] *De Usu et Authoritate Juris Civilis Romanorum in Dominiis Principum Christianorum*, 1653, especially bk. i. ch. ii. (*De Justitia et Encomiijs Legum Romanarum*).

eminent practitioner in the Court of Admiralty, entitled: *The Law of Laws: or, the Excellency of the Civil Law, above all other Human Laws whatsoever. Shewing of how great use and necessity the Civil Law is to the Nation.*[1] The author took it for granted that the authority of Roman law extends to the law of nations, 'under the regulations of which come Embassies, courteous entertainment of foreigners and strangers, Laws of Arms, freedom of Traffique, right of Contracts, free passage through each other's Borders, Reprizalls, the preserving and redemption of captives, Leagues, Truces, Articles and such like.'[2] He admitted that not the whole Roman law may be resorted to, especially not that 'circumstantial and positive part which was a Law to the Romans . . . being made for that people, climate and government only.'[3] 'But,' he says, 'there is in it too a Law whereunto by the light of Reason men find themselves bound in that they are Men . . . a Law that may be applied to the communion and fellowship of all Mankind, or divers Nations . . .'[4] With regard to that law he entertained no doubt that it has been accepted by the general consent of nations as binding in disputes between them.[5] Lord Stowell was only giving expression to a widely held opinion[6] when, in the case of *The Maria,* he professed to act on the view that the law of nations is to a large extent based upon civil law.[7]

§ 13. *Nineteenth-century Writers. Manning, Maine,*

[1] First ed., 1656.

[2] *Ibid.*, p. 60.

[3] *Ibid.*, p. 63.

[4] *Ibid.*

[5] *Ibid.*, pp. 65, 146, 156.

[6] Cf. here the passage in Edmund Burke's *Letters on the Proposals for Peace with the Regicide Directory of France*, 1797 (*The Works and Correspondence of Edmund Burke*, 1852 ed., vol. v. p. 307), where the author, while pointing out that 'It has ever been the method of public jurists to draw a great part of the analogies, on which they form the law of nations, from the principles of law which prevail in civil community,' proceeds himself to construe the relations arising out of the dangers emanating from revolutionary France on the basis of the Roman law of neighbourhood pertaining to the *operis novi nunciatio*.

[7] 1 Chr. Rob. 363.

Phillimore, Westlake.—The attitude of the nineteenth-century English writers does not differ appreciably from that adopted by the above-mentioned representatives of the Oxford school. The traditions of Doctors' Commons had not become extinct. From Manning, Maine, and Phillimore to Westlake, publicists are almost unanimous in their opinion regarding the capacity of Roman law to serve as a source of international law in all cases where there is no customary or conventional rule at hand. Roman law is, indeed, regarded as that general or universal science of law the creation and development of which some continental writers consider to be an urgent task of the jurisprudence of to-day. William Oke Manning, one of the early writers of the nineteenth century, does not hesitate to explain the fact 'of the systematic writers on the law of nations having all been foreigners' by the absence in England of a well-ordered study of Roman law.[1] Sir Henry Maine is even more emphatic. He describes it as an absurdity that England should appear on the stage of international affairs unequipped with the knowledge of Roman law.[2] Sir Robert Phillimore, speaking of the 'reason of the thing' as a source of international law, pays a weighty tribute to Roman law: '. . . To all nations, whatsoever and wheresoever, this Law presents the unbiassed judgment of the calmest reason, tempered by equity, and rendered perfect, humanly speaking, by

[1] *Commentaries on the Law of Nations*, 1839, p. vi.—It is interesting to note how closely the idea of a universal jurisprudence is connected by Amos, Manning's editor in 1875, with the affirmative view on Roman law: 'It may be expected that one of the indirect consequences of the revived study of Roman law in England and of the growing desire to have the Law of Nations republished in a systematic form, will be the introduction of a common language of universal application in the wording of treaties' (p. 129).

[2] He writes in 1856 in the *Cambridge Essays*: 'Englishmen . . . will always be more signally at fault than the rest of the world in attempting to gain a clear view on the Law of Nations. There cannot be a doubt that our success in negotiations is sometimes perceptibly affected by our neglect of Roman law.' See also his *International Law*, 1894, pp. 20, 21, 26-29.

the most careful and patient industry that has ever been practically applied to the affairs of civilized man.'[1] He goes so far as to assert the admissibility of recourse to Roman law in the case of interpretation of treaties between European and Asiatic nations.[2] Westlake enumerates as sources of international law: custom, reason, and Roman law. He says: 'The rules which flowed into international law from this source are now incorporated with the customary law of nations, and such is the respect still generally entertained for Roman law, which has been called written reason, that this part of the customary law is never contradicted even by the seekers after international right.'[3] These publicists may fairly be regarded as representative of the general attitude of English writers on this question. The inquiry, interesting from many points of view, as to why the writers of a nation whose law preserved, with very slight exceptions, its complete independence from Roman law,[4] remained staunch advocates of its applicability to international law, cannot be enlarged upon in this monograph.[5]

[1] *Commentaries upon International Law*, 1879, i. p. 34. Similarly, Creasy, *First Platform of International Law*, 1876, pp. 83-85, 205; and Wildman, *Institutes of International Law*, 1849, pp. 22-24.

[2] *Op. cit.*, p. 36.

[3] *International Law*, vol. i. p. 15.

[4] For whatever may have been the influence of Roman law on Bracton, or on the teaching of law at the universities (the Oxford School of Civil Law), or on the form of legal theory and of the science of law, or in the ecclesiastical courts, or in the Court of Admiralty and on the Law Merchant, and whatever may have been the reasons which were inducing, from time to time, different writers to urge the importance of teaching Roman law in English universities, the overwhelming weight of authority seems to be to the effect that its actual influence on English law as such is exceedingly small. See Pollock and Maitland, *The History of English Law*, 1898, vol. ii. pp. 131-135, 193-197, 333-337; Pollock, *A First Book of Jurisprudence*, 3rd ed., 1911, p. 343; Scrutton, *The Influence of Roman Law on the Law of England*, 1885.

[5] The reason for this affirmative attitude to Roman law so far as international law is concerned lies, if a short explanation may be ventured with diffidence, in the fact that English writers on international law, although following closely the facts of international life and of the practice of States, had never lost sight of what may be called the natural law foundation of international law. Sir Frederick Pollock is quoted below (p. 59) to the effect that to ignore this would mean to ignore the pronouncements of the most authoritative English judges and publicists.

§ 14. *Lorimer.*—It is by James Lorimer, the eminent Scottish international lawyer, that by far the most independent contribution to the question seems to have been made. In an article entitled *Prolegomena to a Reasoned System of International Law*,[1] he discusses the question whether international law may legitimately look for guidance to that department of jurisprudence in which positive law has long been a reality, namely, in municipal law. He concedes that the analogy between the units of private and

This, notwithstanding the fact that the expression 'natural law' is not popular with English lawyers, and that they prefer to use the term 'reason' (see the significant passage in *Doctor and Student*, Dial. 1, c. 5, in Pollock, *The Expansion of the Common Law*, 1904, p. 109; and, by the same author, *Essays in the Law*, 1922, p. 69, and *The League of Nations*, 2nd ed., 1922, p. 28). Bryce expresses the same view in an article on the Law of Nature (*Studies in History and Jurisprudence*, 1901, vol. ii. p. 164). He points to the Indian Code of Civil Procedure of 1882, which lays down that a foreign judgment is not operative as a bar if it is '. . . contrary to natural justice,' and to the Courts in the British Indies, which are directed to apply 'the principles of justice, equity, and good conscience.' But whatever may have been the fate of the 'law of nature' in English law proper, it has never been totally discarded from the British conception of international law. With it, Roman law was being retained as embodying those legal rules which in the formative period of international law were deemed to give expression to the precepts of the law of nature. The fact is also not unimportant that the Court of Admiralty, which came into actual contact with many a question of international law, was engaged in administering the law maritime, a system founded, *inter alia*, upon Roman law, whose authority it successfully defended, for a long time, from the encroachments of the Courts of Common Law. And it is of interest to note that nearly all those writers who stressed the importance of Roman law for the law of nations were either practitioners or judges of the Court of Admiralty. On the whole, it seems natural that the cult and study of Roman law, diverted by historical occurrences and other reasons from influencing English municipal law, should have tended to assert themselves and to justify their existence by pointing to their importance in the field of international law (see Scrutton, *op. cit.*, pp. 170-176; Senior, *Doctors' Commons and the Old Court of Admiralty*, 1922; Holdsworth, *Sources and Literature of English Law*, 1925, pp. 234-235; and also Nys, *Le droit Romain, le droit des gens et le collège des docteurs en droit civil*, 1910, especially pp. 72-102).

Sir John Simon, Attorney-General, while addressing Sir Samuel Evans, the President of the Probate, Divorce, and Admiralty Division, on the occasion of the opening of the proceedings of the Prize Court in 1914 (see *The Chile*, *Lloyd's Reports*, vol. i. p. 6), said: 'A certain part of the law which your Lordship will be applying is what one may call the Common Law of Nations; it depends upon the teaching and learning of civilians and other great authorities, it does not depend upon special treaties or conventional arrangements entered into by the great Powers of the world.'

[1] *Studies, National and International*, 1890 (pp. 148-163).

international law is an imperfect one, and that it breaks down in many directions. But although he admits that caution is necessary, he urges that it must not become the guiding consideration. For, he says,

> 'all analogies are imperfect in this respect, and yet the whole of our reasoning from experience . . . is reasoning from extremely imperfect analogies between past and present occurrences. The question is not, Are the conditions of the two problems the same ?—for that may always be answered in the negative—but, Do they resemble each other closely enough for the old solution to be so modified as to apply to the new problem, or to suggest an analogous solution which may be applied to it ? '

He shows the exaggerations of which the founders of international law have become guilty while giving an affirmative reply to the question, and how frequently they rendered international law 'hidebound' by maxims and subtleties of Roman jurisprudence. This, however, does not affect his final judgment :

> 'But the notion that, as in dealing with international relations they were still dealing with human rights and duties, the definitions which they had received in one class of relations might throw light on those which must be given to them in another class of relations, though differing considerably, was, I believe, a true notion. It is a notion, consequently, on which I have not hesitated to fall back.' [1]

§ 15. *The American Writers.*—The American writers do not appear to have devoted special attention to the subject in question, but they share, on the whole, the view of British publicists. 'The introduction and study of the civil law,' says Chancellor Kent in his *Commentaries on International Law*,[2] 'must have also contributed largely to more correct and liberal views of the rights and duties

[1] *Ibid.*, p. 159. See also pp. 80, 81, *infra*. [2] 2nd ed. by Abdy, 1878.

of nations.'[1] Taylor thinks it impossible to comprehend international law without some understanding of Roman jurisprudence, which he regards as constituting the philosophical basis of the law of nations.[2] Halleck, who, like Manning, connects the problem of Roman law with the demand for a universal jurisprudence, says:

'It will generally be found that the deficiencies of precedent, usage, and express international authority may be supplied from the rich treasury of the Roman Civil Law. Indeed, the greater number of controversies between States would find a just solution in this comprehensive system of practical equity, which furnishes principles of universal jurisprudence, applicable alike to individuals and to States.'[3]

§ 16. *The French and Italian School. Rivier.*—The French publicists, like Bonfils,[4] Despagnet,[5] and others, deal at length with the sources of international law and with its relation to international private law, to constitutional law, to morality, to international courtesy, to politics and diplomacy, but no mention is made of private law proper. The same may be said of Italian writers in the nineteenth century. Recent Italian positivists, however, follow the German lead by either repudiating altogether the application of private law or by favouring the so-called conceptions of general jurisprudence. Thus Anzilotti, the leading Italian positivist, has more than once given expression to his disapproval of any recourse whatsoever to rules of private law.[6] Similar is the attitude of Cavaglieri.[7]

That, on the other hand, the influence of the English conception is not confined to English-speaking countries

[1] *Op. cit.*, p. 26.

[2] *A Treatise on International Public Law*, 1901, pp. 20-21.

[3] *International Law*, 4th ed., by Barker, 1908, p. 61; see also Davis, *The Elements of International Law*, 3rd ed., 1908, p. 22. See, however, Hudson, quoted below, p. 35.

[4] Bonfils-Fauchille, 1922, vol. i., pt. 1, Nos. 63 (4)-70.

[5] *Cours*, 1910, p. 55.

[6] See §§ 60, 123, *infra*.

[7] *Corso di diritto internazionale*, 1925, pp. 100, 101, in *Rivista*, xvi. (1924) p. 29.

may be seen in the treatise of Rivier, the Swiss-Belgian writer, who deals with the matter in a comprehensive manner.[1] He approves of the application not only of Roman law but also of private law rules in general, although he advises a certain amount of caution.[2] When dealing with the meaning of the phrase 'general principles of jurisprudence' used in arbitration treaties, he is clearly of the opinion that in the absence of the declared will of the parties the rules of Roman law, being common to various peoples of the international community, must necessarily be applied.[3]

§ 17. *Examination of the Problem. The 'General Jurisprudence' of the Positivist School as connoting General Principles of Private Law.*—The demand, so persistently put forward by the positivist school, for the complete independence of international law from private law can be regarded as well founded only if it be shown: (*a*) that publicists advocating such independence are able to maintain it in their own writings without introducing the rejected private law in a disguised form or under a different name; (*b*) that this refutation corresponds with the legal conviction of States as manifested in treaties and in international custom; (*c*) that the judicial settlement of international disputes is practicable and in fact takes place without recourse to private law rules and analogies. For, should an *ad hoc* examination of the writings of publicists show that this iconoclasm is only a matter of form and not of substance, and that it is opposed to the practice of States and international tribunals, then, obviously, the doctrine is as inconsistent with the very principles of the positivist

[1] *Principes du droit des gens*, 1896, vol. i. p. 34; vol. ii. p. 123.

[2] 'Il faut procéder avec prudence et *mutandis mutatis*, en tenant compte toujours du motif de la règle et des conditions qu'elle suppose, ainsi que des obstacles que peuvent mettre à son application d'autres principes admis en droits des gens.'

[3] Vol. ii. p. 175. See, however, Nys, vol. i. p. 206; and Calvo, vol. i. p. 165.

teaching as it is misleading. This Section is devoted to a preliminary examination of the first of the three questions ; it will also indicate the manner in which the following chapters will deal with the two other aspects of the problem.[1]

(*a*) It has already been pointed out that there is not

[1] No attempt can be made here at a historical account of the recourse had to Roman law in the formative period of international law. This task, although it cannot be pursued here, is an urgent one. For the usual sweeping statement to the effect that early writers profusely and indiscriminately resorted to private law is of little use. The literature on the subject is certainly exhaustive so far as the seventeenth and eighteenth centuries are concerned, especially in Germany. The problem is there, as a rule, treated in connection with the application of Roman law to public and constitutional law and to the mutual relations of the numerous independent German States, but the monographs in question throw at the same time ample light on the problem of the authority of Roman law in connection with international public law. Triepel mentions, for instance, the dissertation of Bütemeister, *De usu juris Romani aliorumque privatorum jurium in decidendis controversiis liberarum gentium*, 1692. Of a similar character are: Engelbrecht, *De usu Juris Romani in Jure publico Romano-Germanico, huiusque variis Controversiis decidendis*, 1692; M. H. Gribner, *De Præjudicio Principum Imperii ex abusu Juris Justiniani*, 1717; U. Obrecht, *De Usu Juris Civilis in decidendis controversiis publicis* (about 1720).

But even more instructive are the numerous monographs on individual subjects of international law whose number in the seventeenth and eighteenth centuries seems to be much larger than in the two following centuries. Ompteda, for instance, gives in his *Litteratur des gesammten sowohl natürlichen als positiven Völkerrechts* (1785, vol. ii. pp. 512-514) a list of 17 monographs on prescription written between 1710 and 1775, nearly all of them professing to deal with the question whether the private and Roman law institute of prescription has application as between States. Nearly as great is the number of publicists writing on treaties of guarantee. I mention specially the treaties of guarantee as showing how vast are the opportunities which that literature offers to the historian of international law, notably in connection with the subject of this book. How far, for instance, are the *warranti* or *responsales* the result of a conscious application of the institution of *fideiussores* of Roman law and of the principles of suretyship as developed in private law? The answer so far given by modern publicists is conflicting and unsatisfactory. Some elaborate the distinction between guarantee in private and international law, pointing especially to the fact that while the former is of an accessory character, the second is not (see, *e.g.*, Geffcken in *Holtzendorff*, vol. iii. p. 90, or Quabbe, *Die völkerrechtliche Garantie*, 1911, pp. 69-91, who stresses the Gallo-Germanistic character of treaties of guarantee); others insist on the fundamental identity of the two. Cf., *e.g.*, Idman (*Le Traité de Garantie*, 1913, pp. 84-87), who, however, denies the Roman law origin of treaties of guarantee. But it is of interest to note how Neyron (*op. cit.*, p. 80), who cannot be charged with blind allegiance to Roman law, regards the institute of guarantee as an instance of the most beneficial influence of Roman law, although he is quite conscious of the differences in the application of the idea of suretyship in the two spheres of law. It is in a scrupulous investigation of the vast literature of that period, and not in the uncritically accepted catchword on the influence of the patrimonial theory, that the causes of the frequent use of Roman law will be found.

much substance behind the casual rejection of Roman or private law by some of the writers of the classical period. The generally accepted view that they relied largely on that source remains unshattered—although it has been shown to err on the side of imputing to them an uncritical and rather naïve imitation of the example set by private law. For the resort to analogy was, with the majority of them, the result of mature reflection and firmly grounded scientific conviction. In so far, however, as their repudiation of the rules of Roman and private law was genuine and consistent—and it was so to a very small extent—it was counterbalanced by the fact that they were appealing, freely and without reserve, to Roman law as embodying the principles of the law of nature and right reason.

Much more difficult was the position of those modern positivist writers who found themselves rejecting not only private law but also natural law. Being unable to afford the consistency of totally ignoring both private and natural law, they put in their place 'the reason of the thing,' 'the demands of logic,' and 'the principles of general jurisprudence.' It is significant that those writers who are anxious to eliminate the application of private law, regard as essential for the development of international law the creation of a science which would embrace the general concepts of law common to all systems, international and municipal, private and public; this science to be called general jurisprudence. We have seen that it is, *inter alia*, from this source that they explain the identity of the rules governing international treaties and private law contracts. There remains, however, the danger that this general jurisprudence might become a purely abstract philosophy of law—the very natural law from which they wish to purify the science of international law. General jurisprudence must therefore, according to them, be an empirical one, *i.e.* drawn by means of generalising induction from the existing systems of law.

But here the real, and insoluble, difficulty begins. A system of general jurisprudence meant as a generalisation from existing systems of law, national and international, can only have a meaning when there are in existence developed systems of law, private and international, which form the constituent elements of the higher synthesis. Now, it is obvious that in cases in which international publicists resort to so-called general jurisprudence, international law as such does not contribute anything towards this synthesis ; it simply draws from that source when it finds that its own rules, which it was called upon to develop in a comparatively short time and in conditions in which the border-line between law and mere force is often not distinct enough, afford no answer. When, for instance, Liszt says that the *sedes materiae* of condition (treaties under a condition) is general jurisprudence, he needs must mean general jurisprudence of private law.[1] When, in international disputes, rules of general jurisprudence are referred to, what is meant is that not a rule of one particular system of private law is to be applied, but only such a rule—usually a private law rule—as has gained recognition by the general body of civilised nations. This is so for the simple reason that international law has not, in the particular case, developed any rules of its own. In fact, there would be no need to have recourse to general jurisprudence, if there were an international law rule ready at hand. Natural law performed, in the older days, the function of a bridge between international and private law ; it was the cover from under which international

[1] See Rapisardi-Mirabelli, *I limiti, d'obbligatorietà delle norme giuridiche internazionali*, 1922, pp. 86-90, and Liszt, p. 245. See also Werveke in *R.I.*, 3rd ser., vol. i. (1920) pp. 238-251, on acquisition of sovereignty under a resolutive condition in connection with Article 34 of the Treaty of Versailles, and, with regard to the Tacna-Arica dispute, pp. 291, 292, *infra*.

law drew from the rich source of private, notably Roman, law. In the days of the predominance of positivist tendencies it is 'general jurisprudence' which is fulfilling this function.

General jurisprudence is a very useful and necessary notion for the purposes of international law as a science and for the purposes of the judicial settlement of international disputes, so long as it remains clear that what we understand by this conception is rules which international law does not yet possess, but which have been evolved in the various systems of municipal law. Naturally enough, it is of rules of private law that we think in these cases; we do not think in this connection of general principles of criminal or administrative law. Any other meaning of the term is liable to cause confusion and to be grossly abused. Is, for instance, the notion of succession a general conception of all jurisprudence, as is maintained by some writers? [1] What may safely be said is that it is a general notion of municipal, notably of private, law. But its application, in the ordinary meaning attached to it, is denied, in international law, by several positivist writers, even by those who regard it as an universal conception. The principle *res transit cum suo onere* is regarded by the great majority of publicists [2] as an obviously general principle, but even this is doubted by some positivist writers. It has almost become a truism that treaties being contracts (a universal legal conception), they are governed by rules not of private law but of general jurisprudence; but the identification of the two conceptions is now severely criticised from many sides.[3]

[1] See Cavaglieri, *Rivista*, xvi. (1924), p. 29; he calls it 'un concetto generale, pertinente ad un' unica categoria, che si presenta nei vari rami del diritto, assumendo per ognuno di essi atteggiamenti specifici'; see also Guggenheim, p. 43, and Schönborn, p. 3 (both cited at p. 126, *infra*).

[2] Cf. Oppenheim, vol. i. p. 147.

[3] Cf. Niemeyer, p. 126; Mayer in *Archiv für öffentliches Recht*, xxxviii. i. (1918) pp. 8, 9; and Hudson in the *Cornell Law Quarterly*, x. (1925) p. 433.

It would seem that freedom of consent is a condition of validity of contracts which must needs be recognised by every legal system; this, however, is almost unanimously denied so far as international law is concerned. And although the prevalent opinion concedes, in deference to an obvious requirement of general jurisprudence, the vitiating effect of mistake and fraud, there are writers who deny that these rules of private law are applicable to international treaties. The recognition by a Hague arbitration tribunal of interest as a general mode of fulfilment of pecuniary obligations has been subjected to severe criticism by several positivist writers, although others allege that modes of payment and fulfilling of obligations are general juridical categories not confined to private law.[1] Prescription, which is generally regarded as a principle common to all branches of law, is denounced by others as a purely private law notion. It would seem that it is a general principle of law that the claimant party should bear the burden of the proof, but this rule is, according to a widespread opinion, subject in international law to the qualification that the burden of proof rests upon the party alleging some measure of restriction of the sovereignty of another State. The principle that in awarding damages the *restitutio in integrum* should be aimed at, is regarded by many as a rule of universal jurisprudence, but its application in international law is opposed by others. The notions of self-help and necessity, frequently described as belonging to general jurisprudence, are being denounced as having no counterpart in international law.

These instances show with sufficient clearness that there is, as a rule, nothing cogent and well defined in 'universal conceptions of law'—unless, indeed, we agree

[1] So Jellinek, *System der subjektiven öffentlichen Rechte*, 1892, p. 161; see, however, Kohler in *Z.V.*, xii. (1912) pp. 90, 91.

to regard them for most practical purposes as identical with generally recognised principles of private law. This, however, dogmatic positivists refuse to admit, not noticing that, in practice, 'general jurisprudence' is converted into a law of nature in modern garb adopted for the purpose of introducing, with some illusion of consistency, the much denounced private law —in the same manner as some writers in the seventeenth and eighteenth centuries, while rejecting the application of Roman law as such, subsequently introduced it as expressive of the 'reason of the thing' or of the law of nature. It is proposed to discuss in Chapter II., which deals with the general aspects of the relation between private and international public law, the causes leading to these ever-recurring and unsuccessful attempts at self-sufficiency.

§ 18. (*b*) *The Practice of States.*—It is the practice of States that is best suited to throw light on the question under discussion. To the examination of this aspect of the problem, Chapters III., IV., and V. of this monograph will be devoted. An attempt will be made (*a*) to show how, historically, the development of international law has been facilitated by its close connection with private law; (*b*) to inquire to what extent international law of to-day draws from this source. In particular, the theory will be examined which explains the great influence of private law by the patrimonial character of States in the formative period of international law. We shall have to inquire whether the causes are not deeper, and whether they do not obtain to-day with undiminished force.

As to the classification of cases in which recourse to private law occurs, the following appears to be the most suitable arrangement:

(1) We shall discuss, firstly, instances of private law

analogy apart from treaties; for example, the influence of private law on the conception of State territory and on the theory and practice of acquisition of territorial sovereignty, on the development of the conceptions of the freedom of the sea, of the maritime belt, of the sovereignty of the air, and on the questions of prescription, of succession, of State responsibility, of interest and of the measure of damages for international delinquencies.

(2) The second class embraces instances of recourse to private law in connection with international treaties. Here belong cases in which a term of private law is used in a treaty and the answer has to be given as to whether the rules applicable to this term in its original sphere are also applicable in international law.

(3) Thirdly, cases will be considered relating to estoppel, *res iudicata*, and other private law rules of evidence and procedure.

§ 19. (*c*) *International Arbitration and the Problem of Private Law. Enumeration of Instances.*—The most convincing proof, however, of the growing importance of the problem and of the need for its systematic treatment is offered by a long series of cases of international arbitration. In the same measure as municipal courts pass judgment not only upon the claims of the parties but also, incidentally, upon the soundness of legal theories, so there is no better opportunity for testing the value of certain doctrines and conceptions of international law than those cases of international arbitration in which the recourse to these conceptions and doctrines has become relevant. Now, the opinion may be ventured that there are, in the whole course of judicial settlement of international disputes, only few cases in which the tribunal was not called upon to deal in one form or another with the question of application of private law.

The long array of these cases begins with the British-American arbitration commissions constituted under the Jay Treaty of 1794. Some of the main issues in the deliberations of these commissions, namely, the measure of damages and the right of the tribunal to determine its own jurisdiction, receive here solutions which required a century in order to become recognised as established rules of international law. Numerous minor arbitrations in the nineteenth century were dependent for their solution upon application of private law. Thus the cases, *Croft*, *Williams*, and *Fabiani*, may be mentioned as dealing, *inter alia*, with questions of damages, prescription, and admission. It is, however, in the important and well-known arbitrations that evidence in support of the general proposition put forward in these pages will be sought. The Geneva Tribunal in the *Alabama* arbitration of 1871 had to deal not only with the meaning and scope of '*due diligence*' as applied to States, and with the different forms of *culpa* known in Roman law; for the questions also of the measure of damages and of the admissibility of interest proved of no small importance for the decision of the main issues of the dispute. In the Behring Sea arbitration of 1893 between the United States and Great Britain, the question of the application in international law of conceptions of possession and property, as applied to the object of an international right, was widely discussed and answered in the judgment; whilst the problem of the development of international law in its relation to private and natural law occupied counsel for both parties to a considerable extent, as also did the question of damages and of prescription.

In 1899, in the British Guiana Boundary arbitration between Great Britain and Venezuela, the doctrines of prescription, of estoppel, and of title by occupation played a conspicuous part in the written and oral argument. In the Pious Fund case of 1902 between the United States and Mexico, the questions of prescription, of estoppel, and of the extent of the application of the maxim of *res iudicata* in international law were the main points which the Court had to decide. The Delagoa Bay Railway arbitration between Great Britain, the United States, and Portugal of 1900 again furnishes a striking example of a purely private law solution of the question of the measure of damages, as also did, in 1902, the arbitration between Russia and the United States in the Whaling and Sealing Claims. In a series of decisions of the commissions adjudicating, in 1903, claims against Venezuela, the questions of prescription, of interest, and the measure of damages were discussed before the individual commissions. In the Venezuelan Preferential Claim case of 1904 the questions of application of private law rules of bankruptcy, of hypothecation, of *negotiorum gestio*, and of estoppel were in the foreground of the proceedings. The general problem of the applicability of Roman law in international law was here discussed at length in the cases and arguments of several States. In the arbitration, in 1905, between Japan on one side, and Great Britain, France, and Germany on the other, the tribunal was again called upon to decide on a question belonging primarily to the domain of private law—the question of leases. In the Alaska Boundary dispute of 1903 between the United States and Great Britain the problems of prescription, of private law rules of evidence, and of the authority of Roman law were argued at length. In the Orinoco Steamship Company arbitration of 1910 between the United States and Venezuela, private law rules regarding the nullity of judgment and essential error were the real point at issue. The Grisbadarna case between Norway and Sweden, decided in 1909, afforded again an opportunity of discussing and applying the problems of prescription and of Roman law rules of possession.

The important North Atlantic Fisheries arbitration between Great Britain and the United States (international servitudes) showed again, both in the arguments of the parties and in the judgment of the Hague Court, that the question of private law in relation to international public law must be dealt with in a systematic manner. The Russian Indemnity case between Russia and Turkey, decided in 1912 by the Hague Court, is a classical instance of application not only in the pleadings of the parties, but also by the tribunal, of private law rules, especially those governing the question of moratory interest; the case itself was decided by the application of a private law rule amounting virtually to estoppel. The arbitrations between Great Britain and Brazil in 1904 concerning the frontiers of British Guiana, between the United States and Mexico in 1911 (the Chamizal arbitration), and, in the same year, between Great Britain and Germany (the Walfisch Bay arbitration), offer important contributions to the question of prescription.

Two noteworthy awards of the Central American Court of Justice throw ample light on the application of private law constructions in international law: one (between Honduras, Salvador, and Guatemala, in 1908) deals fully with the conceptions of *dolus* and *culpa* in relation to the degree of diligence to be exhibited by the neutral; in the other (between Salvador, Costa Rica, and Nicaragua, in 1917) the Court discussed thoroughly the questions of leases and co-ownership in application to State territory. A number of instructive cases decided by the British-American Claims Arbitral Tribunal constituted under the Convention of 1910 are of special interest in this connection. They deal, *inter alia,* with the question of the measure of damages, especially with damages for prospective profits, and with the problem of admission and estoppel. The Tacna-Arica arbitration (1923-1925) between Chile and Peru affords another typical example of recourse to private law, especially with regard to the nature of condition in international law and to the 'specific performance' character of an international obligation. Finally, a study of the cases decided by the Permanent Court of International Justice, both in the judgments and in the advisory opinions, reveals that such questions as *res iudicata,* the measure of damages, succession and servitudes occupy a prominent place in the pronouncements of the Court and in the pleadings of the parties.

These instances, which will be analysed in the subsequent chapters, show that the problem is not one of a purely theoretical character. They show also, and this may be said partly in anticipation of the results of that analysis, how unjustifiable and superficial is the attitude of indiscriminate repudiation of private law as a source of decision or as an element of development in the law of nations.

CHAPTER II

PUBLIC INTERNATIONAL LAW AND PRIVATE LAW

'The moral sense of humanity, which frequently underlay the much misunderstood "natural law," is asserting itself, and "reason," to use Westlake's term, is showing itself increasingly as a source of International Law, both as a test of principle for the rules established by custom, as well as for the adoption of new rules demanded by the exigencies of international life.'

HIGGINS, Preface to the 8th edition of Hall, 1924, p. viii.

'The duties and rights of States are only the duties and rights of the men who compose them.'

WESTLAKE, *Collected Papers*, p. 78.

I

THE DOGMA OF SOVEREIGNTY, THE POSITIVIST DOCTRINE, AND THE APPLICATION OF PRIVATE LAW

§ 20. *The Two Aspects of the Doctrine of Sovereignty: Positivism and Absolute Supremacy.*—The notion of sovereignty appears in international law under two aspects : (*a*) as the doctrine of rigid positivism according to which only rules expressly recognised by international custom and treaties are the exclusive sources of international law ; (*b*) as the conception of the State as an entity of an absolute legal and moral value, for which international law exists lawfully only so far as it is subservient to its self-preservation and development. The first is a formal statement to the effect that the will of the State is the ultimate and exclusive source of law *pro foro interno et externo* ; the second defines in terms of values this supreme entity as belonging, both legally and morally, to a sphere higher than that which embraces other forms of human organisation. Viewed from either of these two aspects, the recognition of private law as a subsidiary source of international law naturally appears to be mischievous and confusing. It is likely to subject the sovereign will of States to rules which have never received their express consent, and it is liable to make us forget that the interests protected by the State on the international arena are eternal, inalienable, incomparably higher than those governed by private law. It will therefore be of advantage to inquire how far sovereignty thus conceived has become generally accepted, and how far its main postulate, *i.e.* the positivist doctrine, is borne out by the science of international law and by the practice of States.

§ 21. *The First Aspect. The Absolute Character of the International Rights and Interests of the State. Hegel, Lasson, Kaufmann.*—There seems to be no doubt that, with regard to the doctrine of sovereignty, international law stood at the beginning of the present century at the point at which it was left by Hegel with his conception of the State as an absolute end and of international law as external municipal law.[1] He regarded the State as the realisation of the moral idea,[2] as 'the objective spirit,' through which alone 'the individual has his objectivity, his truth and his morality.'[3] 'The State,' he says, 'is the march of God in the world. Its foundation is the power of reason, realised as will. To form an idea of the State we must not have in mind particular States or institutions but consider thoroughly the Idea, the real God.'[4] But this real God stops short of the

[1] It is inaccurate to connect Bodin's theory of sovereignty with the modern Hegelian conception. Bodin's theory does not, in its essence, clash with a working international law—which cannot be said of that of Hegel. See Verdross, *Die Einheit des rechtlichen Weltbildes, etc.*, 1923, p. 13.

[2] *Grundlinien der Philosophie des Rechts*, 1821, § 257.

[3] *Op. cit.*, § 258.

[4] *Ibid.*

frontiers of the State; there is no general rule for the international community. 'With regard to the relation of States among themselves, their sovereignty is the basic principle; they are in that respect in the state of nature in relation to one another, and their rights are not realised in a general rule which is so constituted as to have power over them, but their rights are realised only through their particular wills.'[1] The people conceived as the State is the spirit in its substantial reason and its direct reality; it is therefore the absolute power on earth.[2] There is accordingly no other law for the State but the purpose of its own self, and the treaties concluded by it can be valid only so long as they correspond with this law. Here is the origin of the famous saying of Hegel, that the relation between States is a relation of 'independencies,' which stipulate between themselves but stand at the time above these stipulations.

It is this latter aspect which was stressed two generations later in a picturesque manner by Lasson, who exercised a strong influence upon German political theory of his time.[3] 'The moral person,' he says, 'which we call the State, is at the same time a sovereign person. It is an aim in itself. . . . It is unbounded and unlimited with regard to everything outside itself. . . . The State cannot, therefore, ever be subjected to a legal order or, speaking generally, to another will but its own. . . . It is an unbridled will of selfishness.'[4] The problem of order between States he regards not as a

[1] *Op. cit.*, § 333; see Duguit, *The Law and the State*, in *Harvard Law Review*, xxxi. (1917-1918) pp. 78-102, where Hegel's theory is discussed in detail, and Hobhouse, quoted below, *passim*. Cf. also Meinecke, *Die Idee der Staatsräson*, 1924, pp. 427-460; and Heller, *Hegel und der nationale Machtstaatsgedanke in Deutschland*, 1921, pp. 157-159.

[2] *Grundlinien der Philosophie des Rechts*, § 331.

[3] *Prinzip und Zukunft des Völkerrechts*, 1871, especially the chapter entitled 'States as Sovereign Moral Persons cannot be Members of a Legal or Moral Community' (pp. 12-31); see also his *Das Culturideal und der Krieg*, 1868 (re-edited in 1906).

[4] *Op. cit.*, p. 22.

question of law, but of mechanics. 'Two States are related to each other like two physical forces.'

As an example of the characteristic thoroughness with which Hegel's conception was relied upon by some German writers, the monograph of Professor E. Kaufmann on the *clausula rebus sic stantibus* may be referred to.[1] This book, which appeared in 1911, is no doubt perplexing because of the consistency with which the author draws the logical conclusions from the Hegelian dogma. That not a community of free men, but the victorious war, is the social ideal,[2] the victorious war being the ultimate judge over right and wrong between nations [3]—such a conclusion is likely to shock the majority of international lawyers who know how to express the Hegelian teaching in a more conventional form. But opinions of the kind voiced by Kaufmann, intolerable and repulsive as they may appear owing to the courage with which the author draws the inevitable conclusions from the basic conception of absolute international sovereignty, are well in keeping with the notion, current in and outside Germany, of the almost religious sanctity and absolute value attaching to the international rights of the State. And it must be admitted that the essence of this argument, namely, the adoption of the notorious *clausula*, not merely as a result of supervening impossibility of performance or of fulfilment of an express or implied condition, but as a general and comprehensive principle, is common to almost all writers on international law. Kaufmann does not see any possibility of a law between co-ordinated entities such as States are unless the principle be adopted that might is right.[4] The State must stand above its treaties; the law of co-ordination which is the basis of international law turns otherwise into that of subordination.[5] International treaties

[1] *Das Wesen des Völkerrechts und die clausula rebus sic stantibus*, 1911.

[2] *Op. cit.*, p. 146.

[3] *Ibid.*, p. 153.

[4] *Ibid.*, p. 151.

[5] *Ibid.*, p. 153.

which are based on the interests of the contracting parties must also, so far as their continuous duration is concerned, be determined by these interests.[1] The only objective rule is the right of self-preservation, which is the criterion of the international conduct of States, and which can never come into conflict with international law for the simple reason that international law is based on it.[2]

§ 22. *Its Influence outside Germany (English Idealistic Philosophy, Bosanquet). Its Predominance in International Law.*—Although there is no doubt that it was especially in Germany that these theories gained wide recognition,[3] it would nevertheless be a mistake to assume that they had no influence outside that country. The direct influence, for instance, of Hegelian philosophy upon English political thought cannot, it appears, be disputed. This is nowhere clearer than in the writings of Bernard Bosanquet, one of the most typical modern representatives of English idealistic philosophy, especially in his *Philosophical Theory of the State.* His theory is based on the 'will,' the general will, the objective spirit as distinguished from the volition of individuals. The State is, legally and morally, a supreme being not only in relation to its citizens, but also in relation to everything outside itself; its acts are public acts and cannot be judged by values of private 'organised morality.' 'It has no determined function in a larger community, but it is itself the supreme community; the guardian

[1] *Ibid.*, p. 181.

[2] Also, according to Jellinek, the greatest German jurisconsult in the domain of public law, it is the will of the State, which, through the act of self-limitation, creates international law. His views on this point may best be characterised in his own words defining the *clausula*: 'Whenever the observance of international law is found to be in conflict with the existence of the State, the rule of law retires to the background, because the State is put higher than any particular rule of law. . . . International law exists for States and not States for international law' (*Allgemeine Staatslehre*, 3rd ed., 1914, p. 377).

[3] For a typical exposition of this attitude, see Treitschke, *Politics*, English translation, 1916, vol. ii. pp. 587-670.

of a whole moral world, but not a factor within an organised world. Moral relations presuppose an organised life; but such a life is only within the State, not in relations between States and other communities.[1] The same applies to the sphere of law. In fact, he says, there can be no violation of law by the State, because an act which violates its own law is not an act of State, and, on the other hand, the State is not subject to the law of any other State.[2] Its public acts are acts 'of a supreme power which has ultimate responsibility for protecting the form of life of which it is the guardian, and which is not itself protected by any scheme of functions or relations, such as prescribes a course for the reconciliation of rights and secures its effectiveness.'[3]

With regard to the science of international law as such, it seems that certain historical influences combined, so far as the Latin and British-American group are concerned, to mitigate to a certain extent the rigidity of the Hegelian teaching. It was the idea of the rights of nationality and of human personality which influenced in that direction publicists like Fiore,[4] Bon-

[1] *Op. cit.*, 4th ed., 1923, p. 302. It is obviously misleading to describe (as does, for instance, Duguit in *Harvard Law Review, loc. cit.*) the whole German jurisprudence as identified with this anarchical conception of international law. Such names as Heffter and Bar, or—subject to inevitable war-time deflections—Liszt, Kohler, and Niemeyer, not to mention distinctly pacifistic international lawyers, as Wehberg and Schücking, should be sufficient to prevent too sweeping generalisations. What seems to be true is that the German theory of State was, far more than any other, under the influence of Hegel, and that it did not shrink from giving expression to what is no more than a natural result of a ruthless theory of absolute external sovereignty. This was recognised quite clearly by Sidgwick so far back as 1897 (see his *Lecture on Public Morality*). That these tendencies by no means belong to the past may be seen from a recent work of a distinguished German jurist (Julius Binder, *Die Philosophie des Rechts*, 1925, pp. 550-593), which is written in the best Hegelian vein and ends with the glorification of war as the crowning argument of the author's conception of international law.

[2] *Ibid.*, p. 303, n. 2. For a forcible refutation of the Hegelian conception of the State as represented by Bosanquet, see Hobhouse, *Metaphysical Theory of the State*, 1918.

[3] *Op. cit.*, p. 304.

[4] This does not apply, however, to some modern Italian positivists who follow closely in the footsteps of Hegel and his disciples. Cf., for instance, Anzilotti, *Rivista*, vii. (1913) p. 64, who takes the notorious saying of Hegel that States stand above their stipulations as a starting-point

fils, and Pradier-Fodéré. It was the fact that British-American international law never became completely divorced from the conception of international law as embodying not only positive rules set by sovereign States, but also principles of legal justice, reason, and equity, which considerably modified the current conception of the nature of the legal relations between States.[1] But it would serve no useful purpose to deny that the modern science of international law follows closely the Hegelian conception of State and sovereignty. Accordingly, it will not be found surprising that its expounders did not view with sympathy any larger reception of private law. For private law suggests

of his argument. But see now as to Anzilotti, *infra*, p. 59.

[1] See *supra*, p. 27, n. 1, and *infra*, p. 58, n. 1. Westlake may justly be quoted as the foremost representative of this aspect of modern British international law. Discussing the argument that the special character of the State as an indispensable institution puts it above the ordinary standards of law and morality, he says: 'But although it is certainly indispensable for the welfare of men that they should be associated in some tie, it does not follow that their welfare imperatively requires the maintenance in its actual limits, and with resources entirely unimpaired, of the particular State tie in which they happen to be engaged' (p. 113, *Collected Papers*). The following is his opinion on the right of self-preservation: 'it (self-preservation) is no doubt a primitive instinct and an absolute instinct so far as it has not been tamed by reason and law, but one great function of law is to tame it' (*ibid.*, p. 112).

It is interesting to note how this subjection of the State to a higher legal and moral purpose—and not its identification with these values—finds expression in the writings of T. H. Green, one of Bosanquet's predecessors in the leadership of English idealism. He says in his *Lectures on the Principles of Political Obligation*: 'The wrong resulting to human society from conflicts between States cannot be held to be lost in a higher right which attaches to the maintenance of the State as the institution through which alone the freedom of man is realised. It is not the State as such, but this or that particular State, which by no means fulfils its purpose, and which might perhaps be swept away and superseded by another with advantage to the ends for which the true State exists, that needs to defend its interest by actions injurious to those outside it' (p. 173). We note the important advance made upon Hegel's central idea. The State has, it is true, the highest legal and moral values as its ultimate object, but it is not identical with them. 'Hence there is no ground for holding that a State is justified in doing whatever its interests seem to require, irrespectively of effects on other men' (p. 173). This conception of the State as a moral being subject to legal and moral rules is given clear expression by Woolsey (*Introduction to the Study of International Law*, 1879, sec. 15): 'It would be strange if the State, that power which defines rights and makes them real, which creates moral persons or associations with rights and obligations, should have no such relations of its own—should be a physical and not a moral entity.'

subordination to an objective rule, and not a loose co-ordination of wills; it suggests interests valued by law and measured by it, but certainly not constituting the formal source and the ultimate legal foundation of its validity; it suggests mainly economic interests for the satisfaction of mainly economic wants, and not interests of a 'public,' higher, absolute value. Here lies the first main explanation of the current attitude to private law, and we shall therefore have to examine in further detail this aspect of the problem.[1]

§ 23. *The Second Aspect. The Positivist Doctrine and the Application of Private Law.*—The positivist doctrine, grounded as it is on the conception of international law based on the sovereign will of the State, constitutes, as mentioned above, the second aspect of the conception of international sovereignty. The connection between the positivist doctrine and the problem of private law is obviously a close one. For the will of the State as exclusively expressed by custom or treaty being *ex hypothesi* the only source of international law, the recourse to rules derived from other sources, *e.g.* from private law or natural law or morality, must needs be regarded as inadmissible and dangerous. Processes of juristic analogy are as a rule identical with extensive interpretation, and sovereign States cannot, it is said, be presumed to have agreed to an extension of their obligations (or, what is the same, to limitation of their sovereignty) as a result of recourse had to sources of law other than their express will. Of these sources, private law appears to the positivist mind as the most dangerous. For there is no system of legal rules more imposing and manifold, embodying more legal thought and legal experience, more likely to be called upon to supplement in case of emergency an undeveloped and

[1] See p. 71-75, *infra*.

rudimentary organism of law jealously guarding its own 'positivity' and self-sufficiency. This is the second main reason of the unfavourable reception with which private law has met in the domain of international public law. It is therefore to an examination of the positivist doctrine that we must now turn our attention.

II

THE POSITIVIST DOCTRINE. A CRITICAL EXAMINATION

§ 24. *Are the Positivist Writers truly 'Positivist'? Hall, Oppenheim, Liszt.*—Are positivist publicists in the position to build up a coherent system of international law while remaining at the same time faithful to the basic principle of positivism? When Bluntschli says that it does not depend upon the discretionary will of the State whether it should respect or reject international law;[1] or when Heffter asserts the existence of an international law emanating from necessity and not requiring therefore express recognition;[2] or when Westlake refers to reason as to one of the sources of international law,[3] we know that these writers, although their authority as expounders of existing international law is unimpugned, never regarded themselves, nor ever were regarded, as avowed adherents of the positivist doctrine. But when we see Hall, who is generally regarded as the leading English positivist, beginning the chapter on the 'General Principles of the Law governing States in their Normal Relations' with the statement that 'the ultimate foundation of international law is an assumption that States possess rights and are subject to duties corresponding to the facts of

[1] *Das moderne Völkerrecht*, 3rd ed., 1878, p. 60.
[2] § 3.
[3] Vol. i. pp. 14, 15.

their postulated nature,'[1] we are bound to ask: What is meant by an international law founded on an assumption which is in turn based on a conception of the postulated nature of the State? What have we to think of the positivism of a system which derives international rights and duties from an assumption, *i.e.* from a legal hypothesis, from an obligatory rule independent of the will of the State? It is true, however, that Hall never dogmatised on the necessity of positivism.

This cannot be said of Oppenheim, who states confidently that 'we know nowadays that a law of nature does not exist' and that 'only a positive law of nations can be a branch of the science of law.'[2] It is therefore fair to test the positivist doctrine by a reference to some relevant passages in his writings. Let us consider, for instance, the case of a State entering into the family of nations. Is it asked to consent to the existing rules? May it repudiate all or a part of them? Oppenheim's answer is quite clear: 'It is not necessary to prove for every single rule of international law that every single member of the family of nations consented to it. No single State can say on its admittance into the family of nations that it desires to be subjected to such and such rules of international law and not to the others.'[3] 'On the other hand,' he continues, 'no State which is a member of the family of nations can at some time or another declare that it will in future no longer submit to a certain recognised rule of the law of nations.' There are not many who would disagree with this statement. But then, it is submitted, the mere consent of States is no longer regarded as the necessary condition

[1] § 7.

[2] Vol. i. p. 116.

[3] Vol. i. p. 17; see also his article in *N.Z.*, xxv. (1915) p. 8, where he says: 'A rule is also then a rule of general international customary law, if all States which have come into the position of applying this rule have recognised it by custom, and when the number and the importance of these States is so great that one may assume that cogent interests of the international community are in the background of this rule.'

of the continued validity of a great number of international rules. Acquiescence on the part of a new State is not asked at all. It cannot repudiate a single rule. To this Oppenheim and other writers reply that its consent is implicitly given by the very fact of its applying for recognition. This, however, is no more than a fiction resorted to in order to conceal the objectively binding force of international law as independent of the will of the particular State.[1]

The impossibility of maintaining strictly the positivist attitude is clearly shown by Liszt, whose positivism finds expression in the widely accepted opinion that 'international law is contract, not statute.'[2] However, when dealing with the fundamental rights of nations, he is compelled to have recourse to the 'fundamental conception of international law as to the conception of different States with limited scopes of power and with mutually recognised competencies.'[3] These fundamental principles, he says, are not natural law fallacies, but legal notions which, in accordance with the logical rule of the excluded third, follow from the very conception of the family of nations, and which need not be expressly recognised as law, because without them international law would be impossible. This may be readily admitted, but then it is no longer positive international law, which, as he says, 'is contract, not statute.'

These comments are not meant as a general criticism of the positivist doctrine or of the theory of sovereignty.

[1] Cf. Westlake, *International Law*, vol. i. p. 49: 'Those therefore who lay it down that it is only by virtue of its consent to international law that a State is bound by it, are obliged to infer that consent from incidents in which we may be sure that nothing of the kind was thought of when they occurred. Practically the obligation is always assumed to exist, and it is therefore more reasonable to inquire what is its source than to strain inferences in order to prove that it has been admitted.' Kelsen, a powerful and original thinker, adds hardly anything to Westlake's argument on this question (*op. cit.*, pp. 224-228).

[2] P. 9.

[3] *Ibid.*, p. 115.

What is here put forward is not that States are so interdependent that, in their own interest, they needs must acknowledge the objectively binding force of some legal rules and that the positivist cannot therefore be upheld. The proof of such a thesis may safely be left to others.[1] What is urged here is that the rigid modern positivism as it appears in its current theoretical formulation does not furnish a suitable basis upon which a coherent system of international law can be built, and that positivist writers themselves are unable to follow it in their exposition of international law.

§ 25. *The Logical Necessity of an Objective International Law independent of the Will of the States. The Binding Force of Treaties.*—Is this failure on the part of positivist writers to conform with the chief postulates of their own teaching merely a deplorable lack of consistency, or is it due to a fault inherent in the positivist doctrine? The charge of inconsistency may be ruled out in view of the offence being committed so persistently by leading authorities, of whom Hall, Oppenheim, and Liszt have been mentioned only as typical instances. It is therefore necessary to inquire whether the failure is not unavoidable in the sense that the positivist doctrine is incompatible, in some of its aspects, with the postulates of juridical logic in its application to international law and with the conception of the family of nations as a community of equal [2] States. We are aided in this inquiry by a searching analysis of this side of the problem undertaken by Kelsen and Duguit, two publicists whose influence on the science of international law is now generally recognised. Kelsen points out that the con-

[1] See, for instance, Brierly in *B.Y.* (1924), pp. 4-16; Garner in *R.I.*, 3rd ser., vol. vi. (1924) pp. 36-58.

[2] The term 'equal' is used here in the meaning of equal protection by the law, not as connoting actual equality of rights and competencies. See Dickinson, *The Equality of States in International Law*, 1920, pp. 3-5, and Lorimer, vol. i. p. 171.

ception of a community of States which, notwithstanding actual differences in size, population, and real power, are deemed to be of the same value and possessed of mutually determined competencies, is in the first instance an essentially moral conception. As a legal notion, however, it is possible only with the aid of a juridical hypothesis, namely, that

'There is, above the commonwealth described as the State, a legal order which defines the respective scopes of power of individual States by forbidding the encroachment of one into the sphere of another . . . a legal order which regulates the relations of States by means of rules equally applicable to all. International law does this—but only when its supremacy over the legal systems of individual States is recognised, when . . . it is contemplated as a legal system standing above the States, *i.e.* when the legal systems of individual States are regarded as component parts of a universal legal order.' [1]

Duguit, in an argument almost identical with that of Kelsen, lays stress on the fact that the notion of fundamental rights, which attempts to reconcile the doctrine of sovereignty with the existence of an international law, turns in a vicious circle :

'In order that the personality should be able to possess subjective rights, it is necessary that it should be related to other personalities ; it is necessary that there should be a society subjected to an objective law. It is impossible to explain objective international law by the existence of fundamental subjective rights of States, because such rights cannot exist without there being a society of nations subjected to an objective international law.' [2]

[1] *Der Begriff der Souveränität und die Theorie des Völkerrechts*, 1920, p. 205.

[2] *Traité de droit constitutionnel*, 1921, vol. i. p. 557. This part of Duguit's teaching is quite independent of his rejection of the juristic personality of the State. Compare here the preamble to the *Declaration of the Rights and Duties of Nations* adopted by the American Institute of International Law, January 8, 1916 ('Whereas, the nation is a moral or juristic person,

This reasoning is not a new one. No writer, for instance, realised the theoretical inaccuracy of the positivist conception of the independent will of States more clearly than Lorimer, who saw in the very claim to recognition 'a logical abandonment of independence.'[1]

Similar considerations apply to the question of the binding force of treaties and of the juridical character of the rule *pacta sunt servanda* which constitutes the basis of conventional international law. The explanation usually given by writers, who point either to the fear of the consequences of a wanton breach of a treaty, or to the well-being of the community of nations which would be impossible without the regular observance of treaties, cannot be regarded as satisfactory. The lawyer called upon to answer the question why crime is forbidden obviously leaves his proper field if he answers by referring to the fear of punishment on the part of would-be offenders. The appropriate answer is that which points to the existence of a legal rule commanding or forbidding a certain line of conduct. Now, a legal rule is an objective norm independent of the will of the person who is bound by it. To say that the binding force of treaties is derived from the will of contracting parties who, through an act of self-limitation, give up a part of their sovereignty, is to leave unanswered the query why the treaty continues to be binding after the will of one party has undergone a change. The will of the parties can never be the ultimate source of the binding force of a contract whose continued validity is necessarily grounded in a higher objective rule.

The will of the parties, no doubt, creates law between

the creature of law, and subordinated to law, as is the natural person in political society . . .'). The same is the attitude of Krabbe, *The Modern Idea of State* (English translation), 1919, especially pp. 244-248; and Salvioli, *Rivista*, xiv. (1921-1922), p. 49, n.

[1] Vol. i. p. 140.

them, and if, for instance, Salmond enumerates custom, statute, and agreements as sources of law,[1] one can hardly raise an objection against such an assertion. But from a more general point of view what appears to those directly concerned as an immediate source of the obligation is only a condition under which a higher, more comprehensive rule shall become operative. Thus the will of the parties is only a condition under which the higher rule, *i.e.* that promises should be kept, comes into operation.[2] It is a rule of municipal law which, as between individuals, gives legal force to promises; it is the objective validity, independent of the will of States, of the rule *pacta sunt servanda* which renders legally possible the working of conventional international law.

It is especially in recent years that this elementary truth is being stressed by publicists. But we find already in Bluntschli's treatise a lucid statement of the same problem. He says:

> 'It does not depend upon the discretionary will of the State whether it should respect or reject international law. . . . If international law were only the product of the free will of the individual States, then all international law would really be a law of contract, which means that no State would be under the obligation to another State to respect international law where its rules are not sanctioned by a treaty. Moreover, it is not clear why, in this case, treaties should bind States also after they have changed their mind, and why every change of the will is not a change of the law.' [3]

Later Bar[4] asked the same question and urged the logical necessity of grounding international conventional law

[1] *Jurisprudence*, 6th ed., 1920, p. 119.

[2] Cf. Duguit, *op. cit.*, pp. 562 ff.

[3] 1878, p. 60.

[4] *Grundlage und Kodifikation des Völkerrechts, Archiv für Rechts- und Wirtschaftsphilosophie*, vi. (1912) p. 145.

on an objective rule. Recently the writings of Nelson,[1] Kelsen,[2] Duguit,[3] Krabbe,[4] Salvioli,[5] and Verdross[6] have, it seems, done much to shatter the uncritical dogma of the will of the State as the ultimate foundation of conventional international law. The science of international law, while recognising that it is the business of international lawyers to expound law as it is and not as it should be, is now increasingly realising that dogmatic positivism as taught by a generation of jurists fascinated by the splendour of the doctrine of sovereignty is a barren idea, foreign both to facts and to the requirements of a scientific system of law.[7] Nothing

[1] *Rechtswissenschaft ohne Recht*, 1917, *passim.*

[2] *Op. cit.*, pp. 162-174. It will be observed how clearly the formal basis of Kelsen's theory, namely, the necessity of adopting certain ultimate principles underived from any legal source proper, is set forth in Salmond's *Jurisprudence* (1st ed., 1902; see now 7th ed., 1924, § 48).

[3] *Loc. cit.*

[4] *Loc. cit.*

[5] *Loc. cit.*, and, previously, Perassi in *Rivista*, xi. (1917) pp. 195-223.

[6] *Die Einheit des rechtlichen Weltbildes auf Grundlage der Völkerrechtsverfassung*, 1923, pp. 120-125; *Die Verfassung der Völkerrechtsgemeinschaft*, 1926, pp. 28-33.

[7] It is, perhaps, not yet sufficiently realised that the dogmatic positivism of ten years ago is no longer predominant. The renaissance of natural law is finding its way from legal philosophy and from municipal law into the domain of international law where the influence of the new ideas was facilitated by the depressing consciousness of the inadequacy of rigid positivist method. Needless to say, it is not the old law of nature, it is rather the modern 'natural law with changing contents,' 'the sense of right,' 'the social solidarity,' or the 'engineering' law in terms of promoting the ends of the international society. Cf., in addition to the authors referred to in this paragraph, Pound, *Philosophical Theory and International Law, Bibliotheca Visseriana*, vol. i. pp. 73-90. See also Le Fur in *R.I.*, 3rd ser., vol. vi. (1925) pp. 59-79, Bourquin, *ibid.*, 3rd ser., vol. vii. (1926) pp. 106-110, and Cathrein, *Die Grundlage des Völkerrechts*, 1918, *passim.* It may be useful, for the purpose of illustration of the present position, to refer to a recent inquiry instituted by Prof. Niemeyer (*N.Z.*, xxxiv. (1925) pp. 113-189). In a circular letter addressed to a number of international lawyers, he asked for an opinion whether the law of nature conception of international law as taught by Grotius is valid to-day—that is, whether it may be resorted to by international tribunals as a source of decision for the purpose of supplementing and interpreting customary and conventional international law. It is significant that out of forty-one answers which have reached the editor only eleven were in the negative, whereas seventeen may be regarded as given in the affirmative. There are, in addition, nine answers which, although adhering formally to the positivist principle, give in fact an affirmative reply to the question. Prof. De Louter, for instance, the author of the well-known treatise on *Positive International Law*, says: 'Only in cases where there is no rule or where the law is silent or uncertain is the judicial authority free . . . to decide upon grounds of higher

will illustrate this change more clearly than the following two quotations from the writings of Anzilotti, one of the leading continental positivists. 'States,' he said in 1913,[1] 'are bound because and so far only as they wish to be bound. Even the obligatory force of the rule *pacta sunt servanda* is derived from nothing else than from the collective will of States. . . . The norm which postulates the carrying out of obligations validly contracted ceases to be operative when, logically, the will of States ceases.' However, writing ten years later, he abandons that part of the orthodox positivist doctrine which deduces the rule *pacta sunt servanda* from the will of the State. He conceives of it as of 'a primary norm, over and above which there is no other norm which could explain it juridically (*che ne spieghi la giuridicità*), and which the science of law accepts nevertheless as a hypothesis or an indemonstrable postulate.'[2]

justice—provided always that the source of decision is expressly mentioned.' The answer is so far quite in the affirmative. The restriction which follows is of a more technical character: 'Thus a permanent jurisprudence will gradually evolve which, however, will become law proper only through custom or treaty.' Prof. Politis, while denying that international tribunals are authorised to supplement international law by recourse to principles of the law of nature, says: 'Les principes du droit naturel, d'après la théorie de Grotius, doivent inspirer les juges et les arbitres dans l'interprétation du droit international positif, car ils en sont l'indispensable complément.' This is in fact an affirmative reply to the question, for it is most frequently in the way of extensive interpretation that the supplementing of rules of law by judicial tribunals takes place.

It seems that, quite apart from the doctrine enunciated by Blackstone ('The law of nations . . . is here adopted to its full extent by the common law'), which is in itself an expression of the objective validity of international law,—British (and American) judges and publicists, both positivists and naturalists, were never inclined to commit themselves to the dogmatising tendencies of continental positivism. From Lord Stowell, who regarded the view, that international law depends merely on convention, as adopted only by Barbary pirates (*The Helena*, 4 Rob. 7), through Phillimore to Maine and Westlake, there is in this regard a significant uniformity. 'We must either admit that modern international law is a law founded on cosmopolitan principles of reason, a true living offshoot of the Law of Nature, or ignore our most authoritative expositions of it,' says Sir Frederick Pollock (*Essays in the Law*, 1922, p. 67). See also *supra*, p. 27, n. 5.

[1] *Rivista*, vii. (1913) pp. 64, 65.

[2] *Corso*, 1923, p. 40.

III

THE PRACTICE OF STATES AND THE POSITIVIST DOCTRINE

§ 26. *The Practice of States. 'General Principles of Law,' 'Principles of Justice,' and 'Principles of Equity' in Arbitration Conventions.*—It has been shown that the rigid positivist doctrine inevitably comes to grief on the fact that neither the conception of international law as a whole nor the binding force of conventional international law can consistently be based on the dogma of the will of the States as the exclusive source of international law. However, it is not only theoretical considerations, but also the very practice of States and of international tribunals, that point to an answer in the same direction. Sovereign States, when entering into arbitration agreements, general or particular, frequently define the rules which the international judge or arbitrator is instructed to follow in rendering his decision. What is, in such cases, the law which they wish to see applied ? Is it only such rules as are expressly recognised by conventional or customary international law, or are the judges competent, in the absence of rules of this kind, to decide on the ground of other legal principles ? If it is possible to show that States adopt the latter view, then clearly the theoretical argument advanced above receives corroboration which should be decisive. For there is no better evidence of the legal conviction of governments than those international acts and agreements in which States formulate the law to be followed by international judicial tribunals. These agreements show that almost in all cases in which an international tribunal of arbitration is required to adjudicate, not upon a certain specified claim or the interpretation of a particular convention,[1] but upon a greater number of diverse claims, either specified or as yet undetermined—that is, *prima facie*, in all cases of general arbitration conventions—the law which the arbitrators are instructed to apply is not international law solely and exclusively.

In general arbitration conventions or in treaties establishing international courts and tribunals, the judges and arbitrators are usually instructed to render their decision in accordance either with principles 'of justice, equity, and the law of nations,'[2] or with 'principles of justice, the law of nations, and treaty provisions,'[3] or with 'principles of justice, of equity, and the stipulations of the treaty,'[4] or with 'justice and equity,'[5] or 'in conformity with principles of international law and considerations of equity,'[6] or according to what the arbitrator will deem 'most just,'[7] or, as in the Hague Conventions for the Pacific Settlement of

[1] In these cases the parties either formulate *in concreto* the rules of law to be followed by the tribunal (see British Guiana arbitration, § 101, *infra*, or Alaska Boundary arbitration, § 104, *infra*), or, when the dispute is one as to facts only, refrain from formulating special rules. See, on this point, the award in the Cayuga Indian Claims case before the British-American Claims Arbitral Tribunal, January 1926, *A.J.*, xx. (1926) p. 582. There are, however, many special arbitration agreements in which rules of equity, etc., are referred to as a basis of decision. See, for instance, Agreement of July 1913 between France, Great Britain, Spain, and Portugal (*A.J.*, viii. (1914), Suppl., p. 165), and Agreement of June 1921 between the United States and Norway (*A.J.*, xvii. (1923) p. 362).

[2] Article vii. of the Jay Treaty of 1794 between the United States and Great Britain, Moore, p. 317; United States and Spain, 1795, *ibid.*, p. 999.

[3] United States and Mexico, 1839, Manning, *Arbitration Treaties among the American Nations*, 1924, p. 15. The award in the Cayuga Indian Claims, *loc. cit.*, enumerates twelve other treaties of this kind.

[4] United States and Costa Rica, 1860, Moore, p. 1551; United States and Ecuador, 1862, *ibid.*, p. 1569; United States and Venezuela, 1866, Manning, p. 69.

[5] United States and Colombia, 1857, Moore, p. 1361; United States and Peru, 1868, Manning, p. 79; Guatemala and Mexico, 1888, *ibid.*, p. 174; Guatemala and Great Britain, 1859, Hertslet's *Treaties*, xi. p. 345. For other treaties of this type, see award in the Cayuga Indian Claims, *loc. cit.*

[6] United States, Germany, and Great Britain, 1899, *Treaty Series*, 1900, No. 10 (Samoa Claims arbitration).

[7] Delagoa Railway arbitration, § 28, *infra*; Pious Fund arbitration, § 112, *infra*; Great Britain and United States, 1896, *Treaty Series*, 1896, No. 10.

International Disputes, 'on the basis of respect of law'; or, as in Article 7 of the unratified Hague Convention XII. relative to the Establishment of an International Prize Court, in accordance with treaty provisions, with international law, and, in the absence of rules from these two sources, 'in accordance with the general principles of justice and equity'; or, as in the Convention establishing the British-American Claims Arbitral Tribunal of 1910,[1] in accordance 'with treaty rights and with the principles of international law and equity'; or, as in the Statute of the Permanent Court of International Justice, according to conventional and customary international law and 'general principles of law recognised by civilised States.'[2]

§ 27. *Does this Practice amount to the Creation of a New Customary Rule? Its Bearing upon the Positivist Doctrine.*—These instances, especially the last one, which is the most authoritative, suggest clearly that the ordinary customary and conventional rules of international law are regarded by governments as insufficient for the purpose of judicial settlement of international disputes. Arbitration treaties, either general or particular, in which international law only is referred to as a source of decision, constitute a very rare exception.[3] The importance of these arbitration provisions is enhanced by the fact that the determination of the sources of law to be applied is usually one of the most important items in negotiations preceding the arbitration agree-

[1] § 131, *infra*.

[2] Numerous recent arbitration and conciliation treaties contain the same provision. See, *e.g.*, Germany and Switzerland, 1921, *League of Nations Treaty Series*, xii. p. 281, and Germany and Sweden, 1924, *ibid.*, vol. lii. p. 111.

[3] See, for instance, the Convention of 1907 establishing the Central American Court of Justice (*A.J.*, Suppl., ii. (1908) p. 219). Several arbitration treaties, while mentioning international law only as a source of decision, reserve to the signatories the right to provide the arbitrator with special rules in particular cases (see, for instance, Brazil and Chile, 1899, Manning, p. 259; Argentina and Bolivia, 1902, *ibid.*, p. 316; Argentina and Chile, 1902, *ibid.*, p. 328).

ment,[1] and that it represents therefore the considered judgment of governments.

A convinced positivist will say that these facts do not disprove the positivist doctrine, considering that it is only by virtue of the will of the interested States that those general principles of law become applicable. This may be granted, but what is really granted is that *there is a customary rule of international law to the effect that rules of law otherwise independent of custom and treaty are to be regarded as binding in individual cases.* This sounds paradoxical, but it is the only way in which the practice and the legal conviction of States can be put within the accepted formula. Only with the proviso that it is a customary rule of international law that rules of equity, of justice, of law, or of general principles of law should, in the absence of accepted rules of positive international law, be resorted to as a source of decision, does the usual positivist statement convey a true notion.

§ 28. *'General Principles of Law,' 'Principles of Justice,' and 'Principles of Equity' as connoting Legal Rules* par excellence *in Contradistinction to Decisions* ex aequo et bono.—It would be a grave mistake to assume that in all those cases in which, in contradistinction to rules of international law proper, rules of 'justice,' of 'equity,' and of 'general principles of law' are resorted to, the field of judicial settlement is abandoned, and a settlement *ex aequo et bono* on a non-judicial basis adopted. This is nowhere clearer than in Article 38 of the Permanent Court of International Justice, which,

[1] See the award of October 1922 in the arbitration between Norway and the United States, *A.J.*, xvii. (1923) p. 383. See also the award in the *Cayuga Indian Claims* (January 1926, American and British Claims Arbitral Tribunal), *A.J.*, xx. (1926) p. 585, where arbitration conventions are quoted in which the arbitrators were referred to different grounds of decision with regard to different questions to be decided by them.

after having adopted 'the general principles of law as recognised by civilised nations' as an ordinary source of decision, states in conclusion: 'This provision shall not prejudice the power of the Court to decide a case *ex aequo et bono*, if the parties agree thereto.' Similar provisions are contained in several arbitration conventions.[1] But unless the arbitrator is expressly instructed to settle the dispute *ex aequo et bono*, he is under the obligation to decide according to principles of legal justice.[2] This is generally recognised not only by publicists, but also by arbitrators. The arbitrator in the Walfisch arbitration between Great Britain and Germany[3] says, for example:

> 'Considering that both questions must be solved in conformity with the principles and positive rules of public international law, and, where they fail, in conformity with the general principles of law, since neither the said Agreement of 1890 nor the supplementary Declaration of Berlin the 30th January, 1909, in any ways authorise the arbitrator to base his decision on other rules, and it is notorious, according to constant theory and practice, that such authority cannot be presumed . . .'

The learned arbitrator was no doubt right in assuming that this is the practice followed by international tribunals.[4]

[1] See Manning, pp. 359, 443, 450.

[2] See Lammasch, *Rechtskraft*, pp. 48-55; the same, *Lehre*, pp. 175-186; Oppenheim, ii. p. 27.

[3] Martens, *N.R.G.*, 3rd ser., vi. p. 429.

[4] It is to be regretted that some writers, prompted no doubt by the laudable desire to establish the necessity of a regular court of international justice, thought it necessary to base their argument on the misleading assertion that arbitration as existing before the establishment of the Permanent Court of International Justice was non-judicial and mainly employed in effecting compromises. Nothing could be more open to doubt. It is only in exceptional cases that arbitrators, expressly so instructed by the parties, act as 'amicable referees' (see, for instance, the award in the *Alsop Claim* of July 5, 1911, where King George v. acted as an '*amiable compositeur*' in virtue of the arbitration agreement; *A.J.*, v. (1911) p. 1079). The author ventures to submit that the overwhelming majority of awards hitherto rendered by arbitral tribunals are based on strictly legal considerations in form and in substance. The distinction between arbitration and judicial settlement lies in an en-

Neither does the expression 'rules of equity' mean that the arbitrator is free to deviate from the path of law proper. Although some arbitrators refuse to accept this term in its technical meaning as understood in the English-American jurisprudence,[1] they never confuse it with a settlement *ex aequo et bono*. Rules of equity are rules of law both in municipal law and in international arbitration. Thus the unratified general arbitration

tirely different sphere, namely, in the fact that the Permanent Court of International Justice is, in contradistinction to a tribunal of arbitration, a Court with a permanent body of judges, with a fixed and well-ordered procedure and with rules of law determined once and for all. As an example of this misjudging of the character of international arbitration, Dr. Wehberg's book entitled *The Problem of an International Court of Justice* (English translation, 1918, pp. 16-42) may be mentioned. The author, who is championing the cause of an International Court of Justice, does it by grossly exaggerating the element of compromise contained in the individual arbitral awards. The assertion, for instance, that the Behring Sea award is a compromise is certainly misleading. A perusal of both the minutes of the deliberations of the arbitrators leaves no doubt as to the strictly judicial method pursued by the tribunal. The compromise, if any, is contained in the regulations recommended by the tribunal by virtue of the mandate conferred upon it in Article VII. of the Treaty of February 29, 1892. On the other hand, a writer who criticises the decision in the British-Venezuelan arbitration of 1899 as being a compromise, would nevertheless find it difficult to suggest what would be a strictly legal decision in this case. It is to be regretted that the tribunal failed to give a reasoned decision, but it shows a certain disregard of the extraordinary intricacies of this case to speak of a compromise pure and simple. As to the Savarkar case, the Venezuelan Preferential Claim case, and many others, it is clear that Dr. Wehberg and many others disagree with the decisions arrived at by the arbitrators, but no useful purpose is served in describing as a compromise a decision of which a particular author does not approve. Cf. here especially, as corroborating the view put forward in this note, T. W. Balch, *Legal and Political Questions between Nations*, 1924, pp. 22-35; Moore, quoted by Hyde, ii. 112, n. 2; Ralston, pp. xxxv-xxxvii, and Hedges in *B.Y.* (1926), pp. 110-120. When, therefore, it is being said that 'the Court of Arbitration is equitable, the Court of Justice legal' (Scott, *Sovereign States and Suits*, 1925, p. 242), the saying is to be understood rather as indicating the need of two separate organs for settling disputes than as suggesting that the strictly legal element was entirely lacking in international arbitration prior to the establishment of the Permanent Court of International Justice. It is quite possible, although neither probable nor inevitable, that with the establishment of the Permanent Court of International Justice, which is a judicial court *par excellence*, the Permanent Court of Arbitration and other *ad hoc* established tribunals will gradually assume the character of organs deciding exclusively *ex aequo et bono*. The author confesses to some doubts as to the desirability of such a development. Cf. here Loder, in *Bulletin de l'Institut Interméd. Internat.*, ix., October 1923, pp. 258-285; and Brown, in *R.I.*, 3rd series, vol. v. (1924) pp. 317-332.

[1] See, for instance, the award in the arbitration between the United States and Norway, *A.J.*, xvii. (1923) p. 384.

treaty of August 3, 1911, between Great Britain and the United States describes, in Article 1, as justiciable such disputes as are 'susceptible of decision by the application of the principles of law or equity.'[1] In many cases decided by the British-American Claims Arbitral Tribunal under the Convention of 1910 the arbitrator disallowed claims unsupported by rules 'of international law and of equity' (such being the terms of submission), although he recognised that a judgment governed by considerations *ex aequo et bono* could not have disregarded the claims in question; he appealed in such cases to the respective governments to effect a payment—as an act of grace.[2]

The term 'justice' is used in arbitration conventions in the meaning of legal justice, and it is in this manner that it is interpreted by arbitral tribunals. In the Delagoa Railway arbitration, for instance, the arbitrator had to decide according to what he would deem 'most just.' '*Cette clause*,' says the judgment, '*n'exclut pas, elle implique, au contraire, pour lui l'obligation de déterminer au préalable quelle est la législation qui devra le*

[1] For the text of the Treaty, see *A.J.*, Suppl., v. (1911) p. 254.

[2] Cf. here the award in Claim No. 36 under the British-American Claims Arbitral Tribunal of 1910 (*Eastern Extension, Australasia and China Telegraph Company*): 'As to the contention that, having regard to the terms of Article 7 of the special agreement providing for the settlement of these claims, this tribunal is to decide, "in accordance with treaty rights and with the principles of international law and of equity," compensation in this case should be paid on the ground of equity, the following observations may be made. If the strict application of a treaty or of a specific rule of international law conduct to a decision which, however justified from a legal point of view, will result in hardship unjustified having regard to the special circumstances of the case, then it is the duty of this tribunal to do their best to avoid such a result, so far as it may be possible, by recommending, for instance, some course of action by way of grace on the part of the respondent government' (*A.J.*, xviii. (1924) p. 840). See also the *Cadenhead* case, *A.J.*, viii. (1914) p. 665; the *Home Missionary Society* case, *ibid.*, xv. (1921) p. 297; the *David J. Adams* case, *ibid.*, xvi. (1922) p. 323. Several cases before this Tribunal gave occasion for a learned discussion by counsel on both sides of the question as to the meaning of equity. See, for instance, the discussion in the *Eastern Extension, Australasia and China Telegraph Company Ltd.* case, Nielsen, pp. 51-72. As to the *Hardman* case and the *Cayuga Indian Claims* case, see §§ 133 and 134, *infra*, respectively.

guider dans la recherche de la solution "juste."'[1] The arbitrator called upon to decide in accordance with justice has here recourse to rules of law, more especially to such rules of private law as seem to him most comprehensive and of universal application. We have seen before that 'principles of universal jurisprudence' so frequently resorted to by international publicists prove ultimately to be identical with general principles of private law.[2] The same applies, with even greater force, to those 'principles of justice' and 'generally recognised rules of law' which, in the overwhelming majority of cases, are referred to in arbitration conventions, and without resort to which no regular judicial settlement of international disputes is possible in the present stage of international law. The history of international arbitration supplies, as will be shown later, continuous proof of this contention.

§ 29. *Article* 38 (3) *of the Statute of the Permanent Court of International Justice.*—Article 38 (3) is only the natural result of experience gained in the course of a long period of judicial settlement of international disputes. Concluding, as it does, a chapter of embarrassing uncertainty as to the sources of law to be applied by international tribunals, it is most instructive from many points of view. It signifies the final and authoritative abandonment of the misleading doctrine that international law is a self-sufficing body of rules. The discussions conducted on this subject by the members of the Committee of Jurists charged with the drafting of the Statute show clearly that the authors of the draft were conscious of the importance of the rule adopted ultimately by the Committee.[3] What, until now, was done spontaneously

[1] *Sentence finale du Tribunal Arbitral du Delagoa*, 1900, p. 154; see also § 128, *infra.*

[2] See pp. 33-37, *supra.*

[3] See *Proceedings of the Committee of Jurists*, pp. 293-339, and especially the speech of the Chairman, Baron Descamps, '*On the Rules of Law to be Applied*,' p. 323.

by individual arbitrators and in individual arbitration conventions, received here the sanction of practically the whole family of nations. What was, until now, exposing international arbitration to the reproach that it was not judicial, has here been included as a source of decision of the international judicial tribunal *par excellence.*

That international law is still incomplete and leaves unanswered many a problem, was the unanimous opinion of the whole Committee. But while the minority insisted that the Court should in such cases pronounce a *non liquet* and declare itself incompetent, the view prevailed that such a declaration would in particular cases amount to a denial of justice.[1] The result of the lengthy discussions, although embodying a compromise,[2] constitutes a definite rejection of the dogmatic positivist view. The Article as proposed by the Committee and as incorporated in the Statute runs as follows:

'The Court shall apply—

'1. International conventions, whether general or particular, establishing rules expressly recognised by the contesting States;

'2. International custom, as evidence of a general practice accepted as law;

'3. The general principles of law recognised by civilised nations;

[1] See *Proceedings*, pp. 296 (Hagerup), 311 (Loder), 317 (Lapradelle); on the other side, Root, p. 308.—It is illustrative of the attitude of governments that among the official proposals for the establishment of an international court, which the Committee took to a large extent as a basis for its discussions, there was none which restricted the source of law applicable by the Court to customary and conventional international law. Thus the five Neutral Powers proposed that in the absence of treaty provisions and of recognised rules of international law the arbitrator should enter judgment according to its own opinion of what the rule of international law on the subject should be; Switzerland proposed for that event 'principles of justice and equity,' and Germany 'principles of law and equity' (see Annex to the *Proceedings*).

[2] The expression 'general principles of law recognised by civilised nations' was, at the instance of Mr. Root and Lord Phillimore, substituted for the term 'legal conscience of civilised peoples' as proposed by the Chairman of the Committee.

'4. Subject to the provisions of Article 59, judicial decisions and the teachings of the most highly qualified publicists of the various nations, as subsidiary means for the determination of rules of law.

'This provision shall not prejudice the power of the Court to decide a case *ex aequo et bono*, if the parties agree thereto.'

The will of States as expressed in treaties, or, failing that, in international custom, remains thus the primary source of law. If, however, these sources are silent, the Court, far from having to declare its incompetence, is bound to pronounce on the basis of general principles of law which are thus definitely recognised as a subsidiary source of international law. What remains now is to answer the question, What is the exact meaning of those 'general principles of law as recognised by civilised nations'? Bearing in mind that they are not identical with decisions *ex aequo et bono*, which are dealt with separately, we may point to three sources from which the answer to the question may be drawn. (*a*) It may be drawn, firstly, from the study of international arbitration before the establishment of the Permanent Court of International Justice. Such an investigation, to which the last part of this monograph is devoted, shows that whenever international tribunals have recourse to 'general principles of law' they apply, as a rule, a general principle of private law, *i.e.* a principle not belonging to the system of law prevalent in one country, but expressing a rule of uniform application in all or in the main systems of private jurisprudence.

(*b*) The query may be answered, secondly, on the ground of a simple logical inference drawn from the context of Article 38 (3). The Statute refers here to such general principles of law as are neither international law proper nor considerations *ex aequo et bono*. This means that although the Court may apply, for the purpose of a particular case, a rule of criminal or administrative law of sufficient generality, it is of general rules of private law that, on the whole, we must needs think in this connection.[1] For it is, as a rule, private law which gives shape and definite form to those general sources. Here lies the organising and ordering part played by it. Those 'general principles' threaten otherwise to degenerate into altogether subjective natural law or legal philosophy.[2]

(*c*) Thirdly, the utterances of jurists drafting the Statute do not fail to throw some light on the meaning of the clause in question. Thus the Chairman of the Committee, from whom the substance of the clause originated, explained its meaning by reference to the principle of *res iudicata* adopted by the tribunal in the Pious Fund case; and another member suggested, while referring to that case, that this was a rule which had the same character of law as any written law, and that all such general principles of common law, being a part of international law, are applicable to international affairs.[3]

[1] The proposition put forward in the text is corroborated by the following passage contained in the resolution of the Institute of International Law, adopted at its meeting of September 1925, and dealing with the question of extinctive prescription (limitation of actions): 'Practical considerations of order, of stability and of peace, long accepted in arbitral jurisprudence, should include the limitation of actions for obligations between States among the general principles of law recognised by civilised nations, which international tribunals are called upon to apply.' See also Anzilotti, *Corso*, 1923, p. 64: '. . . essi non sono, o almeno non sono soltanto, i principî generali dell' ordinamento giuridico internazionale sono, in genere, i principî giuridici ammessi dai popoli civili; una specie . . . di novissimo *ius gentium* nel senso classico.'

[2] It may or may not be accurate when some authors say that, to mention one instance, the adoption of rules governing fluvial accretion is not analogy to private law, but simply application of common sense. But even granting the accuracy of such a statement, it does not say anything else than that it is a rule of private law which embodies here a principle of common sense. Most rules of law embody a principle of common sense, but frequently it takes, within the society of nations, decades or centuries of strife to bestow upon an obvious principle of common sense the authority of a rule of law. It is private law which, by supplying in many cases the formulation of principles of legal reason and legal justice, smoothes the way and suggests the solution.

[3] Lord Phillimore, p. 316, *op. cit.* He pointed out in another place (p. 335) that the general principles of law were those accepted by all nations *in foro domestico*, such as certain principles of procedure, the principles

Thus Article 38 not only shows, upon analysis, a refutation of extreme positivist tendencies, but also indicates what is the true nature of those general principles of law to which it refers. It corroborates the conclusions reached in this section, namely, that the rejection of private law is, in so far as it is prompted by current positivist notions, hardly warranted by facts; that the positivist doctrine can be accepted, if it is accepted at all, only when it is understood that there is a customary rule of international law to the effect that the actual will of States as evidenced by custom and treaty may, when necessary, be supplemented by such rules and principles as correspond to the nature of the legal relations between them, to rules of justice, and to general principles of law; and, finally, that those general principles of law are for most practical purposes identical with general principles of private law.

IV

THE POLITICAL ASPECT OF THE DOCTRINE OF SOVEREIGNTY. THE 'SPECIAL CHARACTER' OF INTERNATIONAL LAW

§ 30. *The 'Special Character' of International Law and the Application of Private Law.*—Although the positivist argument for the repudiation of private law is most frequently resorted to, it is not the only one in the field.

of good faith, of *res iudicata*, etc. On Article 38 (3), see Salvioli, *Rivista*, xvi. (1924) pp. 276-284; Llanas, in *R.I.* (Geneva), ii. (1924) pp. 295-298 — "Estos principios de Derecho Natural, no solamente son la piedra de toque del Derecho positivo, y la norma subsidiariamente imperativa, cuando faltan los tratados o la costumbre, o cuando es necesario suplir sus lagunas y deficiencias, sino que influyen notablemente en la interpretación del derecho positivo'; Verzijl in *R.I.*, 3rd ser., vol. vi. (1925) pp. 738-742; Anzilotti, *loc. cit.*; Kosters, *Les Fondements du Droit des Gens, Bibliotheca Visseriana*, vol. iv. (1925) pp. 214-216; and Verdross, *Die Verfassung der Völkerrechtsgemeinschaft*, pp. 60-67, 69-75.

For the rejection of private law is, to a considerable extent, prompted by the conviction that the interests protected by international law are fundamentally different from those regulated by private law. It is the conviction embodied in that conception of the absolute value of the State which, under the influence of the idealistic philosophy and political theory, was determining the trend of modern international law.[1] The possibility of private law playing any part at all in the development of international law is therefore conditioned by a previous abandonment of that political aspect of the doctrine of sovereignty and by the acceptance of the view that acts of States and of their organs are actions of men, for ordinary human purposes, governed by standards of justice and morality accepted by States and their peoples within their territories, and that the interests of States are only in degree different from those protected by other collective bodies or from interests of individuals. It is also dependent upon the realisation of the fact that the well-known argument on the inadmissibility of analogy to private law because of the absolute difference of the subjects and objects of law in the two branches of jurisprudence is stronger in its dogmatic formulation than in its substance.

§ 31. *The Alleged Supremacy and Heterogeneity of Interests protected by International Law.*—It is now gradually being recognised that there is nothing in the interests protected by international law which is fundamentally different from those protected by municipal and private law. The conception of their being 'eternal and inalienable' in the sense that they are exclusively creative of rights and not amenable to duties is rightly being repudiated. It might be said that interests of individuals are chiefly economic, whereas those of States

[1] See pp. 44-50, *supra*.

are political in their character; but even if this be so, it ought not to be forgotten that, as a rule, the political activities of States in the field of international relations are primarily devoted to safeguarding collective economic interests, no matter under what disguise they happen to appear. What gave to them, and still gives, that mysterious aspect of absolute heterogeneity and supremacy is the deeply rooted conviction that the special sanctity attaching to them justifies, *pro foro externo*, the State's independence of those common standards of law and right which govern the relations of individuals under the sway of municipal law.[1] In the measure in which the necessities of international intercourse or public opinion force the governments to give up this postulated independence of law, international law advances and develops. Along with this, the conviction must gain in strength that between individuals, autonomous groups, and States there is a legal difference of degree only.

§ 32. *The Alleged Fundamental Difference of Subjects of Law. (A Note on the Present Position of the Doctrine of*

[1] How great is the influence of that common conception of the 'public' character of international law, and of the necessity of establishing different standards—legal and moral—for the purposes of international law, may be seen from the following opinion of a leading legal authority: '. . . To think of the moral responsibility of the British Empire in terms of the moral duties of a single man . . . is to put morals in terms of law, not law in terms of morals, as we did in the classical era. In truth, a moral order among States is not the simple matter which the analogy of the individual mind has made it appear. There are many difficulties, psychological, economic, and biological, that make the analogy of politically organised society to the individual human being wholly misleading' (Pound, *Philosophical Theory and International Law, Bibliotheca Visseriana*, vol. i. (1923) p. 79). It is submitted, with deference, that this is the view which underlies the modern theory of international law, and the results of which are, also according to Dean Pound, by no means reassuring. We ought certainly to put law in terms of morals; but to put different standards of morality for individuals acting as such, and for individuals acting as members of a family, of a corporation or of a State, is destructive both of those moral standards and of the legal value of the principles which are derived from them. The moral responsibility of States is co-extensive with the moral responsibility of their citizens, or of those elected by them. Cf. here § 33 and the authors there cited.

It is, therefore, not surprising that the conception, hitherto predominant, of States as the only possible subjects of international law is now being abandoned

also Picciotto, *The Relation of International Law to the Law of England and of the United States*, 1915; Pitt Cobbett, *Leading Cases*, 1922, vol. i. p. 22). It might therefore be of advantage to examine the two main propositions put forward by Triepel in support of his thesis. The first is the well-known case of the *Franconia* (*R.* v. *Keyn*, 2 Ex. Div. 63). The decision in this case has been severely criticised by some authors. It is, on the other hand, carefully quoted by others. But if all the circumstances are taken into consideration, it cannot be said that this judgment amounts to a rejection of the rule that international law is a part of the law of England. Writers seem to forget that the main issue of the controversy in this case was not the question whether a rule of international law can be enforced without an Act of Parliament; what *was* in dispute was the existence and the extent of a rule of international law relating to jurisdiction in territorial waters. The majority judges gave their judgment on the ground that '. . . by the principles of international law, the power of a nation over the sea within three miles of its coast is only for certain limited purposes; and that Parliament could not, consistently with these principles, apply English criminal law within those limits.' It may be said without exaggeration that four parts out of five of the bulky judgment are concerned with that question of international law. There is a significant passage in the main judgment, that of Cockburn, C.J. After stating the divergent views of writers, the learned judge proceeded as follows: '. . . Looking to this, we may properly ask those who contend for the application of the existing law to the littoral sea independently of legislation, to tell us the extent to which we are to go in applying it. Are we to limit it to three miles or to extend it to six? Are we to treat the whole body of criminal law applicable to it, or only so much as relates to "police and safety" . . . ? What is there in these conflicting views to guide us, in total absence of precedent or legal sanction, as to the extent to which we may subject foreigners to our law?' (at pp. 193-192). Clearly, the unsettled position of international law with regard to this particular question guided the learned judge when he emphasised the necessity of an Act of Parliament. The two subsequent cases, in which the question became relevant, namely, that of the *West Rand Central Gold Mining Co., Ltd.*, v. *Rex*, (1905) 2 K.B. 391, and that of *Porter* v. *Freudenberg*, (1915) 1 K.B. 857, do not allow an unqualified acceptance of the dualistic view. (As to the first, see Westlake, *Collected Papers*, pp. 498-518; as to the second, Picciotto, *op. cit.*, p. 72-74.)

Neither does Triepel lay sufficient stress on the only appropriate explanation of the necessity of an 'act of transformation' in the form of an Act of Parliament whenever the law of the land is being modified by a treaty, namely, the fact that the treaty making power rests, in Great Britain, exclusively with the Crown and not with Parliament. This is the true explanation. 'If it were not so (that is, if all treaties were directly binding upon the subject),' says Anson, 'the King, in virtue of his prerogative, might indirectly tax or legislate, without the consent of Parliament' (*The Law and Custom of the Constitution*, 3rd ed., 1908, vol. ii. p. 103). It may be said with some justification that the enabling Act of Parliament partakes not so much of the character of an 'act of transformation' as of that of a ratification. There are Acts in which the legislative function modifying the existing law is unequivocally combined with the expression of general assent to the treaty (without such an assent being required by the stipulations of the treaty). The Act, for instance, enabling Her Majesty to carry into effect the International Convention for the Protection of Submarine Cables

by positivist writers as being at variance with facts of international life, and as incapable of including the new institutions of international organisation. The recent

(48 & 49 Vict. c. 49) contains the passage: 'the Convention of the 14th March 1884 is *hereby confirmed*, and subject to the provisions of this Act the articles of such Convention shall be of the same force as if they were enacted in the body of this Act.' The same is the form of the Acts carrying into effect the Conventions concerning the North Fisheries (46 & 47 Vict. c. 22), the liquor traffic in the North Sea (51 & 52 Vict. c. 18), and the sea fisheries between France and Great Britain (31 & 32 Vict. c. 45). None of these Conventions contains provisions rendering necessary the ratification or confirmation by Parliament. This double function of the enabling Act, namely, of giving assent to ratification (although, in strict law, ratification is an act of the Crown), and of effecting the necessary changes in municipal legislation, finds expression, to some extent, in the fact of several treaties having been laid before Parliament for the purpose of passing the enabling Act before the treaties in question have been ratified by the Crown. The series of recent peace treaties furnishes a striking example of such a procedure. The Treaty of Versailles was signed on June 28, 1919; the enabling Act was passed on July 31 (9 & 10 Geo. v. c. 33); the formal act of ratification (the signing by the King) took place on October 10, 1919, and the ratifications were exchanged on January 10, 1920. The same sequence of events occurred with regard to the treaties of Trianon, St. Germain, and Neuilly, as well as with regard to the Air Navigation Convention of 1919 (10 & 11 Geo. v. c. 80). And although the submitting of treaties of Parliament after, and not before, their ratification forms now a clear rule followed by the present British Government (the attempt of the former Government to introduce a contrary practice having been expressly repudiated; see *B.Y.*, 1924, p. 190, and 1925, p. 188), the instances quoted above clearly establish the element of ratification contained in the enabling Acts.

That the provisions of the American constitution are a clear refutation of the dualistic theory should be clear to every one who does not confuse the issues in question. The fact that a conflicting Act of the Congress may derogate from a rule of international law means simply that the absolute supremacy of international law is not recognised by the United States (but even here, see Hyde, vol. i. p. 12; Wright, *The Enforcement of International Law through Municipal Law in the United States*, 1916, pp. 225-226; and Potter, *A.J.*, xix. (1925) pp. 315-326). The decisive point is that a rule of international law embodied in a treaty binds directly the courts and private individuals. However, positivist writers continue to see in the Promulgation by the President of the United States that act of transformation of which the dualistic theory is so badly in need (see, recently, Triepel in *Recueil des Cours, Académie de Droit International*, 1923, p. 90).

It is not surprising that Article 4 of the new German constitution is severely criticised by the dualistic school still predominant in Germany. 'The universally recognised rules of international law,' says Article 4, 'are valid as binding constituent parts of the German Federal Law.' Universally recognised international law becomes *per se* a part of the law of the land. It supersedes conflicting municipal law without any further legislative action being necessary. The framers of the article did not leave any doubt as to their intentions. They were not satisfied with an express declaration that they intended to adopt the English-American conception; they stated clearly their intention to discard the accepted dogma that international law binds States only, and not individuals. Minister of the Reich, Dr. Preuss, said, while defending the wording of the Article as it stands

writings of prominent Continental positivists like Anzilotti, Cavaglieri, and Strupp are strikingly illustrative of this change of opinion. Says, for instance, Anzilotti, pointing to the uncritical attitude hitherto adopted by publicists: 'Instead of demonstrating that States *are* subjects of international law, it is being maintained that only States *may become* subjects of international law.' This assertion he refuses to accept.[1] Says Strupp, with even greater clearness: 'The opinion is to be rejected that according to the conception of international law (*begrifflich*) States alone can be subjects of international law. Such an opinion is the logical consequence of a wrong premise, which maintains that international law is a law obtaining between States only, whereas what is true is that till now States alone are the organs of international legislation.'[2] Also writers

now (Minutes of the Constitutional Committee, 3rd Meeting, p. 7): 'The prevailing opinion in international law is that it binds States only and not organs and subjects. But Article 4 goes beyond that. I am of the opinion that the dogma that international law can bind subjects only through municipal statute is not unconditionally true.' Similarly von Simson, speaking in the name of the Foreign Office: 'Article 4 intends to express the rule of the practice adopted by England and America to the effect that the universally recognised rules of international law bind not only States but also subjects.'

[1] *Corso di diritto internazionale*, 1923, p. 67.

[2] *Grundzüge des positiven Völkerrechts*, 1923, p. 37; see especially Cavaglieri, *Corso di diritto internazionale* (*parte generale*), 1925, where he defines international law as 'a body of juridical norms set by the concordant will of a number of States for the purpose of regulating the relations either between themselves or, by way of exception, with those other persons to whom they have conceded the character of international personality,' and the same in *Rivista*, xvii. (1925) pp. 18-32, 168-187. But see Kosters, in the *Bulletin de l'Institut Interm. Internat.*, 1923, July, pp. 1-31, who quotes a recent decision of the Swiss Federal Court (February 2, 1923; *ibid.*, pp. 31-51) as fully accepting the view of the predominant doctrine. See also the same author, *Les Fondements du Droit des Gens*, *Bibliotheca Visseriana*, vol. iv. (1925) pp. 253-261, and Lord Phillimore in *Recueil des Cours*, *Académie de Droit International*, 1923, pp. 63-67, who rejects the view that the individual is a *civis mundi*. Similar is the provision of Article 34 of the Statute of the Permanent Court of International Justice. But it is instructive that in the course of the discussions in the Commission of Jurists charged with the drafting of the Statute, lawyers of the authority of Lapradelle and Loder strongly urged the necessity of the Court being open to private parties. However, the arguments based on the principle of sovereignty prevailed. (See *Proceedings*, pp. 196 ff.) On the other hand, the General Claims Commission between the United States and Mexico denied in a recent award (March 31, 1926) that the rules of

whose work lies in the field of philosophy of law, and whose influence upon international publicists is by no means insignificant, strongly urge the same view. Duguit, Kelsen, and Krabbe may be mentioned in this connection.[1] Gradually a consensus of opinion is evolving to the effect that although it is States which are the normal subjects of international law, there is nothing in international law which is fundamentally opposed to individuals and other legal persons becoming subjects of international rights and duties, *i.e.* subjects of international law.

§ 33. *The Personification of the State.*—Thus the current argument on the dangers of analogy to private law because of the fundamental difference of subjects must be received with appropriate caution. But the result reached so far is of importance also from another point of view. It shows the theoretical shortcomings of that current personification of the State which is one of the characteristic features of modern international law and which has become one of the main factors that impeded its progress by weakening, as it was bound to do, the sense of international duty in those responsible for the conduct of the external affairs of the State. The State, it is said, the metaphysical and mystical State, is the subject of duties, if any, not men. Again, therefore, no rules of law obtaining between individuals can be applied to the State. It was inevitable that publicists who did not see in the positivist formula the last

international public law apply only to States, and described as antiquated the view that individuals cannot under any circumstances have a personal standing under it (Ralston, No. 88).

[1] 'International law,' says Krabbe (*op. cit.*, p. 240), 'lays obligations upon those individuals or groups of individuals—judges called upon to give effect to a treaty, the legislature which must appropriate money for the execution of a treaty—who by the constitutional law of their country are entrusted with the care of the respective interests.' At the same results arrive Duguit, *Droit constitutionnel*, 1923, vol. i. p. 560; Kelsen, *op. cit.*, pp. 130-134, 162-167; and *Allgemeine Staatslehre*, 1925, p. 122.

word of international jurisprudence should regard the personification of the State as a source of grave danger and stagnation. The emphasis which, for instance, Westlake lays upon the fact that it is men upon whom international law imposes rights and duties, and not the mystical entity called State, is perhaps the most important and hope-inspiring feature of his teaching.[1] Sir Henry Maine shows how the assumed individuality of sovereigns enabled the founders of international law to regard States as moral beings bound by rules of morality.[2] And Bryce, who no doubt was well acquainted with the movement which, under the influence of Dicey and Maitland, stressed the real personality of corporations, saw clearly that, whatever may be the merits of these doctrines in the field of political theory, any exaggerated conception of the juristic personality of the State is disastrous for the progress of international law.[3] Thus the rejection of the uncritically adopted slogan that States only are subjects of international rights and duties must ultimately prove fatal to the theory of personification of States and, with it, to one of the reasons most commonly adduced in support of the sweeping repudiation of recourse to private law.[4]

[1] See *International Law*, pp. 40, 197; *Collected Papers*, Preface, p. xix; pp. 1, 2, 266, 282, 411, 412, 498-503, 532, 617, 618. Cf. also Lorimer, p. 29, *supra*.

[2] *International Law*, p. 57.

[3] He says in 1922 in *International Relations* (p. 202): 'Though some continental writers have treated it (the State) as a sort of mystical corporation, greater and wiser than the sum of the citizens who compose it, there is nothing in the State but what its members give it. It is that aggregate of the minds and wills of the citizens to which we give a collective name.' (See also the suggestive remarks by Maitland himself in *Collected Papers*, 1911, vol. iii. pp. 304-319.) For what is believed to be the best modern criticism, both from the juridical and the philosophical point of view, of the personification of the State, the reader is referred to Kelsen, *Der soziologische und der iuristische Staatsbegriff*, 1922.

[4] The founders of international law addressed the precepts of the law of nations to individuals, and here lies to a large extent the reason for their historical success. This is beginning to be recognised by modern authorities, although they are inclined to explain it by pointing to the patrimonial theory which caused the classical publicists to address themselves to princes and kings—an ex-

§ 34. *The Formal Analogy between Individuals and States. International Law as 'a Higher Private Law' regulating Interests of Co-ordinated Legal Persons.*—Even if personified States are regarded as the exclusive subjects of international rights and duties, the view cannot be lightly dismissed which urges that notwithstanding the difference of subjects of the two branches of law, there is a close formal analogy between them. We find this opinion repeatedly expressed in the writings of Grotius, who stresses the broader analogy between States and individuals. He says: '*Civitates respectu totius generis humani privatorum locum obtinent.*'[1] Many modern writers take up the same line. Fricker refers to international law as to 'a higher private law,'[2] and Holland calls it 'private law writ large.'[3] Gerber,[4] Gierke,[5] and Heilborn[6] all express the same view. It would be a mistake to assume that these expressions are meant to convey nothing more than a simile. They help us to realise that if the main distinction between private and public law is that the first regulates the relations of legal entities in a state of co-ordination, and the second the relations of those in a state of subordination to one another, then, formally, international public law belongs to the *genus* private law. There is also another, even less formal, resemblance between the two groups of legal rules. If, as many assume,

planation which seems hardly to be satisfactory. Vattel, for instance, says (Introduction, § 7) the law of nations 'contains the obligations which the law of nature imposes upon States, and on them this law is not less obligatory than on individuals, because States are composed of men; their deliberations are the deliberations of men, and the law of nature is obligatory on all men, whatever may be the relations in which they act.'

[1] *Mare Liberum*, ch. v. See also L. ii. c. 9, s. 2 (1).—Montesquieu describes international law as '*le droit civil de l'univers dans le sens que chaque peuple est un citoyen.*'

[2] *Vom Staatsgebiet*, 1867, p. 6.

[3] *Studies in International Law*, 1898, p. 152; see also Pollock, *A First Book of Jurisprudence*, 3rd ed., 1911, p. 99.

[4] *Öffentliche Rechte*, 1852, p. 40.

[5] *Deutsches Genossenschaftsrecht*, 1868, vol. i. p. 843.

[6] *Das System des Völkerrechts*, 1896, p. 413; *Grundbegriffe des Völkerrechts* (in Stier-Somlo's *Handbuch des Völkerrechts*), 1912, pp. 102, 105, 106.

the main distinction between public and private law lies in the fact that, to use Ulpian's words,[1] the first *ad statum rei publicae spectat*, and the second *ad singulorum utilitatem*, then again the analogy between international and private law is a striking one. For, however public and collectivistic may be the character of the State's activities on the international arena when judged from the point of view of persons composing the State, it is, from the point of view of the members of the international community, distinctly individualistic.[2] Of course, in order to fully understand this formal analogy, it is necessary to discard the misleading notion that whereas private law is above the subjects of law, international law is a law between them, and that therefore every analogy is inadequate. Both international and private law are composed of external rules of conduct which, once given their formal existence as law, are independent of the will of the parties, and, as such, above the subjects of law. It is true that there is a difference in the manner in which, in the two spheres, law is created. Individuals give their consent, apart from custom, through the machinery of municipal legislation; States, their number being small, give their consent directly, in treaties, particular or general. But even this is not always the case. Frequently States are subject to international rules in the creation of which they have had no part whatsoever.[3] They are certainly co-ordinated legal entities, but this co-ordination presupposes logically subordination to a higher rule.

[1] *D.*, I. i, *de iustitia et iure*, i. 2.

[2] However, it is probable that with the legal development of international organisation and the creation of central authoritative institutions, a body of rules will evolve which, as regulating the relations between individual States and the authoritative organs of the international community, will closely correspond to public law within the municipal sphere, for instance, to constitutional and administrative law. In fact, there are already now rudiments of international rules of this kind.

[3] See pp. 52, 53, *supra*.

§ 35. *The Nature of Analogy.*—The formal analogy between international and private law as between two branches of jurisprudence regulating interests of co-ordinated individual or collective persons, is no doubt apt to throw some light on the nature of analogy in its application to international law. For over-emphasis of the heterogeneity of subjects and interest was certainly not conducive to a clear understanding of this problem. What is analogy? It is 'identity or similarity of proportion.'[1] This definition is an application to the domain of law of that conception of analogy which logicians and scientists necessarily apply in their respective disciplines. Kant defines analogy as a complete similarity of relation between two quite dissimilar objects;[2] Jevons, who regards analogy as at a deeper-lying correspondence, which is of a purely conceptional nature, expresses agreement with the view that it denotes a resemblance not so much between things as between the relations of things;[3] Mach points out that although no particular quality in two objects may be similar or identical, they may nevertheless be perfectly analogous.[4] It is so also in the domain of law. The *analogia proportionis* is of decisive importance, not the external similarity of the attributes of the objects or the subjects of the legal relation. Thus, given the exclusive right of use and disposition over a part of the surface of the earth—one as against other individuals, the other as against States—no difference of subjects will warrant the exclusion of analogy between private property and territorial sovereignty. It is true that neither in law nor in natural science do we find such perfect analogies as, for instance, in

[1] See Wharton's *Law Lexicon*, 13th ed., 1925, p. 52.

[2] Quoted after Eisler, *Wörterbuch der philosophischen Begriffe*, 3rd ed., 1910, vol. i. p. 39.

[3] *Principles of Science*, 1892, p. 627.

[4] *Erkenntnis und Irrtum*, 3rd ed., 1917, p. 221.

geometry, where the elements of two triangles, one having been constructed by a line drawn parallel to one of the sides of the other, although different in size, are nevertheless in complete proportion.

There is accordingly no absolute logical cogency in the process of juridical analogy, as there is none in natural science. It is an inductive and experimental method subject to correction. But its foundation is sound, based as it is on the solid rock of juridical logic and the principles of legal justice common to all law. As such, it is a vehicle of progress, and the jurist may well paraphrase Kepler's eulogy and call them '*fidelissimi magistri omnium iuris arcanorum conscii.*' It is especially in an undeveloped system of law that it would be most unreasonable to sacrifice scientific progress and efficiency of interpretation on the altar of positivist formulas. Of course, the process of analogy is in the first instance a means of interpreting and supplementing the law in accordance with its own principles. That means that in resorting to analogy for the purpose of interpreting and construing rules of international law, we must so far as possible take into account its actual rules and its spirit. Should, however, no help be forthcoming from those sources, the recourse to a subsidiary source is the proper way for an international judge or jurist to choose.

§ 36. *The Limitations of Analogy.*—The recourse, in the domain of international public law, to private law sources is no doubt fraught with dangers. Some of them lie in its abuse, frequent and deliberate, for the purposes of special pleading, and it is both unnecessary and unprofitable to discuss them in detail. But it may be of some use to mention four *bona fide* sources of confusion.

There is, firstly, the tendency on the part of many

writers to resort to notions peculiar to their own municipal law or to some other system of private law regardless of the fact that conceptions of that kind cannot, owing to their technical character or the altogether special reason of their creation, claim that degree of cogency which is conditioned by the actual universality of a legal rule, from the point of view either of juridical logic or of legal justice, and which alone may reasonably serve as a basis of analogy. Only general principles of private law recognised by the main systems of jurisprudence, ascertained by comparative study and, if possible, declared by scientific legal opinion as fit objects of any future attempt at unification of private law, are a suitable object of analogy.

Secondly, it is frequently being forgotten that not every relation between States has its counterpart in private law. It would be futile to engage in extracting analogies with a view to applying them in the domain of extradition or the laws of war. And yet, that is what frequently happens.

Thirdly, recourse is repeatedly had to analogy of private law, although the solution of a difficulty may easily be found in individual cases by filling the gap by means of logical deductions from existing rules of international law or of analogy to them. There is no need to resort to rules of an extraneous system of law so long as other avenues are open. For international law, deficient and undeveloped as it is in many respects, constitutes nevertheless a system of law to which by necessity the general rules and methods of scientific interpretation and construction resorted to in other systems of law must apply.[1]

[1] Cf. here especially Windscheid, *Pandekten*, 9th ed., 1906, vol. i. §§ 20-24; Geny, *Méthode d'interprétation et sources en droit privé positif*, 2nd ed., 1919, vol. i. pp. 303-314; Salmond, *Jurisprudence*, 7th ed., 1924, pp. 202-204. Austin's rather discursive and not completed *Excursus on Analogy* in vol. ii. pp. 1036-1055 (4th ed., 1873) is neverthe-

Fourthly, not sufficient regard is paid to the fact that although there is a law above the States, there is not yet in existence a universally compulsory judicial tribunal to determine what that law is, or a central authority to enforce it. This circumstance undoubtedly causes certain analogies to be inaccurate. However, caution on this account need not be pushed too far. For if the recourse to analogy is in such cases misleading, it is so not because the corresponding legal relation differs in international law from that in private law, but because the international community has not yet attained that stage of legal organisation at which law is in all cases stronger than the individual will, or at which the rule of law is powerful enough to extend to all the essential aspects of the international relations.

Accordingly, although inferences drawn by way of analogy may, in the last-mentioned class of cases, be misleading, they are never dangerous. They do not falsify or distort a rule of international law; they only assume, rather prematurely, the existence of a legal regulation where, in fact, no such regulation yet exists. It is true that such inaccuracies should not be indulged in more than is necessary, but, on the other hand, they are not the worst that may befall international law. The false or partial use of analogies between the State and the individual is, to quote Lorimer once more, 'a fault which, scientifically at least, is less heinous than that of not knowing that there is a necessary law at all, either for States or for men, or any analogy between its manifestations in the various branches of jurisprudence.'[1] If a summary, in one sentence, of the conclusions reached in this Chapter were needed, the above quotation from Lorimer may suitably be regarded

less suggestive. On the problem of gaps in international law, cf. Verdross, *Verfassung der Völkerrechtsgemeinschaft*, 1926, pp. 69-75, and especially Cavaglieri, *Lo stato di necessità nel diritto internazionale*, 1918, pp. 104-118.

[1] Vol. i. p. 80.

as such. What, however, was to Lorimer the result of a philosophic naturalism, is here put forward as corroborated both by a theoretical investigation in the principles of the positivist doctrine and by a most instructive and almost uniform practice of governments.

PART II

THE PRACTICE OF STATES AND THE SCIENCE OF INTERNATIONAL LAW

CHAPTER III

PRIVATE LAW ANALOGIES APART FROM TREATIES

I

THE LEGAL NATURE OF TERRITORIAL SOVEREIGNTY

§ 37. *The Territory as an Object of the State's Right. The 'Object Theory.'*—The part of international law upon which private law has engrafted itself most deeply is that relating to acquisition of sovereignty over land, sea, and territorial waters. This influence, which dates from the formative period of international law, is now, it is believed, unduly minimised by the reaction against the so-called patrimonial conception of State. It is proposed, therefore, to inquire how far the part played in this connection by private and Roman law may be explained by the peculiarities of one historical period, and what, if any, is its function in the modern law of nations. The inquiry must necessarily start from the question, What is the legal nature of the relation between the State and the territory within which it exercises *imperium*?

'According to a theory which is commonly held,' says Hall,[1] 'either the term "property," when employed to express the rights possessed by a State over the territory occupied by it, must be understood in a different sense from that which is attached to it in speaking of the property of individuals, or else its use is altogether improper.' He does not, however, agree with that

[1] P. 53.

theory, and what he is willing to concede is no more than that this distinction might perhaps be of importance for the purposes of municipal public law. With regard to the main question, he says:

'As between nations the proprietary character of the possession enjoyed by a state is logically a necessary consequence of the undisputed facts that a state community has a right to the exclusive use and disposal of its territory as against other states. . . . When a person in law holds an object with an unlimited right of use and alienation as against all other persons, it is idle to say that he does not legally possess complete property in it.' [1]

This opinion of Hall, at which he arrives after a careful consideration of the opposing view, is unquestionably predominant in modern international law. It is true that the proprietary right of the State over its territory is now generally conceived as being of a public character, as *imperium* rather than *dominium*, the latter being regarded as an anachronistic relic of conditions which passed away long ago.[2] In both cases, however, the territory is construed as an *object* of the State's right. And it is this 'object theory' which regards the relation of the State to its territory as identical with or as analogous to the private law right of property, that is now, after prolonged discussion among publicists, no less predominant than at the beginning of the nineteenth century.[3]

[1] P. 53.

[2] It will be observed, however, that Hall's argument has nothing to do with the patrimonial conception of the State. Individuals not being, in his opinion, subjects of international law, 'any rights which belong to them must be clothed in the garb of state rights before they can be put forward internationally' (p. 53).

[3] Cf. Klüber, *Droit des Gens*, 1861, p. 160; Wheaton - Dana, § 161; Heffter - Geffcken, p. 148. As to recent publicists, cf., *e.g.*, Fenwick: 'It is a convenient and not wholly arbitrary rule of international jurisprudence to regard the territory of the state as something distinct from the state itself, and to treat it as if it were national property possessed by the state in much the same way that property in land is held by individual citizens within the state' (p. 219). To the like effect, Hyde, vol. i. p. 162: 'The existence of an exclusive right of property and control over territory necessarily implies the existence of a possessor whose

§ 38. *The 'Space Theory.'*—If the 'object theory' still holds the field, it does so owing to its intrinsic merits, and not to the absence of alternative attempts at juridical construction. Thus it has been subjected to adverse criticism on the part of the so-called 'space theory,' which repudiates not only the conception of *dominium*, but also that of *imperium* as exercised by the State over its territory. The adherents of this view point out that *imperium* over a lifeless object of nature, such as territory, is impossible. The territory, it is said, is an *element* of the State, and it can no more be regarded as the object of a State's right,[1] than the body of a man can be said to be his property. The territory is the space within which the jurisdiction of the State is exercised, it is the theatre of the State's rule. The State rules *within* the territory, not *over* it.[2]

Before the space theory was able to influence international law to any appreciable extent, a new attempt at an explanation of the juridical nature of territorial sovereignty was launched, and received wide attention. It is the so-called 'competence theory,' which conceives of territorial sovereignty as of a sum of competencies *ratione loci* which international law concedes to international persons.[3] It is not intended to discuss here

capacity to possess is recognised by the family of nations'; and Fauchille, No. 482 (2).

[1] See especially Fricker, *Vom Staatsgebiet*, 1867, *passim*; Zitelmann, *Internationales Privatrecht*, 1897, i. p. 91; Heyland, quoted below, pp. 58 ff.

[2] Laband (*Das Staatsrecht des deutschen Reiches*, 1911, vol. i. pp. 190 ff.) and others try to reconcile the opposing doctrines by having recourse to analogy between territorial sovereignty and landed property. Property in land, they say, may be conceived either as the space within which the owner may exercise his exclusive right, or as the object of the owner's right. For a bibliography and discussion of this and other theories on territorial sovereignty, see Heyland, *Die Rechtsstellung der besetzten Rheinlande* (Stier-Somlo's *Handbuch des Völkerrechts*), 1923, pp. 55-63; Henrich, *Kritik der Gebietstheorien*, *Z. V.* (xiii.), 1924, pp. 28-63 and 194-232; and the same author, *Theorie des Staatsgebietes*, 1922, *passim* (especially pp. 8-14); and above all, Donati, *Stato e territorio*, 1924, *passim*.

[3] See Radnitzky, *Archiv für öffentliches Recht*, vol. xx. (1905) pp. 313 ff., and Henrich, *op. cit.* For a short, but by no means clear and in-

this doctrine in detail. Unrelated as it is to the practice of States, it is not likely to be of lasting influence. It possesses, however, the merit of having clearly demonstrated that the view which regards the territory as an *element* of the conception of State is untenable.

§ 39. *Recent formulations of the 'Object Theory.' Donati.* —It is not surprising, therefore, that a recent writer revives, in a scholarly examination of the theories of territory, the purely private law conception of State territory.[1] He not only regards the territory of the State as an object attributable to the State in its own right ('*cosa attribuita allo Stato in suo diritto*'), but maintains that that right 'constitutes a right of property in the strict meaning of the word' ('*costituisce un diritto di dominio in senso stretto*').[2] This right of property, he points out in an argument strikingly reminiscent of that used by Hall, is not inconsistent with the private right of property exercised by individuals, because the two rights are valid in different spheres of law.[3] The relation of the State to its

telligible, statement of the theory, see Henrich in Strupp's *Wörterbuch*, vol. ii. pp. 600-604. He takes the conception of 'competency' as the basis of the 'only juridical construction of State territory.' He conceives of the latter as of the sum of local competencies of State organs. The law, he says, regulates the conditions under which acts of certain persons acting as organs of the State should be attributed to it. One set of these conditions determines where these acts should be performed. The sum of these local competencies is territorial sovereignty. Every provision which changes these local competencies is a change of territory: cession itself is nothing else than a contractual replacing of local competencies. But, continues the author, international law recognises as States only such juridical persons as have at their exclusive disposal 'a territory in the narrower meaning,' that is, a material basis whose extent is defined by international law and within which the legislative, judicial, and administrative acts of the organs of the State are performed (p. 601). It may be doubted whether this construction differs appreciably from the rejected 'object theory.'

[1] Donati, quoted above; see especially pp. 53, 59, 60.

[2] P. 59.

[3] He says: 'Il diritto internazionale di dominio è un diritto spettante allo Stato *in confronto agli altri Stati in base all'ordinamento internazionale*; la proprietà individuale, e cioè il

territory is, *pro foro interno*, of a public character in contradistinction to that obtaining under the influence of the patrimonial conception, but this does not exclude — on the contrary, it implies — that in relation to co-ordinated units, of which each in turn exercises an equal right over its territory, the right *quoad imperium* exhibits, *pro foro externo*, those formal characteristics which we attribute to *dominium* in private law.[1]

There is, in fact, no ground for assuming that the science of international law will discard the analogy between territorial sovereignty and property in private law, even if it does not go the length of identifying the two conceptions. The reaction against patrimonial ideas cannot obliterate the fact that the two notions are essentially analogous on account of the exclusiveness of enjoyment and disposition which is in law the main formal characteristic of both private property and

diritto *interno* di dominio degli individui, è un diritto spettante al singolo *in confronto* agli altri consociati e allo *Stato in base all'ordinamento interno.* Perciò l'uno può perfettamente coesistere con l'altro, cioè non vi è contraddizione logica e giuridica, ma assoluta conciliabilità, fra il fatto che lo Stato sia proprietario di tutto il territorio, e quindi anche delle parti soggete alla proprietà individuale, *in confronto agli altri Stati in base al diritto internazionale*' (p. 60, *op. cit.*).

[1] Donati rejects the assertion that the territory is an essential element of the conception of State. He disposes especially of the argument that the State cannot be imagined without a territory. There is a difference, he says, between a certain relation to an object being an essential part of the concept and the object itself constituting a part of the concept. Thus it is difficult to think of an individual as detached from a part of the surface of the earth. But this does not justify us in regarding the earth as an essential part of the concept 'man' (p. 27). Also a nomad State has a territory, but the territory is not a permanent one; it is not therefore an essential element of the nomad State (p. 30). He discusses the Athenian State, reduced during the Persian occupation to ships; the Vaal Republics, which, although they abandoned their original territory, did not thereby change their state; and the legal position of Belgium and of Serbia during the war (see Preface, p. iii). Similar is the opinion of another recent Italian writer of authority. He says: 'La stessa osservazione che lo stato non può concepirsi senza territorio no prova di più che l'osservare che l'individuo, almeno nella sua vita, non può concepirsi senza mezzi di sussistenza' (Gemma, *Appunti di diritto internazionale*, 1923, p. 180). He is also clearly of the opinion that the relation of the State to its territory is a real right *par excellence*: 'Possiamo dunque dire che ogni Stato abbia sul proprio territorio di fronte agli altri State un diritto di natura reale sia nello stretto significato di un *ius in re* sia in quello più assoluto di un diritto esclusivo di attività statuale exercitato *erga omnes*' (p. 181).

territorial sovereignty.[1] They belong, in juridical logic, to the same class of rights.

§ 40. *The Practice of States. Exchange, Purchase, Pledge, Lease.*—A cursory survey of the practice of governments with regard to modes of cession of territory will show that they have never ceased to regard the territory as an object of the State's right. The position in this regard is to-day not essentially different from that obtaining two or three hundred years ago, *i.e.* in the time of the reign of the patrimonial conception. It is true that disposition of territory by way of gift, of testamentary arrangements, or of marriage settlements is no longer practicable.[2] But it must not be forgotten that these modes of cession were highly infrequent even in the time of the patrimonial State—certainly less frequent than some writers are apt to assume. They were, on the whole, confined to those tiny kingdoms and duchies which did not in fact differ much from private estates.[3] And there are in existence, so far back as the fourteenth and fifteenth centuries, express constitutional provisions or statutory enactments limiting considerably the freedom of French or Spanish monarchs to dispose of the territory of the State.[4] On the other hand, cases of exchanging, of pledging, and especially of selling, territory are as common (or rather as rare) to-day as before. It seems even that they are more frequent in the present century and in the second half of the nineteenth century than at the beginning of the latter. Some instances will illustrate this.

[1] This is admitted also by writers who approve of the 'competence theory'; see, for instance, Verdross, *Die Verfassung der Völkerrechtsgemeinschaft*, 1926, p. 185. In addition, there is nothing to prevent a juridical construction of the right of property as of a sum of competencies granted by law in relation to the object of property.

[2] For historical instances, see Phillimore, vol. i. pp. 379-380 (gift), pp. 383-384 (marriage settlement), pp. 384-387 (testamentary disposition).

[3] See Ward, *Inquiries, etc.*, vol. i. p. 258.

[4] See, for details, Neyron, *Essai historique et politique sur les Garanties*, 1777, p. 69.

The purchase of Alaska by the United States from Russia in 1867 is a clear example of cession of territory in the form of a purely private law transaction.[1] There was in this case no preponderant influence of a powerful neighbour threatening to take possession of the territory by force should a peaceful purchase be refused. The negotiations between the two Powers show that the question of the price was of the essence of the agreement, and a minority of the Congress recommended the rejection of the purchase on the ground that the territory to be acquired seemed to them worthless. The purchase of the Danish West Indies, ratified in January 1917, furnishes another instructive example. The Danish flag was removed and that of the United States raised at the moment at which the Secretary of State handed over to the Danish ambassador treasury bonds to the value of 25,000,000 dollars.[2] In numerous recent treaties territories or spheres of influence have been mutually ceded in a way which vividly recalls to mind their character of exchange.[3] The treaty of July 1890 between Great Britain and Germany relating to territory in East Africa and to Heligoland, and the agreement between France and Great Britain of April 1904 relating to Morocco and Egypt, may be quoted as examples.[4]

[1] See Moore, *Digest*, vol. i. pp. 462-476, vol. v. pp. 226-229; and Hill, quoted below, pp. 258, 259.

[2] The treaty provides for the cession by Denmark to the United States of 'all territory, dominion and sovereignty, possessed, asserted or claimed by Denmark in the West Indies . . . in consideration of twenty-five million dollars' (see the Convention of August 1916, printed in *A.J.*, Suppl., xi. (1917) p. 53*a*). Article 2 provides that Denmark guarantees that the cession made by the preceding articles is 'free and unencumbered by any reservations, privileges, franchises, grants or possessions. . . .' See also on the purchase of Louisiana by the United States from France in 1803, Moore, *Digest*, vol. i. pp. 433-439; Howard, *The Louisiana Purchase*, 1902, and especially Charles E. Hill, *Leading American Treaties*, 1922, ch. v. The legal character of the transaction is, naturally, quite unimpaired by the kind of motive animating the parties.

[3] See on this subject Rapisardi-Mirabelli, in *R.I.*, 3rd ser., vol. iv. (1923) pp. 663-665.

[4] See Rapisardi - Mirabelli, *ibid.*, p. 664, n. 3.

The occupation of the territory of a State for the purpose of securing the execution of international obligations has occurred as frequently in the last fifty years as ever before; and although the patrimonial theory has been discarded, modern publicists construe occupation of this kind after the analogy of pledge (or hypothecation) in private law.[1] Three recent instances may be mentioned. In virtue of the Peace Treaty of Shimonoseki, of April 1895, Japan occupied Wei-hai-wei 'as a guarantee of the faithful performance of the stipulations of this Act';[2] in virtue of the Peace Treaty of December 1897, Turkey remained in occupation of Thessaly as a security for the payment of the war indemnity by Greece;[3] and last, but not least, Article 428 of the Treaty of Versailles provided that, in order to secure the performance of the Treaty, the Allied and Associated troops will occupy for a period of fifteen years the German territory situated west of the Rhine.[4] The construction of these treaty provisions as a pledge admittedly offers serious difficulties. For it is an *essentiale* of a pledge in private law that it may be sold by the creditor should the satisfaction of his claim not be forthcoming. But this means of obtaining satisfaction is obviously not practicable in international law, and some writers suggest that the right of satisfaction should be modified in the direction of allowing the creditor to appropriate the object of the pledge. There are, in fact, precedents to this

[1] See Phillimore, vol. ii. p. 83; Heffter-Geffcken, p. 209; Bonfils-Fauchille, No. 842; Bluntschli, § 428. For further bibliography on the subject and a detailed discussion of the problem of pledges, see Heyland, quoted above, pp. 27-66.

[2] Martens, *N.R.G.*, 2nd ser., xxi. p. 646.

[3] *Ibid.*, vol. xxviii. p. 633. The Convention between Great Britain and Tibet, signed at Lhasa, September 7, 1904, provides in Article 7 that 'as a security for the payment of the above-mentioned indemnity . . . the British Government shall continue to occupy the Chumbi valley until the indemnity has been paid. . . .' (Hertslet's *Treaties*, vol. xxiv. p. 1046).

[4] For many earlier instances, see Heyland, *op. cit.*, p. 38.

effect.[1] It is also of importance that the term ‘ pledge ’ is not solely a construction introduced by publicists, but that it is actually used in modern treaties.[2] But even if the special circumstances accompanying the granting and realisation of security in international law necessitate a thorough modification of the corresponding rules of private law, there is no doubt that in all these cases the territory of a State is regarded as an object of its right. It will also be seen from an examination of international leases that whatever may be the legal nature of the so-called political leases, like those granted at the end of the last century by China, there is another type of international lease adopted in several recent treaties for economic and administrative purposes, and to which a strictly private law interpretation must needs be applied.[3] All these cases show that too hasty and too general inferences drawn from the obsolescence of the patrimonial idea are not corroborated by the modern practice of States.

II

ACQUISITION OF TERRITORIAL SOVEREIGNTY. PRIVATE LAW RULES OF PROPERTY AND POSSESSION

§ 41. *The Requirement of Form in Acquisition of Territorial Sovereignty. The Requirement of* animus *and* corpus.—The analogy of legal relations existing between the conceptions of property and territorial sovereignty finds, *inter alia,* clear expression in the fact that the two main principles of the law of original acquisition of territorial sovereignty constitute at the same time a

[1] See especially Phillimore, *loc. cit.*

[2] See Article 3 of the Peace Preliminaries of February 1871, and Article 7 of the Peace Treaty of Frankfurt of May 1871, between France and Germany.

[3] See pp. 183-187, *infra.*

general rule of private jurisprudence. There is, first, the principle that the *forms* of acquisition of territory are regulated and defined by international law. The number of modes of acquisition of territory is limited, although it may be a matter of dispute whether, for instance, accretion or subjugation or prescription each forms a class by itself, or ought to be included as a sub-division of another group.[1] International law will not recognise acquisition of territory accomplished in disregard of the accepted forms. Not every acquisition is a lawful one. The dictum '*Besitzstand gleich Rechtszustand*' (possession is law) has no validity in international law.[2] Mere force unaccompanied by a legally recognised form of acquisition does not confer a legal title. Even the title by conquest is regulated by international law. The second principle, dominating the theory and practice not less to-day than a hundred or two hundred years ago, is that based on the Roman law rules of possession, *i.e.* on the connection of *animus* with *corpus*, of the bodily act with the mental attitude. From Grotius,[3] Vattel,[4] and Bynkershoek,[5] through the long series of disputes following the discoveries of new parts of the world, to the Berlin Declaration of 1885, which, in Articles 34 and 35, gave a modern formulation to the requirement of *corpus* and *animus*, it is the same principle which ultimately asserts itself both in the theory and in the practice of original acquisition of territory.[6] The history of nearly all modern boundary

[1] With regard to accretion, see Jerusalem, *Ueber völkerrechtliche Erwerbsgründe*, 1911 (reprint from *Festgabe für A. Thon*), p. 418. With regard to subjugation, Pradier-Fodéré, vol. ii. p. 392; Twiss, vol. i. p. 227 (title by conquest resolves itself juridically into title by cession); and p. 105, *infra*.

[2] That mere facts are of constitutive value in acquisition of territorial sovereignty is maintained by Jerusalem, *op. cit.*, p. 423; by Liszt, p. 241; and Gareis, p. 88. See also Fischer Williams, quoted below, p. 105, n. 1.

[3] See passages in *Mare Liberum*, quoted below.

[4] Bk. i. § 208.

[5] *De Dominio Maris*, ch. i.

[6] See Westlake, i. pp. 111-113, for extracts illustrating the opinions of leading authorities on the question of effective occupation.

disputes and arbitrations could be written in terms of the recourse to and application of this set of rules by States and international tribunals. It was of the greatest importance as an ordering element in the development of international law and international relations in the period following the discovery of the New World.

§ 42. *Its Historical Function. The Formative Period of International Law. The Modern Practice.*—Two opposing principles confronted governments and publicists in the two centuries following that period: that of full recognition of title given by mere discovery, and that of combination of *animus* and *corpus* as a condition of acquisition of title. Claims based on discovery pure and simple were soon abandoned, and governments sought to fortify them in a different way. Thus Pope Alexander VI. granted in 1493 to Ferdinand and Isabella of Spain the territories lying farther west than a line drawn from north to south a hundred leagues west of the Azores, of which no Christian Power had taken possession before Christmas Day 1492, and to Portugal the lands east of that line; and the two States appealed frequently to that confirmation of their original right based on discovery. But even this was hardly sufficient. Vattel says that when explorers have discovered uninhabited land through which the explorers of other nations have passed, leaving some sign of their having taken possession, they have paid no more regard to such empty forms than to the regulations of Popes.[1] In fact, modern European history shows how great was the need for a comprehensive rule able to command the respect of navigators and statesmen in a greater degree than the regulations of the Popes and the principles of fictitious discovery. This rule has

[1] Bk. i. § 208.

been found in private law. The principles of contiguity, of the middle-distance, of the mouth of the river and of the watershed, are the milestones which mark the way of the recognition of the requirement of effectiveness of occupation; they stand half-way between the doctrine of discovery and that of effectiveness of possession. They are the bridge leading from the arbitrariness of pure assertion towards the relatively well-defined principles of the Berlin Declaration; the State had to possess at least the basic territory in order to be entitled to claim the rights of contiguity. It is only natural that Roman law was not able to cope with all the contingencies arising out of the discovery of the New World, but this fact is of minor importance in comparison with the weight of the service it had rendered.[1]

It was in the nineteenth century, when the claims accumulated in the two preceding centuries had to be adjusted in arbitrations and protracted negotiations, that the value of effectiveness as a principle of order and moderation became generally recognised. The Oregon controversy, the Louisiana dispute, the two British Guiana arbitrations,[2] and the Delagoa Bay arbitration of 1875,[3] offer instructive instances of constant and successful recourse to this principle of private law. Lord Stowell had, it seems, no hesitation in applying it to questions of territorial sovereignty. He says in his judgment in *The Fama*:[4] 'All concur . . . in holding it to be a necessary principle of jurisprudence, that to complete the right of property, *the right to the thing* and *the possession of the thing* itself should be united . . . this is the general rule of property, and

[1] It must not be forgotten that the question of effectiveness is also in private law a question of fact and, frequently, of legal fiction.

[2] For reference to these disputes, as well as for a lucid exposition of the question, see Hyde, vol. i. §§ 99, 101. See also pp. 229, 230, 275, 276, *infra*.

[3] For details, see Lindley, *The Acquisition and Government of Backward Territory*, 1926, pp. 135-136, 140, 142.

[4] 5 C. Rob. at p. 115.

applies, I conceive, no less to the right of territory than to other rights.' In the course of the negotiations, in 1824, between the United States and Russia with regard to certain disputed territories in North America, the United States contended that 'the dominion cannot be acquired but by a real occupation and possession, and an intention (*animus*) to establish it is by no means sufficient.' [1] Thirty years later Twiss, a fairly positive writer, disapproves of a claim to territory based on mere discovery by simply stating that the latter is not recognised either by Roman law or by Grotius or Pufendorf.[2, 3] The principle of effectiveness is firmly embedded in the international law of to-day, and the great majority of writers do not hesitate to use the terms *corpus* and *animus* for the purpose of explaining the rules of occupation as a title of acquisition of territorial sovereignty.

We see thus that the analogy to private law with regard to original acquisition of territory is not due merely to the prevalence of the patrimonial conception. It has been called into life by the necessities of international intercourse, and it is owing to these necessities and to the identity of the legal relations that a close analogy of rules has been established. To reproach international publicists, as some authors do,[4] with having taken over purely private law, is to disregard the fact that many of its rules are now an integral part of the practice of States. Even dogmatic positivists admit

[1] Lindley, *op. cit.*, 141.

[2] Vol. i. p. 197; *The Oregon Question*, 1846, p. 156.

[3] The Duke of Wellington demanded repeatedly, in the course of his negotiations with Russia, to be supplied with the opinion of civilians on the legal questions connected with the claims of Russia. This, it seems, was done, for he writes in a note to Count Nesselrode, in October 1822, referring to the claims put forward in the Russian Ukase of 1821: 'Thus, in opposition to the claim founded on discovery . . . we have the undisputable claim of occupancy and use for a series of years, which all the best writers on the law of nations admit is the best founded claim to a territory of this description' (Appendix to the *Case* of the United States in the Alaska Boundary arbitration, pp. 113-117).

[4] Henrich, *op. cit.*, p. 121.

that the private law origin of a particular rule does not constitute an obstacle to its recognition as a part of international law, provided that its adoption has been sanctioned by custom and actual observance.[1]

§ 43. *Analogy in other Modes of Acquisition and Loss of Territory.*—The same intrinsic similarity of relation explains also why the branch of international law which deals with acquisition of territorial sovereignty has, in addition to the requirement of effectiveness, retained both the classification and a number of other rules of the Roman law of property and possession. The division into original and derivative acquisition, and the three modes of original acquisition, namely, *occupatio, accessio, praescriptio,* have been taken over. The rules concerning accession have been retained *in toto,*[2] and their application has been extended from fluvial accessions to those arising on the seashore.[3] As recently as 1911, the Roman law terminology and Roman law rules on this subject were appealed to in the Chamizal arbitration between the United States and Mexico not less freely than in the formative period of international law.[4] With regard to prescription, it is no longer disputed that, at least so far as acquisition of territorial property is concerned, it is a rule of international law.[5] The same applies to the corresponding modes of loss of territory. It is especially with regard to abandonment (dereliction) of territory that frequent recourse to private and Roman law conceptions is most conspicuous in the utterances of statesmen and in pleadings before international tribunals.[6]

[1] See Strupp, *Delikt*, p. 57, n. 1.

[2] See Fenwick, p. 229; Taylor, p. 273.

[3] That many of these rules are simply the embodiment of common sense (see, *e.g.*, Hall, p. 146, and Triepel, *op. cit.*, p. 225) does not alter the fact that they have been taken over from private law (see p. 70, n. 2, *supra*).

[4] See award in *A.J.*, v. (1911) p. 794.

[5] See pp. 116-117, *infra*.

[6] See especially *Proceedings before the Tribunal in the British Guiana Arbitration*, § 101, *infra*, and the

§ 44. *Where Analogy is Lacking. Conquest. The Tendencies (Note on Adjudication).*—The analogy to private law with regard to original acquisition of *imperium* breaks down in one vital point. International law recognises the title by conquest; private law does not know of any such mode of acquiring property.[1] It is of interest, however, to note how the realisation of the idea of law within the community of nations is, also with regard to conquest, co-extensive with the approach to standards generally accepted in municipal law. The recognition of conquest as conferring *per se* a legal title is no doubt the unavoidable consequence of the circumstance that a weak international law recognises as law-creating certain facts of international life over which it has no control. International law does not create or countenance war, but it recognises and regulates it; consequently, it is unable to declare null and void acts of force; consequently, it is not in the position to disallow contest as a mode of acquisition of territory. All this in no way alters the fact that the principle involved in the recognition of title by conquest is on the face of it repulsive to the idea of law. This is the reason why many international lawyers who as a rule confine themselves to registering the practice of States are not too eager to recognise title by conquest.[2] It is therefore not surprising that, recognition of conquest

note addressed on July 21, 1895, by the Brazilian Minister for Foreign Affairs to the British Minister, and cited in full by Moore, *Digest*, vol. i. pp. 299-301.

[1] This seems to be the accepted doctrine. In so far, therefore, as the learned author of a recent Article (Sir John Fischer Williams, *B.Y.* (1926), pp. 24-42) is at pains to prove that international law does not prohibit the use of force in acquisition of territorial sovereignty, his argument challenges no contradiction. In so far, however, as it purports to show that definitive possession is the only deciding factor in acquisition of title, it is open to serious question with regard both to conquest and to other modes of acquisition of territory. See § 41, above.

[2] See the long array of publicists cited by Fauchille, No. 557 (11); see also Hyde, vol. i. p. 175. It is interesting to note how writers who recognise title by conquest have recourse to fictions based on private law. The conquered territory is simply regarded as *res nullius* (see Heimburger, *Erwerb der Gebietshoheit*, 1888, p.125; Nys, vol. ii. p. 52).

and the conception of a community of nations governed in its entirety by law being mutually exclusive, the attempts at a legal organisation of all or of certain groups of States usually start from or involve the repudiation of conquest. The first official attempt to effect a closer association of American States was accompanied by a solemn act of a partial repudiation of the title by conquest. The delegates of the sixteen American States to the first Pan-American Conference of 1889 and 1890 agreed unanimously, with one abstention, to accept the following resolution proposed by the United States:

'1. That the principle of conquest shall not, during the continuance of the treaty of arbitration, be recognised as admissible under American public law;

'2. That all cessions of territory made during the continuance of the treaty of arbitration shall be void if made under threats of war in the presence of an armed force.'[1]

The repudiation of the principle of conquest was one of the main features of President Wilson's addresses in which he formulated the foundations of the coming international order. Article 10 of the Covenant of the League of Nations, in which 'the Members of the League

[1] Moore, *Digest*, i. 29. The resolution supported by a majority of States taking part in the Conference proposed: 'that the principle of conquest shall never hereafter be recognised as admissible under American public law'; it did not, however, secure the support of the United States (see Moore, *loc. cit.*). See also the draft of the Convention on Conquests prepared by Professor J. B. Scott for adoption by the Pan-American Commission of Jurists set up in connection with the proposed codification of international law and printed in an Editorial Note by Professor Scott in *A.J.*, xix. (1925) p. 336: 'The American Republics . . . solemnly declare as a fundamental concept of American international law that, without criticising territorial acquisitions effected in the past, and without reference to existing controversies,

'In the future territorial acquisitions obtained by means of war or under the menace of war or in presence of an armed force, to the detriment of any American Republic, shall not be lawful,

'And that, consequently, territorial acquisitions effected in the future by these means cannot be invoked as conferring title; and

'That those obtained in future by such means shall be considered null in fact and in law.'

undertake to respect and to preserve as against external aggression the territorial integrity and political independence of all Members of the League,' and which, to use President Wilson's expression, constitutes the backbone of the Covenant, is essentially a prohibition of acquisition of territory by force. The discussions within the Assembly of the League, the opinion of writers, and the plain meaning of the Article itself show clearly that, at least so far as the Members of the League are concerned, the title by conquest has been abolished.[1] It seems that even the territory of the aggressor State against whom the League proceeds with sanctions is safe from conquest.[2, 3]

[1] See Komarnicki, *La question de l'intégrité territoriale dans le Pacte de la Société des Nations*, 1923, pp. 164-170. The Commission appointed in 1924 by the Council of the League of Nations to investigate and to report on the question of the frontier between Iraq and Turkey did not accept the view that conquest may be regarded as conferring a title (C. 400, M. 147, 1925, vii. pp. 84, 85). See also pp. 37, 38 of the *Counter Case* of Peru in the Tacna-Arica dispute, 1924.

[2] Article 15 of the unratified *Geneva Protocol* of September 1924 provided: '. . . in view of Article 10 of the Covenant, neither the territorial integrity nor the political independence of the aggressor State shall in any case be affected as a result of the application of the sanctions mentioned in the present Protocol.'

[3] The indirect prohibition of conquest by Article 10 of the Covenant, the necessity of avoiding such an interpretation of its provisions as would point to a stereotyping of the international order, as well as Article 19 of the Covenant, suggest the probability of international law eventually taking over the only Roman law mode of acquiring dominion which has not been adopted by international publicists, namely, adjudication. *Adjudicatio* (*I. de off. jud.*, 4, 17) was in Roman law a derivative mode of acquisition by virtue of the award of a judge in a partition suit. Whereas a judgment was only declaratory of a pre-existing right, the *adjudicatio* had a constitutive effect. It transferred to a party the right of ownership which it had not before. Adjudication is, so far, unknown to international law. Decisions of international tribunals are, according to the better opinion, solely declaratory of existing rights (see Fauchille in *R.G.*, xxvii. (1920) pp. 192-193, and the writers there cited). Thus the questions whether an arbitral award is constitutive or declaratory, as well as the applicability of Roman and private law in this respect, formed one of the main issues in the Boundary Dispute between Colombia and Venezuela, decided in 1922 by the Swiss Federal Council. Both parties admitted that the effect is declaratory, although they seem to have drawn opposite conclusions from the same premise. See *Premier Mémoire de Venezuela*, 1918, p. 26; *Premier Mémoire de la Colombie*, 1918, p. 63; Venezuelan *Réplique*, 1920, pp. 188-193; the opinions of Alvarez, Borel, Burckhard and Fauchille in the Colombian *Réplique*, 1920, pp. 181-304. It must, on the other hand, be admitted that such decisions as that of the Concert of European Powers in 1913 concerning Skutari, which was given

III

SOVEREIGNTY OVER THE SEA, THE TERRITORIAL WATERS, AND THE AIR

§ 45. *The Influence of Private Law upon the Development of the Conception of the Freedom of the Sea. Grotius, Bynkershoek. Modern Writers.*—The influence of the private law principle of intention coupled with actual possession was not limited to acquisition of sovereignty over land. It is not too much to say that it has been the chief legal argument on both sides [1] in the theoretical battle for and against the freedom of the sea. The *Mare Liberum* bristles with quotations from the Digest and the Institutes showing the necessity of actual occupation in order to obtain a clear title.[2] Its author, speaking of the sea and the seashore, says:

'If any part of these things is by nature susceptible of occupation, it may become the property of the one who occupies it only so far as such occupation does not affect its common use. . . .[3]

to Albania, or of the Council of the League of Nations concerning the award of Memel to Lithuania (see *League of Nations*, Doc. C. 159, M. 39, 1924, vii.), or of Mosul to Irak, were more than declaratory of existing rights. Moreover, Article 19 of the Covenant of the League, which provides that 'The Assembly may from time to time advise the reconsideration by Members of the League of Treaties which have become inapplicable, and the consideration of international conditions whose continuance might endanger the peace of the world,' may lead to situations in which the League will, in a quasi-judicial process, adjudicate territorial rights. This development, however, seems far off. On the question of adjudication, cf. Schätzel, in Strupp's *Wörterbuch*, vol. i. p. 6, and the same, *Völkerbund und Gebietserwerb*, 1919, pp. 30-32.

[1] For the opponents of the principle of the freedom of the sea, far from denying the applicability of the private law rule of effective occupation, were attempting to prove that the claim to sovereignty over the sea does not clash with the respective principles of private law. Cf. Selden, *Of the Dominion, or, Ownership of the Sea Two Books. In the First is shew'd that the Sea, by the Law of Nature, or Nations is not common to all men, but capable of private Dominion or Proprietie, as well as Land*, 1635 (title as in Nedham's translation of 1652).

[2] *Mare Liberum*, translation by Magoffin, 1916, pp. 13, 25, 29.

[3] *Ibid.*, p. 30.

'The nature of the sea, however, differs from that of the shore, because the sea, except for a very restricted space, can neither easily be built upon, nor enclosed. . . .'[1]

The argument that occupation and possession are necessary for acquisition of sovereignty is taken up by Bynkershoek,[2] who, however, holds that the sea can be actually occupied by maintaining there an efficient fleet. He adduces ample evidence proving the right of dominion over the sea on the part of such nations as have gained possession of it; but he denies that any European nation of his time has actually acquired such possession: 'We have said above that no sea is held to-day under the dominion of any prince, and we have proved it according to the rules of ownership.'[3] He agrees with Grotius so far as the ocean itself is concerned: 'The fact is certainly patent that this is not occupied and clearly cannot be possessed; for all the ships of the rulers would not in any way be sufficient for holding it in possession . . . wherefore no one can justify a legal individual right over it.'[4] Also Vattel follows Grotius' lead.[5]

The appeal to the private law rule of effectiveness of possession remained in the course of the nineteenth century the leading legal argument in favour of the freedom of the sea. Ortolan, the author of the classical treatise on the law of the sea, appealed to it[6] in much the same manner in which the founder of international law availed himself of it two hundred years before. He says, quoting Savigny's treatise on possession:

'Le fait sans l'intention ne suffirait pas pour constituer cette possession, encore moins l'intention sans le fait. Il

[1] *Ibid.*, p. 31.

[2] *De Dominio Maris Dissertatio*, 1702, translated by Magoffin, Classics Edition, 1923.

[3] *Op. cit.*, p. 60.

[4] *Op. cit.*, p. 77.

[5] Bk. i. § 280.

[6] *Règles internationales et Diplomatie de la mer*, 3rd ed., 1856.

faut l'un et l'autre réunis. . . . Décuplez, centuplez toutes les flottes du monde réunies, metront-elles la mer à la discrétion d'un peuple ? . . . La mer n'est pas susceptible de tomber dans la propriété des hommes, parce que la mer ne peut pas être possédée.' [1]

Nearly all publicists writing in the nineteenth century follow the same argument. Hall is only giving to the doctrine a modern form when he makes the following statement: 'It being recognised that states are unable to maintain effective control over large spaces of sea, so as to be able to reserve their use for themselves, it is a principle of international law that the sea is in general insusceptible of appropriation as property.' [2] There is no reason to suppose that this line of argument will totally disappear in the future, owing to the fact that the recourse to this principle of private law may now in turn prove destructive to the idea of the freedom of the sea as a result of the development of modern navies, which, it is alleged, renders possible the effective occupation of large parts of the sea.[3] For, firstly, the occupation of the sea continues to remain precarious even for the most powerful fleet, and this precariousness will naturally increase with the technical development of submarines, contact mines, and sea aircraft. Secondly, it must not be forgotten that to-day the legal basis of the freedom of the sea, whatever may have been its origin, is exclusively the fact that it has become universally recognised as a part of customary

[1] *Op. cit.*, pp. 126-127.

[2] P. 70.—He says in another place (p. 189): 'The true key to the development of the law is to be sought in the principle that maritime occupation must be effective in order to be valid'; Hautefeuille, *Des droits et des devoirs des nations neutres en temps de guerre maritime*, 3rd ed., 1868, vol. i. p. 43; Heffter-Geffcken, pp. 164-166, also p. 166, n. 2; Twiss, i. § 172; Westlake, vol. i. p. 164 ('The true foundation of the rule that the open sea is not the subject of sovereignty is the fact that it is not capable of occupation').

[3] See, for instance, Oppenheim, vol. i. p. 420, and especially Stier-Somlo, *Die Freiheit der Meere und das Völkerrecht*, 1917, pp. 39-56.

international law, and that it cannot therefore be seriously affected by a change of external conditions rendering possible the occupation of the sea. But be that as it may, the publicist, while explaining to the student the *ratio legis* of the rule at the time when it was being fought out, in battles at sea and in theoretical battles among publicists, will continue to refer to the private law principle of effective occupation.[1]

§ 46. *On the Conception of Territorial Waters.*—While this private law doctrine of effectiveness of occupation succeeded, so far as legal theory is concerned, in finally silencing the claims to sovereignty over the sea, it contributed, on the other hand, to the general acceptance of the rights of States over their territorial waters. Bynkershoek is commonly regarded as the publicist who laid the foundations of the modern conception of territorial waters. As a matter of fact, he was only taking up the argument of Grotius, who admits that if a portion of the sea can be occupied the occupation should be recognised.[2] Bynkershoek follows him closely, although, as observed, he does not agree with him in the application of the rule. He points out that his views concerning the ownership of the sea are derived solely from the law of ownership and from those rules for acquiring or losing possession which are identical in the law of nations and in the civil law of the Romans.[3] Hence the rule on the extent of the maritime belt, 'as far as cannon will carry'; 'for that is as far as we seem to have both command and possession.'[4] The possession of a thing, he says, is vested in him 'who so holds it that another cannot hold it against his will . . . for there can be no

[1] It is of interest to note how increasingly useful the Roman law conception of *res omnium communis*, substituted for that of *res nullius*, is proving for the purpose of determining the legal position of the high sea.

[2] *Mare Liberum*, p. 31; see p. 108, *supra*.

[3] *De Dominio Maris*, p. 53.

[4] *Op. cit.*, p. 44.

reason for saying that the sea which is under some one man's command and control is any less his than a ditch in his territory.'[1] A cursory survey of the opinions of writers on the legal nature of the maritime belt shows clearly how great was the influence of private law on this point. Whether it be Vattel,[2] Wheaton,[3] Fiore,[4] or Hall,[5] who attribute to the State dominion over territorial waters, or Bluntschli,[6] Despagnet,[7] Rivier,[8] and many others, who stress the State's rights of sovereignty over the maritime belt, the starting-point, so far as legal construction is concerned, is the same, namely, that it is an accessory of the territory over which the State exercises the rights of *dominium* or *imperium*. To quote one instructive instance, Westlake's very lucid treatment of the subject[9] is in every detail reminiscent of that of Grotius, Bynkershoek, and Vattel. He points out that whereas the sea is not under the *imperium* of the State because it is incapable of occupation, the maritime belt is so partly, owing to the forts and batteries on shore. That, however, he says, is not enough. *Corpus* is not sufficient; there must be *animus possidendi*: 'For the establishment of sovereignty, motive and occupation must be combined.'[10] The motive he finds in reasons of utility, security, and defence. The analogy is thus completed.

§ 47. *On the Conception of the Freedom of the Air. The Adoption of Analogy to Private Law by both the Champions and the Opponents of the Freedom of the Air.*—The private law principle of connection of intention with actual possession was destined, once more, to play an important

[1] *Op. cit.*, p. 43.
[2] Bk. i. § 287.
[3] § 189.
[4] *Code*, Nos. 265, 1029.
[5] P. 190.
[6] § 302.
[7] No. 403.
[8] Vol. i. p. 145.
[9] Vol. i. pp. 187, 188.
[10] *Ibid.*, p. 188.

part in the theoretical battle centring round the problem of the sovereignty of the air. '*L'air par sa nature même, ne se prête à aucune appropriation ; il ne saurait être occupé d'une façon réelle et continue ; il ne peut donc être un objet de propriété,'*—it was in this manner that Fauchille defended before the Institute of International Law the principle of the freedom of the air.[1] A thing which cannot be occupied cannot become an object of property or sovereignty,—that is the main legal argument invoked by the champions of the freedom of the air not less freely than by the defenders of the freedom of the sea two and three hundred years ago. And in the same way as the principle of effective occupation from the coast led to the idea of measuring the extent of territorial waters by the range of cannon, so some jurists adopt the idea of establishing horizontal zones in the air space above State territory and territorial waters.[2] The State should, according to them, have full sovereignty over the air from the earth to a certain height which it is able to control, the zone above that line remaining free from the interference of State regulations. On the other hand, publicists asserting the full sovereignty of the State over the whole air space above its territory base themselves, in their legal argumentation, on certain private law rules of ownership,[3] notably on the rule of Roman law expressed in the maxim *cujus est solum ejus est usque ad coelum*, and adopted by many systems of private

[1] See *Annuaire*, xix. (1902) p. 32; see also the report of Nys, *ibid.*, p. 104. Attention may be drawn here to the masterly exposition by Fauchille of the theories of the sovereignty of the air (No. 531 (2) and following Nos.). It will be observed how strikingly the arguments put forward by him resemble those used by Grotius in *Mare Liberum* (see especially pp. 585-588). For an account of these theories, see Hazeltine, quoted below, pp. 40-46.

[2] See Mérignhac, *R.G.*, xxi. (1914) p. 223.

[3] See Sir H. Erle Richards, *Sovereignty over the Air*, 1912, p. 10; see also Hazeltine, *The Law of the Air*, 1911, pp. 72-76; Liszt, p. 140. For a summary of the air controversy, see Garner, *Recent Developments in International Law*, 1925, pp. 141-148.

jurisprudence. The inference drawn by way of analogy from that maxim is the existence of a full right of sovereignty of the State over the air space above its territory.[1]

§ 48. *The Principle of Effective Possession as the Regulating Principle.*—Is it possible to reconcile the two opposing standpoints, or is the fact that the two contentions are to a large extent based on private law a clear instance of the barrenness of the attempts to bring into closer contact problems of the two branches of law ? The second part of the question must, it is submitted, be denied. It is not only in the domain of international law that the two principles clash. They clash with no less force in private law, where the problems arising out of the conquest of the air urgently require a readjustment of some well-established rules. The German Code[2] states expressly that the right of the owner of land extends over the entire air space above the surface of the land as well as to the entire soil beneath the surface ; but the second part of the same Article states no less explicitly that the owner may not forbid interference which takes place at such a height or depth that he has no interest in its prevention. Similar is the corresponding provision of the Swiss Code.[3] And although there is no doubt that the English common law adheres to the *usque ad coelum* rule,[4] it is significant that Sir Frederick Pollock, while admitting that on the principles of common law an entry above the surface constitutes trespass, adds : 'Unless indeed it can be

[1] It is obvious that behind legal formulas there lie in this theoretical battle considerations of a quite different order. The principle of sovereignty and the needs of the self-preservation and security of States are here confronted by the necessities of international intercourse and by the development of aviation and radio-telegraphy.

[2] Article 905.

[3] Article 667.

[4] See especially per Fry, L.J., in *Wandsworth Board of Works* v. *United Telephone Co.*, (1884) 13 Q.B.Div. 904, 927.

said that the scope of possible trespass is limited by that of possible effective possession, which might be the most reasonable rule.'[1] In fact, the common law rule has been seriously impaired by the Air Navigation Act of 1920. It is submitted that the principle which regulates the right of property over the air space by the application of the postulate of effective possession, and which a leading authority, in a very guarded passage, recommends as 'the most reasonable rule,' cannot be in the long run disregarded by international law.

The rule *usque ad coelum* is undoubtedly a rule of several systems of private law; but it is frequently urged in this monograph that only rules of universal application, or at least such as are adopted by the main systems of private jurisprudence, are suitable for the purpose of analogy in international law. The maxim *usque ad coelum* has now ceased to be a rule of this kind. The analogy of effective occupation which influenced deeply the theory and the practice of acquisition of sovereignty over land, sea, and the maritime belt has not, therefore, entirely lost its importance for international law. This is so notwithstanding the fact that the practice of States and conventional international law seem, under the stress of abnormal war and post-war conditions, to adopt the opposing rule. Article 1 of the Convention,[2] relating to the Regulation of Aerial Navigation, of October 13, 1919, says: 'The High Contracting Powers recognise that every Power has complete and exclusive sovereignty over the air space above its territory.' However, Article 15 provides that 'every aircraft of a contracting State has the right to cross the air space

[1] *The Law of Torts*, 12th ed., 1923, p. 352.

[2] The fact should not be lost sight of that the Convention of 1919 was strongly influenced by the World War, and that since August 1914 the frontiers of neutrals were closed to belligerent aircraft.

of another State without landing.'[1] This seems to contain an indication that the rigid principle of exclusive sovereignty over the air is capable of thorough modifications. It is believed that reasons of convenience and the necessities of international intercourse will cause the private law principle of effective possession to assert itself ultimately, in substance if not in form, also in the domain of international aerial law.[2]

IV

PRESCRIPTION, ACQUISITIVE AND EXTINCTIVE

§ 49. *Acquisitive Prescription.*—Prescription appears in international law either as a mode of original acquisition of territorial rights or as a rule limiting the time in which both contractual claims and those arising out of an international tort may be put forward. With regard to the first-mentioned aspect of the question, it appears that prescription has become a well-recognised rule of international law. The modern practice of States has recognised it in arbitration conventions [3] and in proceedings before international tribunals.[4] With regard to the latter, the British Guiana arbitration of 1904,[5]

[1] *League of Nations, Treaty Series*, xi. p. 174; cf. also the resolution of the 28th Conference of the International Law Association. See, however, in favour of the principle of the freedom of the air, the resolution of the Institute of International Law of 1911, *Annuaire* (1911), p. 346; and, for further references, Spaight, quoted below, p. 5.

[2] Cf. here Blewett Lee in *Harvard Law Review*, xxxiii. (1919 - 1920) pp. 23-38, and especially Catellani, *Le Vie del Mare e dell' Aria e il diritto internazionale*, 1919, p. 32.

[3] See the treaty preceding the British Guiana arbitration of 1897, p. 229, *infra*, and, previously, the treaty between Guatemala and Mexico of January 26, 1888 (Manning, p. 174). See also Moore, *Digest*, vol. i. p. 296, on the implied recognition of prescription in several British-American treaties.

[4] See Hyde, vol. i. p. 194, n. 4, on the recourse by Great Britain to the doctrine of prescription in the Passamaquoddy Bay dispute; for other instances, see Fauchille, vol. i. pt. 1*b*, No. 557(5).

[5] See pp. 275, 276, *infra*.

the Grisbadarna case before the Hague Tribunal in 1909,[1] the Walfisch Bay arbitration of 1911,[2] and the Chamizal arbitration of 1911[3] may be mentioned as four relatively recent cases of the application of the doctrine.[4] The science of international law follows this practice closely. Even such publicists as are usually quoted as rejecting the doctrine[5] admit that, although it does not create the title, it allows the presumption of it. Stubborn opposition against this rule of private law could only come from writers who emphasise the fundamental difference between international and private law. In a community in which force constitutes right, and in which actual possession, regardless of time, confers a title, the institute of prescription is unnecessary. If no possession is illegal, if every possession is lawful, then clearly there is no need for a jural principle calculated to legalise an originally illegal position. This is, for instance, the view of Liszt, who speaks of the direct law-creating influence which mere force, especially conquest, has in the domain of international law.[6] This opinion, although generally rejected, is nevertheless instructive as showing the theoretical sources from which the opposition to private law arises.

[1] See p. 264, *infra*.

[2] See p. 277, *infra*.

[3] See p. 276, *infra*.

[4] The reason given by some writers against the adoption of prescription, namely, that there is no rule of international law fixing the period necessary for its completion, has now been dismissed in a similar way to the argument opposing the awarding of interest on account of there being no settled rule of international law regulating the rate of interest and the *dies a quo* (see p. 146, *infra*). Nevertheless, this argument, originally propounded by Vattel, proved powerful enough as an obstacle in the way of a more searching treatment of the problem. The important question how far the private law requirements of prescription, for instance, that possession should be undisturbed and uninterrupted, are recognised in international law is seldom, if ever, approached, although international tribunals are frequently confronted with it (see, for instance, the Chamizal arbitration, p. 277, *infra*, the two British Guiana arbitrations, pp. 229, 276, *infra*).

[5] See, for instance, Ullmann, § 92, and Rivier, vol. i. p. 183.

[6] P. 241; and especially Jerusalem, *Die völkerrechtlichen Erwerbsgründe*, 1911, p. 422 (in *Festgabe für A. Thon*).

§ 50. *Extinctive Prescription.*—While the field of application of acquisitive prescription is naturally a limited one, extinctive prescription, corresponding to limitation of actions in municipal law, is becoming of ever-growing importance in international arbitration. The *Williams* case, in which umpire Little, after a detailed discussion of the problem, adopted the doctrine of prescription, marks the beginning of its full recognition in international law.[1] This development had been checked for a while by the much misunderstood award in the Pious Fund arbitration,[2] but the balance was soon restored. In 1903 extinctive prescription was again fully adopted in a learned award which has since been followed by other international tribunals.[3] The Institute of International Law was fully justified in stating, in 1925, in its Resolution on Limitation of Actions in International Public Law, that the principle itself is 'long accepted in arbitral jurisprudence.'[4] Where

[1] See Moore, pp. 4181-4199; see also the *Mossman* case, *ibid.*, p. 4180.

[2] See pp. 249, 250, *infra*.

[3] See the *Gentini* case, *Ralston's Report*, p. 720 and p. 274, *infra*. See also Ralston in *A.J.*, v. (1911) p. 133; and the same, Nos. 683-687. There is, however, a comparatively recent arbitral award which states that 'the principle of limitation of actions does not . . . operate as between States.' The argument of the arbitrator, who in this case was an '*amiable compositeur*,' is not very convincing (see *Award* in the *Alsop Claim*, *A.J.*, v. (1911) pp. 1079-1107).

[4] The resolution wholly confirms the view put forward in the text. It regards the limitation of actions as 'a general principle of law recognised by civilised nations,' and urges the necessity of its adoption in arbitral jurisprudence (Article 1). 'In the absence of a conventional rule in force in the relations of the litigant states, fixing the limit of the prescription, its determination is a question left entirely to the decision of the international judge . . .' (Article 2). Article 3 (2) provides that the judge has to take into consideration 'whether the delay in the claim applies to its original presentation or simply to its renewal, as prescription ought to be excluded in the second hypothesis except if it is established as a fact that the subsequent inaction of the claimant State is not imputable to the adverse party or to a case of *force majeure*.' The Institute acted consistently in refusing to disallow prescription in cases relating to public or contractual debts (in contradistinction to debts of a private origin or tortious debt; see Politis, *R.I.* (*Geneva*), iii. (1925) p. 4). It states only (Article 3 (1)) that, as a rule, it is more difficult to admit prescription for debts of the first kind. The resolution is printed in *A.J.*, xix. (1925) p. 760. Cf. also Montluc in *R.I.* (*Geneva*), iii. (1925) pp. 195-197; Niboyet in *R.I.* (1925), 3rd ser., vol. vi. pp. 659-665; and Cavaglieri in *Rivista*, xviii. (1926) pp. 169-204.

international tribunals refuse to recognise the plea of prescription, the refusal can, as a rule, be traced to the special circumstances of the particular case. Thus, when a claim has been brought in time before the respondent Government, and the delay has been occasioned by its inability or unwillingness to respond to the claim, the tribunals refuse, for obvious reasons of justice and convenience, to give effect to the plea of prescription.[1]

V

STATE SERVITUDES

§ 51. *The Present Position of the Doctrine.*—It may be said with some justification that of all attempts to apply to relations between States conceptions taken from private law, none has caused more confusion or has brought the recourse to analogy into more disrepute than the efforts made to introduce the conception of servitudes into international public law. This is certainly not a result of lack of interest bestowed upon the matter. Few questions of international law have in the past twenty years been treated in more detail. Thus the problem of servitudes constituted the central issue of one of the outstanding arbitrations, namely, of the North Atlantic Fisheries arbitration, and hardly ever has a question of international law been discussed before an international tribunal by abler lawyers or been backed by more learning and research. The answer given by the

[1] See the *Butterfield* claim of the U.S. against Denmark (award, Moore, p. 1205); the *Stevenson* case (*Ralston's Report*, p. 327); the *Roberts* case (*ibid.*, p. 142). See also Lapradelle-Politis, *note doctrinale*, on the case of *The Macedonian*, vol. ii. pp. 205-209; and Politis, *loc. cit.*, pp. 7-9. See also Ralston, *op. cit.*, Nos. 688-694.

tribunal was not conclusive, although it is regarded by many as having rejected the doctrine of servitudes,[1] and was, in part, so regarded by a commission of jurists appointed in 1920 by the Council of the League of Nations for the purpose of reporting on the question of the Aaland Islands.[2] The Hague Court rejected the doctrine as a rule of legal construction, but was prepared to accept it if so stipulated by the parties: 'It [the doctrine of servitudes] could therefore . . . be affirmed by this Tribunal only on the express evidence of an international contract.'[3] The tribunal, which disapproved of the view that the creation of an international servitude may lightly be inferred, adopted the conception of servitudes as such, and thus intimated that should the parties avail themselves of this institution of law international law will recognise it and give effect to the will of the parties by applying rules generally accepted as applicable to this conception. It is only to be regretted that the tribunal did not explain what is meant by 'the express evidence of an international contract.' Is it necessary to use the term 'servitude,' or may the express evidence be inferred from unmistakable provisions of the treaty? The Permanent Court of International Justice confined itself in its first judgment[4] to the statement that the question whether there really exist in international law servitudes analogous to servitudes of private law is a controversial one.

In so far as the literature of international law is concerned, it appears that although the necessity of getting rid of a doctrine which, it is alleged, is likely to be abused or at least to cause further confusion, is strongly urged by some writers,[5] the great majority of

[1] See, for instance, Oppenheim, vol. i. p. 365.

[2] *Official Journal*, League of Nations, Special Suppl., No. 3, October 1920, p. 16.

[3] Award, Scott's *Reports*, p. 160.

[4] Publications of the Court, Series A, No. 1, p. 24.

[5] Strupp, p. 77; Niemeyer, p. 104; to a certain extent Hyde, i. p. 276. See also McNair, in *B.Y.* (1925), p. 126.

publicists are not disposed to jettison the conception of international servitudes.[1]

§ 52. *International Servitudes Proper.*—If the view be accepted that it is the business of international lawyers to clarify conceptions by sifting the chaff from the wheat, and not to abandon that task prematurely merely because it is too difficult, then there should be no doubt that the attitude adopted by the majority of writers is the correct one. For it cannot be denied that there are in international law relationships which present an analogy to prædial servitudes of the Roman law or to easements of the common law almost amounting to identity, namely, those relationships in which a part or the whole of the territory of one State is made to serve the economic needs of another. There exists in such cases not only a dominant tenement (*praedium dominans*) and a 'servient tenement' (*praedium serviens*), but also the possibility of most of the formal requirements of the private law of servitudes being fulfilled. An instance taken from the recent Peace Treaties may be quoted as an illustration: Article 358 of the Treaty of Versailles provides that France shall have on the whole course of the Rhine included between the two extreme points of the French frontier the right to take water from this river to feed navigation and irrigation canals, or for any other purpose, and to execute on the German bank all works necessary for the exercise of this right. In the same article France is granted the right of support on and the right of way over all lands situated on the right bank which may be required in order to

[1] See, for instance, Hatschek, p. 155; Fleischmann in Liszt, p. 133; Fenwick, p. 284; Fauchille, No. 339; Verdross, *Die Verfassung der Völkerrechtsgemeinschaft*, 1926, pp. 189-192; Visscher in *R.I.*, 3rd ser., vol. ii. (1921) p. 256; Staël-Holstein, *ibid.*, 3rd ser., vol. iii. (1922) p. 431; Brown in *A.J.*, xv. (1921) p. 271.

build and to operate weirs. In order to ensure the execution of the first-mentioned provision, Germany assumes the negative obligation not to undertake or to allow the construction of any lateral canal on the right bank of the river. The Article contains detailed provisions as to the exercise of the above-mentioned right of support and way, and the indemnification of the proprietors 'whose property will be burdened with such servitudes.' Thus the treaty not only actually contains provisions reproducing a typical servitude in private law, but also, as if to leave no doubt, adopts the formal terminology of private law.[1]

It is submitted that, quite apart from the terminology adopted in this and similar international agreements, relationships of this kind resemble closely servitudes in private law, and that it is convenient to classify them as such also in international law. Of course, the classification as servitudes carries with it all the implications of a real right;[2] the term itself would otherwise serve no useful purpose, and would only encourage a laxity of language which international law has special reasons to avoid. On the other hand, the grave consequences attaching to the construction of an international

[1] See, for other examples of economic servitudes in the Treaty of Versailles, the Articles 89, 98, 104.

[2] It may perhaps be pointed out that the *real* character of the right implies that the servitude survives a change of sovereignty not only over the servient, but also over the dominant territory. In addition, according to several publicists (Clauss, *State Servitudes*, Scott's compilation, p. 165; Heilborn, pp. 30-34), and to an outspoken decision of the Cologne Court of Appeal, the grant of a servitude implies the existence of jurisdictional rights exercised by the grantee in his own name. The Court said:

'. . . This means . . . not what might be termed a mining concession to the Dutch Government granted by Prussia according to civil law, but the exclusion of certain sovereign rights in the ceded parts. . . . A sort of international servitude has arisen by which Holland as a State is entitled, now as previously, in the matter of this mine to exercise its own legislative authority and police and supervision—that is, it has real sovereign rights with respect to the object situated within the territory of the foreign State' (Ullmann, *Völkerrecht*, p. 320). The award is printed in *A.J.*, viii. (1914) p. 907.

Exactly the same was the contention of the United States before the Hague Tribunal (see p. 240, *infra*).

obligation as a servitude require that it should be resorted to only when there is no doubt that the parties intended it to be a permanent relation independently of who is the sovereign of the entitled or encumbered territory. Such an intention may be inferred :

(*a*) from the term 'servitude' having been expressly used in a treaty ;[1]

(*b*) from other clear provisions of the treaty ; for instance, to the effect that the restriction should last for all time, or that it should remain unaffected by changes of territorial sovereignty ;[2]

(*c*) from the character of the international agreement in question, *i.e.* if the number of signatories is such that the Convention assumes the character of an act of international legislation creating a rule of universal international law ;[3]

(*d*) from the fact that a certain restriction has been repeatedly taken over by successive sovereigns, so that the question as to its real character has been answered in the affirmative by actual observance.[4]

It would be of advantage if international lawyers could be induced to exercise a greater measure of restraint in classifying as servitudes different restrictions of sovereignty, preferably to the extent of recognising as servitudes only economic or quasi-economic restrictions of territorial sovereignty, and confining themselves to the

[1] See Article 358 of the Treaty of Versailles mentioned above, and the Treaty of Stettin of 1570, mentioned by Staël-Holstein, *op. cit.*, p. 436.

[2] See, for instance, Article 4 of the Hay-Pauncefote Treaty between the United States and Great Britain, of November 18, 1901 ('no change of territorial sovereignty, or of international relations of the country or countries traversed by the before-mentioned canal, shall affect the general principle of neutralisation or the obligation of the High Contracting Parties under the present Treaty'), Hertslet's *Treaties*, vol. xxiii. p. 1151.

[3] See on this point McNair, *op. cit.*, p. 126.

[4] For a clear example of an economic servitude of this kind, see Staël-Holstein, *op. cit.*, pp. 439-448. The repeated taking over of the obligations concerning the neutralisation of the provinces of Chablais and Faucigny (see Fauchille, No. 368) may, if regarded as a servitude, be mentioned as another example.

four above-mentioned modes of ascertaining the intention of the parties. Thus it may be doubted whether the widely adopted class of military servitudes, especially the negative ones, admits of any analogy to servitudes of private law, or whether it can be defined at all with any approach to exactitude.[1] While, however, it may be difficult to discard this kind of servitudes by reason of their being well established in the literature, it is difficult to approve such statements as that the Monroe doctrine imposes a servitude upon other American States in the sense that they may not alienate their territory in favour of a European power;[2] or that Article 49 of the Versailles Treaty, in which Germany renounces her sovereignty over the Saar territory, constitutes a servitude in favour of the League of Nations;[3] or that the provisions of international mandates are servitudes restricting the sovereignty of the mandatory.[4] Here, as in many other cases, conceptions of private law prove to be vicious and misleading only if resorted to for purposes of metaphor or when made to support certain debatable political assertions. But the conception of State servitudes, when approached from the point of view of giving effect to the will of the parties—which is in the bulk of cases expressive of objective economic conditions and of the necessities of intercourse and neighbourly adjustments—and not from the point of view of the current arguments on the obsolescence of patrimonial ideas or the dangers of recourse to private law, is bound to remain, within its necessarily limited scope, a useful part of international law.

[1] See on this point, Visscher, *op. cit.*, p. 256.

[2] Fenwick, p. 284.

[3] Fleischmann in Liszt, p. 132; Hatschek, p. 161.

[4] See the speech by Mr Amery, the Minister for the Colonies, *The Times*, June 12, 1926.

VI

STATE SUCCESSION

§ 53. *State Succession. The Problem Identical in International and Private Law.*—There is, perhaps, no question more typical of the relation between private and international law than that of State succession. The notion of State succession has been created and developed in close connection with the corresponding conceptions of private, and especially Roman, law. From Grotius to the end of the nineteenth century there is, with rare exceptions, no hesitation among publicists in applying them for the purpose of answering the question as to how far, in the case of change of sovereignty, the rights and obligations of the former sovereign are taken over by his successor. Patrimonial ideas played a certain part in that development, but the adoption of analogy is not entirely, or even predominantly, due to them. It is due to the fact that the problem of succession, so far as it is treated as a problem of law, is identical in private and international law. The fundamental fact in both cases is that there take place both substitution and continuation of rights and duties, and that legal stability and acquired rights are not destroyed in consequence of the subject of law ceasing to exist. There are, no doubt, circumstances which give to State succession an aspect somewhat different from the passing over of rights and duties in municipal law, and which exclude the rigid application of the principle of unlimited succession. But it will be seen that unlimited succession is, as a rule, unknown to private law, and that the essential aspects of the problem are the same in international and in private law. The main question in State succession is: Is the international legal order strong enough to regulate facts arising out of a change of sovereignty, or does this change take place in a legal *vacuum*? Does the new sovereign acquire rights because it pleases him to take them, or because international law confers upon him the title? Is he bound by the obligations of the former sovereign because he finds it convenient to be so, or because international law imposes upon him that duty?

§ 54. *The Positivist Theories basing State Succession upon the Will of the State. Huber, Keith, Gidel, Cavaglieri, Schönborn. The Necessity of a Comprehensive Rule.*—The modern opposition to the application of analogy to this branch of international law originates from writers who regard the process accompanying changes of sovereignty as a fact lying completely outside the sphere of law. Such are the theories of Huber, Gidel, Keith, Cavaglieri, and Schönborn.[1] According to Huber, the States which belong to the family of nations have the individual right to change the personal rights of other members of the community of nations. They have the right to put themselves in the place of other States; the successor makes the rights and the duties of the predecessor to his own by his own will.[2] The law of the changes thus effected is the law of succession of States. Keith expresses the same theory in a less abstract form:

'Another power attacks a state, defeats its armed force, occupies its seat of government, appropriates its revenue, annexes it, counts its citizens as its nationals, and legislates for it. What takes place is a substitution of authority;

[1] Huber, *Die Staatensuccession*, 1898; Keith, *The Theory of State Succession*, 1907; Cavaglieri, *La dottrina della successione di Stato a Stato e il suo valore giuridico*, 1910; Schönborn, *Staatensukzessionen*, 1913; Gidel, *Des effets de l'annexion sur les concessions*, 1904.

[2] *Op. cit.*, p. 25.

there is a break with the past. The state seizes whatever thing of value it can obtain, but it certainly did not conduct the war for the sake of assuming onerous obligations.' [1]

There is, according to him, no legal obligation to take over either contractual debts, or debts secured on local revenues, or even such real rights as local servitudes of passage, although the last-mentioned may be taken over as a matter of expediency.[2] Gidel supplies the theoretical construction for the case of cession: The State, he says, which cedes the territory abandons its rights over it, and the acquiring State establishes over the territory, now free from any other domination, its own authority in the manner in which it pleases, and only with such restrictions as it thinks proper.[3] Schönborn goes the length of denying that the rule *res transit cum suo onere* has application in relations between States,[4] and Cavaglieri draws the inevitable logical conclusion from this theory of the complete break of legal continuity by stating that the problem is not one of international law but of municipal regulation.[5]

Although these theories are rejected by the majority of writers,[6] and although, as will be seen later, the above-mentioned authors themselves are not in the position to maintain in its entirety their negative attitude, it appears nevertheless that their influence upon some international publicists is not inconsiderable.[7] As to the practice of States, it is true that it follows, on the whole, the principle of succession not only in rights, but also in obligations. There are, however, remarkable exceptions showing the contrary. Treaties, for the

[1] *Op. cit.*, p. 5.

[2] *Ibid.*, p. 4.

[3] *Op. cit.*, p. 64. See also pp. 12-14.

[4] *Op. cit.*, p. 47.

[5] *Op. cit.*, p. 135; see also Schönborn, pp. 100-106.

[6] For a concise and clear review of authorities on the question of succession, see opinion of Prof. Struycken on the question of German settlers in Poland, printed in *Studien zur Lehre von der Staatensukzession, Drei Gutachten*, 1923, pp. 26-40; see also Guggenheim, cited below, pp. 29-42; and Keith, *op. cit.*, pp. 1-7.

[7] See especially Gemma, pp. 71-77; Strupp, p. 52.

most part, affirm the principle of succession, but some deny it.[1] A vicious circle is involved in the question whether treaties providing for the taking over of obligations conform to the rule, or state an exception; or whether treaties which exclude succession do so as an exception to a generally recognised principle. Clearly, if unanimity is the test of a customary rule, then no customary rule of international law has yet been evolved on the question of State succession. Moreover, the taking over of financial and other liabilities independently of a treaty is always liable to be interpreted as an act of grace or of political convenience, and not as a matter of legal obligation. It is clear, therefore, that only a comprehensive general rule which could serve as a basis for legislative international enactments or pronouncements of authoritative judicial

[1] For a review of the practice of States, in the nineteenth century, see Huber, *op. cit.*, pp. 55 ff., and Struycken, quoted above, pp. 42-50. The recent Peace Treaties signify a full recognition of the principle of succession. The Treaty of Versailles provides in Article 254 that the Powers to which German territory is ceded shall undertake to pay a portion of the debt of the German Empire as it stood on August 1, 1914, and of the German State to which the ceded territory belonged. In those exceptional cases where no burdens are taken over (see, for instance, Articles 157, 255, 257), the reason for such a course is as a rule indicated in the treaty itself. Cf. especially Articles 255 (1) and 255 (2). The same applies to the Treaty of St Germain. Article 203 contains detailed provisions with regard to taking over both the secured and the unsecured debt. The war debt constitutes an exception (see Article 205, s. 4). Similar are the provisions of Articles 186-188 of the Treaty of Trianon, of Article 141 of the Treaty of Neuilly, and Article 46 of the Treaty of Lausanne. See also Article 8 of the Treaty of October 28, 1920, between the Principal Allied Powers and Roumania respecting Bessarabia (*A.J.*, Suppl., xviii. (1923) p. 7), and Article 21 of the Treaty between Poland and the Associated and Allied Powers of June 28, 1919 (Hertslet's *Treaties*, vol. xxix. p. 1010). With regard to private rights, concessions, and contracts, it is sufficient to compare the well-known report of the Transvaal Concessions Commission (see Westlake, vol. i. p. 74) with the detailed provisions of Article 4 of the Treaty of May 15, 1922, between Germany and Poland concerning Upper Silesia, in order to ascertain how far a modern treaty goes in the direction of securing private rights (Strupp, *Documents*, vol. iv. pp. 722-726). Of special interest is section 3 of the mentioned paragraph: 'Si des concessions ou des privilèges . . . sont supprimés ou diminués par l'application des lois générales ou par d'autres dispositions, l'État qui applique ces lois, ou prend ces dispositions sera tenu à l'indemnisation complète.' See also Advisory Opinion of the Permanent Court concerning German settlers in Poland, pp. 294, 295, *infra*.

tribunals can supply a final answer to the question. It is believed that the following general considerations must underlie any such final solution.

§ 55. *The International Order as securing Continuity of Rights. Succession and Revolution.*—The basic function of law is protection of acquired rights. Municipal law protects them, as a rule, from the consequences of the death of the debtor. International private law safeguards rights acquired under foreign municipal law, and the execution of foreign judgments is, subject to slight modifications, a recognised rule. While preserving the peculiarities and the individuality of the different systems of municipal law, the international community gives thus expression to the unity of law among the members of the family of nations. Only in the case of States being mere agencies of force unfettered by the rule of law, can this recognition of acquired rights be disregarded by the events of international life. It is not only the sense of right that is *prima facie* violated in this case ; it is the sense of legal order overstepping the borders of State which is being violated. The death of the individual and the changes in State sovereignty are, in relation to legal rights and obligations, crises which must be regulated by a rule of law independent of the will of the actual successor. Private law does it with the help of the institute of inheritance and succession. It is by accepting this broad principle of private law that international law will most effectively strengthen the element of law within the international community.

The idea of international law filling a gap caused by events which threaten otherwise to destroy the continuity of the international legal order is not a new one even to orthodox positivist publicists. It is generally accepted as a truism that the change of the internal constitution of State by way of revolution does not affect the duties of the State as an international person. And yet, there is no legal continuity between the old and the new constitution, between the old and the new government. The latter originates in a revolutionary act, from which, and from which alone, is derived the legal validity of the new order. From the point of view of the new government there is no legal obligation whatsoever to regard itself as bound by the acts of its predecessor, which, legally, do not exist for it. It is the objective international legal order which imposes this duty upon the new government and which constitutes the bridge between two facts otherwise totally disconnected. It is international law which fills the void and provides for a succession of rights and duties.[1] The same applies to the rights and duties of States in the event of changes of sovereignty. A legal order, independent of the will of States, is the link securing legal stability and recognition of acquired rights.

§ 56. *The Problem of Continuation and Substitution. Roman and Modern Law Modifications of the Rigid Principle of Continuation.*—The inquiry as to the extent to which the analogy to succession in private law is admissible has hitherto been hindered by the widely and uncritically accepted assertion that succession in private law is based on the conception of the continuation of the personality of the deceased, an idea which must, in international law, lead to untenable consequences. It would be embarrassing, says a recent writer, to inquire how far Italy is a continuation of the Papal State, or

[1] Cf. Guggenheim, *Beiträge zur völkerrechtlichen Lehre vom Staatenwechsel*, 1925, pp. 1-29, 42-46, and Kelsen, *op. cit.*, p. 238. The contrary opinion is that the changes take place outside the sphere of law. Clear expression is again given to this standpoint in a recent article by Cavaglieri in *Rivista*, xvi. (1924) p. 33: 'Tra l'estinzione del vecchio Stato e l'apprensione dei suoi elementi costitutivi da parte di uno Stato nuovo o già preesistente vi è un *hiatus*, che il diritto è incapace di colmare.' See also Schönborn, *op. cit.*, p. 82.

Czechoslovakia of the Austrian Empire.[1] It seems, however, that the importance of the *dictum* that whereas in private law succession takes place *quoad defunctum*, in international law it does this *quoad iura* only,[2] has been grossly exaggerated. The close connection between the personalities of the *cuius* and the heir is not a general principle of private law. Modern law has made a decided advance upon early Roman law in this connection in so far as it stresses the transmission of rights and property, whereas in Roman law the continuation of the personality of the deceased person was, until Justinian,[3] the main feature of the conception of inheritance.[4] Grotius' statement, '*heredis personam, quoad dominii tam publici quam privati continuationem, pro eadem censeri cum defuncti persona, certi est juris*,[5] can therefore be modified without the necessity of abandoning the broad analogy to private law. The non-transference of political treaties, which correspond to merely personal obligations in private law, the equitable limitation of the financial obligations to be assumed by the new State,[6] and the exclusion of

[1] Gemma, p. 73.

[2] See Huber, *op. cit.*, p. 18. This view is generally adopted by publicists, and it is cited by Westlake, vol. i. p. 69, who seems to approve of it.

[3] With the introduction of inventories, the legal personalities of the *heres* and the deceased were no longer regarded as one.

[4] See Sherman, *Roman Law in the Modern World*, 2nd ed., 1922, § 662.

[5] L. ii. c. 9, s. 12.

[6] See Westlake, vol. i. p. 76, whose statement of the theory of succession is in full accord with the general proposition put forward in these pages. He discards the argument that, in contradistinction to private law, it is the will of the State which is creative of rights in case of change of sovereignty; he points out that 'a private successor is not bound to accept the succession, so that he also comes in by his own will.' See also *Collected Papers*, ch. viii. p. 475. Keith, in order to prove the impracticability of succession as a general rule in international law, is forced to take as a basis of comparison a very abstract type of absolutely universal succession admitting of no exception or relaxation. There is in reality no such private law in existence. On the contrary, private law shows an increasing tendency to modify the stringent rule of universal succession in accordance with equity and convenience. The Roman *beneficium inventarii*, and the exclusion of succession in obligation for torts, may be quoted as examples (with regard to the latter, see p. 283, *infra*). Even the exclusion of obligations with regard to war debts does not destroy the broad principle of succession.

responsibility for tortious acts of the predecessor, are well compatible with the adoption of the general principle of succession.[1]

§ 57. *The Ultimate Adoption of Succession in Obligations.*—The impossibility of completely divorcing the problems accompanying changes of sovereignty from the legal and moral considerations underlying the doctrine of succession, is shown clearly by the fact that the authors who deny the validity of the principle of succession in international law, and to whom the will of the State is in this respect the exclusive source of law, do not go the length of denying any legal obligation whatsoever on the part of the successor. Thus Schönborn, who is of the opinion that it is only reasons of convenience, *e.g.* the necessity of avoiding too great a disturbance of the existing legal relations and of taking into consideration the interests of other States, that influence the attitude of governments in matters of succession, admits that the international practice shows that States adhere, on the whole, to the private law principle of succession.[2] Keith urges the legal obligation of the new government to recognise private rights *in rem* as against the old State.[3] Huber recognises the existence of a customary rule of international law imposing the obligation to take over financial debts,[4] an obligation which he construes as a kind of 'real burden' (*Reallast*) as between State and State. Creditors, he says, lend money not to a corporation which is incidentally in

[1] See Hurst, in *B. Y.* (1924), pp. 163 *et seq.*

[2] *Op. cit.*, p. 100, and again in Strupp's *Wörterbuch*, vol. ii. p. 580.

[3] *Op. cit.*, p. 7. The right *in rem*, he says, 'is good against all the world as well as the sovereign, and there is no reason why a change of sovereign should alter the right. If the right is *ex contractu*, the case is different. The change of Government destroys one of the parties to the contract, and therefore the contract falls utterly to the ground.' It is submitted that the distinction is not cogent, unless the contractual rights against the old State are of such a nature that they cannot reasonably be fulfilled by the new one.

[4] See pp. 81 ff.

possession of a certain territory, but to the territorial entity endowed with economic means and represented by State organs.[1] Cavaglieri, who is emphatic in denying State succession proper,[2] arrives nevertheless at the conclusion that there is a legal obligation on the part of the new government to give effect to such principles as *bona non intelliguntur nisi deducto aere alieno*, and *nemo locupletari potest cum alterius iactura*.[3] 'Between two States,' he says, 'there exists with regard to succession no legal relation . . . except that of enrichment.'[4] This relation he regards in the first instance as a postulate of equity and of political expediency. But if the State fails to pay attention to these considerations, the equitable obligation turns into a juridical one, and the creditors who have failed to obtain satisfaction may now seek redress in the courts of the successor State by means of an action '*per indebito arrichimento*.'[5] Thus the legal obligation is being based on the fact of unjustified enrichment, which the author construes in accordance with the respective private law theories obtaining in Italy.[6] Gidel, who asserts a total substitution of sovereignties, arrives in the end at the similar conception of '*l'enrichissement sans cause aux dépens de l'autrui*.'[7]

[1] *Op. cit.*, p. 88.

[2] *Op. cit.*, p. 108; according to him, succession, if any, is due 'unicamente al fatto che lo Stato Successore vi aveva acconsentito, ed è avvenuto soltanto nella misura di tale consenso; mancavano quindi in realtà i caratteri proprii della successione erediteria.'

[3] *Op. cit.*, pp. 131-134.

[4] *Op. cit.*, p. 141. Cf. also Focherini, *La succesione degli Stati*, 1910. The author is in favour of the theory of substitution. But the absence of succession, he says, is moderated by the protective function of the State and by a juridical order higher than States (p. 104).

[5] *Op. cit.*, p. 139.

[6] They are to some extent akin to the Roman *condictiones ex iniusta causa* and *causa data causa non secuta*; partly also to the *actiones de in rem verso*.

[7] *Op. cit.*, pp. 92-100.

VII

STATE RESPONSIBILITY

§ 58. *The Question of Analogy to Private Law in the Theory of State Responsibility.*—It is not possible, within the limited compass of this monograph, to consider in detail the various modifications of the doctrine of succession when applied to different aspects of change of sovereignty (as annexation, cession, dismemberment) or to different kinds of rights and obligations (political obligations, local debts, public debts, concessions, etc.). However, it is clear that, with regard to all of them, the gist of the problem is the acceptance or rejection of the private law principle of succession as such. The fact that it is accepted by the growing practice of States, evidenced particularly in the recent Peace Treaties, and by the vast majority of writers; that it is ultimately adopted even by those writers who attack it vigorously; and that even those who cast doubt on its existence as a rule of law accept it as a rule dictated by justice, equity, and the necessities of the intercourse of nations,[1] proves that in this as in many other cases the principles of private law, far from fettering the development of international law, are an important element in its development to a higher stage of law. The necessity of adopting the corresponding principle of private law is shown, with still greater clearness, in the theory of State responsibility for international delinquencies. Here again no clear-cut rule can be laid down with regard to all cases in which the international responsibility of the State becomes engaged. It varies largely with the

[1] See Schönborn, *op. cit.*, pp. 82, 106, 107; Keith, *op. cit.*, p. 102. Cf. also Hyde, vol. i. p. 205.

position of the State organ responsible for the commission of the injurious act and with the circumstances in which the act has been committed.[1] But the central problem in all cases is again that of rejection or acceptance of a principle of private law, to wit, of the principle of fault. Is an international delinquency committed by the mere fact of the legitimate interests of one State having been injured within the territory or by the organs of another? Or is it an essential condition for the existence of such responsibility that malicious intent or culpable negligence should be proved? A historical survey of the treatment of this problem shows again the usual characteristic features: the adoption of the private law principle in the formative period of international law, its beneficial effect upon international relations, its acceptance by the common opinion of writers and by the practice of States, and, lastly, its rejection as a misleading private law analogy by a number of positivist writers on the ground of the special character of international law.

§ 59. *Grotius and the Practice of Collective Responsibility.*—It was Grotius who introduced the conception of fault into this branch of international law. 'That any one,' he says, 'without any fault of his own, is bound by the acts of his agents, is not a part of the law of nations.'[2] 'A civil community, like any other community, is not bound by the act of an individual member thereof, without some act of its own, or some omission.'[3] This 'fault of his own' lies in *patientia* and *receptus*, *i.e.* in the sharing in the crime by 'allowing' or 'receiving.' The principle thus introduced by Grotius into international law was based on the Roman law doctrine of liability as dependent on *culpa*. It is, subject to modi-

[1] See Oppenheim, vol. i. pp. 251-263.

[2] L. ii. c. 17, s. 20.

[3] L. ii. c. 21, s. 2.

fications and exceptions, the foundation of the doctrine of liability in modern systems of private law. There are in international law few examples of both theory and practice following so closely in the footsteps of the founder of international law as in the case of this private law principle of culpability.[1] The opposing theories do not arise before the end of the last century.

The great historical service rendered to international law by the introduction of this principle can only be fairly estimated by considering the state of affairs to which the *culpa* theory was originally opposed. It was directed against the Germanic doctrine of reprisals based on collective responsibility for wrongs done to a State or its subjects by a foreign State or its subjects.[2] There was an element of perpetual strife and anarchy in this reversal of the Roman principle of '*si quid universitati debetur singulis non debetur, nec quod debet universitas singuli debent,*' an element so rooted in the habits and usages of Grotius' time that the great lawyer himself was not free from a partial justification of some aspects of this practice.[3] However, it is obvious that by the adoption of the principle of *culpa* he dealt a death-blow to the doctrine of collective responsibility.

[1] For an ample bibliography, see Schön, quoted below, pp. 9-10, and Strupp, p. 45 n. Cf. especially Heffter, §§ 100-103, whose recourse to private law proved here, as in many other cases, fruitful and stimulating. Cf. also Creasy, pp. 314-328; Rivier, vol. ii. p. 407; Lawrence, 5th ed., p. 539.

For cases illustrating the practice of States and international tribunals, see Moore, *Digest*, vol. vi. pp. 787-883; Borchard, *Diplomatic Protection of Citizens Abroad*, 1916, pp. 213-245; Ralston, quoted above, Nos. 578-647. Cf. also the opinion of the Committee of Jurists appointed by the Council of the League of Nations after the Greek-Italian dispute (Monthly Summary of the League of Nations, vol. iv. p. 53, April 1924). Cf. also para. 18, annex ii. pt. viii., of the Treaty of Versailles ('The measures which the Allied and Associated Powers shall have the right to take, in case of voluntary default by Germany . . . may include . . .').

[2] Nys, *Les origines du droit international*, 1894, pp. 62-68; for an historical exposition, see Goebel, *A.J.*, viii. (1914) pp. 802-808.

[3] 'And this rule has been established by a certain necessity, in that otherwise there would be great licence for the commission of injury, since the goods of the rulers often cannot so easily be got at as those of private persons, who are more numerous.' L. iii. c. 2, s. 2.

It is not possible to expatiate here upon the merits of the doctrine introduced by him, but it may be stated with confidence that it became a part not only of the science of international law but also of the practice of governments. It is believed that it corresponds with the conception of States as moral entities accountable for their acts and omissions in proportion to the *mens rea* of their agents, the real addressees of international duties—a conception which must form the foundation of any legal theory of responsibility.[1]

§ 60. *The Theory of Absolute Liability. Anzilotti.*—The attack upon the orthodox theory, launched by Triepel[2] and carried on by Anzilotti, was coupled with the usual argument on the inapplicability of private law to relations between States.[3] It is especially Anzilotti who is of the opinion that it is the theory of State responsibility which has been, to its own disadvantage, influenced more than any other part of international law by private and Roman law.[4] His argument is based upon the dualistic conception of the two branches of law. In private law, he says, the juridical precept imposing upon the individual a certain line of conduct emanates from a will other than that of the individual, who, as a rule, is not in a position to influence the scope of duties imposed upon him; but the legal precepts of the international community are a result of the direct will of the State, which is not bound to a greater extent than it wishes.[5] As, therefore, the will of the State is the only source of

[1] Attempts have been made to prove that the recent practice of States dispenses with the requirement of culpable negligence, and that it adopts the principle of absolute liability; see, for instance, Goebel, quoted above. It seems, however, that in all these cases the indemnities demanded have been paid under external pressure.

[2] See p. 142, n. 5, *infra.*

[3] *La teoria generale della responsibilità dello Stato nel diritto internazionale*, 1902, pp. 143-152, 179-180.

[4] '. . . Non vi è forse altro argomento in tutto il diritto internazionale in cui l'influenza delle teorie romanistiche sia cosi profondamente radicata come in questo' (p. 154).

[5] *Loc. cit.*, pp. 179, 180.

its obligation, it is not necessary to make its responsibility conditional upon a particular connection between the injurious act and a certain state of mind. Besides this, it is said, the ordinary conception of fault can hardly be applied to acts of State organs. For if they act within the scope of their competence and in accordance with their municipal duties, no fault can reasonably be attributed to them. On the other hand, if they act outside their competence, it is impossible to attribute fault to the State which has not sanctioned their actions.[1] Anzilotti thus arrives at the following conclusion:

> 'The State is responsible not for the direct or indirect connection between its will and the action of the individual, not for a possible culpable or malicious intention, but for not having fulfilled the obligation imposed upon it by international law, for having violated a duty to other States, a duty consisting in the non-toleration of the fact or in its punishment if it has occurred. It is not fault (*culpa*), but a fact contrary to international law, which creates responsibility.'[2]

§ 61. *The Doctrine of Absolute Liability analysed.*—This statement is the *locus classicus* of the positivist opposition to the established doctrine. The argument that not *culpa*, a subjective state of mind, but the mere fact of an international obligation having been violated, is the source of responsibility, is being quoted with unqualified approval by recent writers. But in what does this violation of an international duty consist? It consists, apart from actual malice, in not showing proper care. No one, not even Anzilotti and his followers, asserts that a State is responsible for every injury done on its territory

[1] For a critical exposition of these arguments, see Schön, quoted below, pp. 36-42.

[2] *Op. cit.*, p. 172, and especially in *R.G.*, xiii. (1906) p. 291. A different formulation of the theory of absolute liability is contained in Fauchille's theory of *risque étatique* (*Annuaire*, xviii. (1900) p. 234).

to another State. It is responsible for not showing a proper degree of care. But then, 'care' and 'due care' are conceptions indissolubly connected with the idea of fault.[1] Undoubtedly, the State bears in many cases responsibility for injuries caused by unauthorised acts of its agents,[2] but even in this case its responsibility, apart from being a vicarious one, *i.e.* limited to redressing the wrong by way of punishing the offenders or making reparation, is conditioned by the *mens rea* or by negligence of the offending official. And when, as a result of acts and omissions of higher organs, the responsibility of the State becomes directly engaged, it is again clear that neither theoretical considerations nor the practice of States dispense with the requirement of fault. Apparently Anzilotti and his followers, while maintaining that fault cannot reasonably be attributed to State organs acting in accordance with their municipal duties, do not attach sufficient weight to the fact that a person acting in accordance with his duties as an official of the State may nevertheless, by this very act or omission, be at fault from the point of view of inter-

[1] This part of Anzilotti's theory is recently expounded *in toto* in Lapradelle-Politis, vol. ii. pp. 973-975. It is interesting to note the attempt to support the theory of absolute responsibility by reference to the new tendencies denying the juridical personality of the State (Lapradelle-Politis, *ibid.*, p. 974). As there is, says the author, no separate juridical entity, there is no subject to whom *culpa* can be attributed. But he forgets that these new tendencies replace the mystical State by real persons, by individuals who are subjects of international duties and to whom *culpa* and *dolus* may no doubt be attributed. It is maintained by some writers (see, for instance, Strupp, *Delikt*, p. 50) that the Three Rules of Washington being closely connected with the conception of fault, have been discarded by Article 8 of the XIII. Hague Convention, which substituted the expression 'means at their disposal' for that of 'due diligence.' As a matter of fact, however, *both* expressions are indissolubly connected with the idea of fault. The statement of Prof. J. B. Scott (*Sovereign States and Suits before Arbitral Tribunals and Courts of Justice*, 1925, p. 246), to the effect that the Three Rules of Washington 'are to be found in their entirety in the Convention of the Second Hague Conference relating to the duties and rights of neutral Powers in maritime war,' seems to be quite justified. See, however, Oppenheim, vol. ii. pp. 535, 536.

[2] It is responsible for them in the same measure as the employer is responsible for the acts of his servant committed in the course and within the scope of the latter's employment. To this extent it may be said that the State is absolutely responsible.

national obligation. It is impossible to discuss here the technicalities of Anzilotti's theories, but it is believed there is no relation between them and problems of State responsibility arising from actual occurrences. Whatever the theory of absolute responsibility may say, the international judge or arbitrator will never be in a position to disregard such questions as: Was there or was there not fault with the respective officials of the State in whose territory an outrage has been committed against the representatives of a foreign State or its nationals? Could they have prevented it if acting with due care or without malice? Could they have apprehended the offenders if proceeding with diligence and care? Attempts to deal with problems of international liability without reference to questions of this kind are not only to be deprecated as impairing, in the last resort, the consciousness of international duty in those responsible for the international conduct of the State, but they are also utterly unknown to the ordinary practice of States or of international tribunals.[1]

The attitude of writers urging absolute responsibility was to a large extent prompted by the great difficulties in dealing with the responsibility of many turbulent States, especially in America, for acts of their agents and private persons in the course of frequent revolutions occurring within their borders. The requirement of culpable negligence, no doubt, helped many of them to escape responsibility for damage done to the life and property of foreign residents. But the acceptance of the

[1] It is to be regretted that this problem, which has recently in the domain of private law given rise to searching and fruitful investigation, namely, with regard to the extent to which exigencies of social life call for extending, by way of exception, the range of absolute liability, has been obscured by the method of putting forward technical and ingenious queries as to the applicability, in international law, of the conception of fault. The question is of paramount importance for international law, but it must be treated from an aspect much wider, namely, that which takes into account the analogous developments in private law from its very inception.

principle of absolute responsibility oversteps the mark. For absolute liability is in the last instance tantamount to divorcing legal responsibility from the moral one. It may be necessary, having regard to considerations of intercourse and safety, to introduce it here and there, but to proclaim it as a sole rule is even more dangerous in international law than in private law. The legitimate interests of foreign residents can be safeguarded by reasonably extending the responsibility of States not only to the suppression of wrongs perpetrated in the course of revolutions, but also to the prevention of such revolutions as far as possible.[1, 2]

§ 62. *The Ultimate Adoption by Positivist Writers of the Principle of Fault. Schön, Strupp, Jess, Visscher.*—It is neither possible, nor necessary, to discuss here in more detail the theories of those positivist writers who, while strongly opposing the influence of private law, put forward the doctrine of absolute liability. It may, however, be pointed out that that theory is now being abandoned, in its essence, even by positivist writers. The condemnation of private law commends itself *a priori* to the positivist mind, but when confronted with the practice of States it does not prove a working theory. The last ten years have produced four monographs on the question of State responsibility, and in all of them

[1] Cf. here Oppenheim, 2nd ed., vol. i. p. 222, and 3rd ed., vol. i. p. 260.

[2] The consideration might also have been present in the mind of the expounders of this theory that the unorganised character of international law does not permit subtle distinctions between liability based on fault and absolute liability. But such a point of view should, it is submitted, never be made a starting-point for a juridical treatment of problems of international law. International publicists, when putting forward suggestions with the view of influencing the practice of States, should visualise the international community as proceeding gradually to a stage of organisation with a normally functioning judicial authority. In our case, we ought not to accept absolute liability, because there is no superior to judge whether negligence (or *dolus*) has taken place; we ought to think in terms of a Court of International Justice deciding in each particular case whether a breach of international duty has been committed.

the private law principle of fault has been adopted to a large extent. Schön,[1] a thoroughly positivist writer, arrives, after a careful analysis of the practice of States, at a rejection of Anzilotti's and Triepel's theories so far as the responsibility of the State for acts of private persons is concerned. The conclusion which he reaches is that the State is responsible if it omits, negligently or maliciously, to prevent or to punish the injurious act of private persons.[2] He does not shrink from applying the private law principle, the current prejudices notwithstanding. He says : ' Although problems of international law cannot be solved by a simple application of private law, recourse to it should not be banned where the legal situation, apart from the difference of subjects of law, is the same, and where there are no special doubts arising out of the fact that it is to States that the corresponding principles of private law have to be applied.'[3] Schön adheres, however, to the principle of absolute liability with regard to acts and omissions of State organs. Strupp[4] goes a step farther. He admits that an international delinquency is conditioned by fault in all cases of omission, although he asserts absolute liability in cases of commission of internationally injurious acts by State organs. Jess[5] adheres strictly to the classical doctrine of fault in so far as principal responsibility (moral and political satisfaction) is concerned, but regards the duty of material reparation as independent of guilt.[6]

[1] *Die völkerrechtliche Haftung der Staaten aus unerlaubten Handlungen*, 1917.

[2] P. 57.

[3] *Op. cit.*, p. 58.

[4] *Das völkerrechtliche Delikt*, in Stier-Somlo's *Handbuch des Völkerrechts*, 1920, pp. 54-60.

[5] *Politische Handlungen Privater und das Völkerrecht*, 1923, pp. 116-134. On the other hand, Triepel (*Völkerrecht und Landesrecht*, 1899, pp. 334-339), from whom the attack against the private law doctrine of culpability originated, while rejecting the principle of fault so far as political and moral satisfaction is concerned, urged the necessity of retaining it with regard to the duty of material reparation.

[6] As an illustration of this theory, see the declaration of Greece before the Council of the League of Nations in the course of the dispute with Italy (*Official Journal*, vol. iv. (1923) p. 1300).

Professor De Visscher's attitude[1] is similar to that adopted by Schön.[2]

A survey of instances in which the responsibility of States has become involved reveals that the modifications thus introduced deprive the doctrine of absolute liability of its sting. For it is mainly cases of omission in connection with acts of private persons that give rise to international delinquencies, and it is in them that the question of fault is of real importance. With regard to responsibility for positive acts of State organs the problem of fault is of less consequence. The *culpa in eligendo,* so violently rejected by Anzilotti, is, after all, a legal fiction not only in international law but also in private law, where the responsibility of individuals and corporations for acts of their agents performed within the scope of their employment is a recognised principle. It is unimportant whether we justify it by adoption of the fiction of *culpa in eligendo* or by recourse to reasons of security and good faith. However, if necessities of international life lead us to the adoption, in certain instances, of the principle of absolute liability, such cases will nevertheless, as they do in private law, constitute an exception to the generally recognised principle of responsibility based on fault

VIII

INTEREST AND THE MEASURE OF DAMAGES

§ 63. *The Question of Moratory Interest in International Law. The Positivist Attitude.*—Does the general rule of private law,[3] that in case of default on the part

[1] *La Responsabilité des États, Bibliotheca Visseriana,* 1924, vol. ii. pp. 89-106.

[2] Similarly Ruegger, *Die völkerrechtliche Verantwortlichkeit des Staates für die auf seinem Gebiete begangenen Verbrechen,* 1924, pp. 7, 11.

[3] The position of the English common law will be considered later. See p. 261, n. 3, *infra.*

of the debtor to fulfil a pecuniary obligation the creditor is entitled to moratory interest without further proof of actual damage, apply in international law? And, further, is interest to be adjudged on sums awarded as damages for an international tort? Does the fact that all systems of private law recognise in this or some other form the obligation to pay interest entitle it to recognition by international law? It may be, and has been,[1] argued in this connection that nothing is more dangerous and unjustifiable than application by analogy of the rules of one system in the field of another; that, although there are similar situations calling for recourse to analogous rules, such rules cannot derive obligatory force from a source other than the collective will of the States.[2] It is being maintained that a rule of private law, even if identical in all municipal systems, remains nevertheless a rule of private law, unable by itself to govern relations between States, and that, moratory interest not being a logical consequence of responsibility, the awarding of sums under this head is not admissible in international law.

§ 64. *The Practice of International Tribunals.*—It will be seen that in the course of the important arbitration in which this question constituted the main issue, namely, in the Russian indemnity case before the Hague Court,[3] arguments were put forward designed to show that the position is not analogous, and that payment of moratory interest cannot be regarded as an established rule of international law. The Court, however, adopted the view that the non-fulfilment of an obligation by one contracting State constitutes a delinquency entitling the other to compensation, and that in the case of a

[1] See Anzilotti, *Rivista*, vii. (1913) pp. 63-67.

[2] *Op. cit.*, p. 60 ('Nessuna applicazione analogica è possibile dall' un all' altro campo, perchè l'applicazione analogica presuppone che i subietti del rapporto sieno sottoposti alla norma da applicare analogicamente, e gli Stati non sono sottoposti alle norme del diritto civile').

[3] See pp. 255, 256, *infra*.

pecuniary debt this compensation assumes, in accordance with the generally recognised principle of private law, the form of moratory interest.[1] In fact, the adoption of the contrary view leads, in the long run, to mischievous consequences. To maintain that a legal relation between two States, *prima facie* identical with a corresponding relation between individuals, cannot be governed by a generally recognised rule applicable to the matter in question, because it has not been expressly recognised by international law, is to make such a relation impossible or to render it ineffective. The postulate of positivism is complied with by the fact that States entering into legal relations may stipulate for special rules derogatory of the general principle, but it cannot mean that a legal relation should be rendered abortive because there are no rules of international law on the subject. International law and private law differ from each other mainly in respect of the subject-matter which they regulate. If the subject-matter is the same or analogous, then the rules to be applied must be the same or analogous, unless there is an express or customary provision to the contrary. It is true that a generally recognised rule of private law is not *per se* a part of international law; but it becomes so impliedly by States entering into such legal relations as can only be maintained or rendered effective by the application of this generally recognised rule.

The practice of allowing interest in international arbitrations is generally recognised,[2] and special reasons

[1] See p. 258, *infra*.

[2] See Ralston, Nos. 212, 213, 219, and Lapradelle-Politis, vol. i. pp. 529, 624, and vol. ii. pp. 222, 567, 635. See also cases quoted in the award in the Russian Indemnity case, Scott's *Reports*, p. 314, and Venezuelan Arbitrations, *Ralston's Report*, pp. 425, 658. For another enumeration of cases where interest has been allowed, see case of the *Cape Horn Pigeon* and others, *U.S.A. For. Rel.*, 1902, Appendix I. (U.S. *Argument*, Russian *Counter-Memorandum*, and Decision, p. 451). Cf. also the award of the Permanent Court of Arbitration in the matter of French Claims against Peru of October 11, 1921, *A.J.*, xvi. (1922) p. 483 ('Whereas, since this credit is liquid and payable, interest at 5 per cent. is due from the date of the payability of each of the

are adduced by arbitrators in those cases in which interest is disallowed—for instance, if the claimants are guilty of delay in the prosecution of their claim, or if the award of interest is expressly excluded by the arbitration convention.[1] Only in one case has interest been disallowed on the ground that 'there is no settled rule as to the payment of interest on claims on countries or governments.'[2]

There is no cogent reason for objecting to awarding interest in international law because of the absence of a settled rule as to the rate of interest or the date from which it begins to run.[3] This circumstance can no more prevent the awarding of interest than the application of the principle of prescription can be excluded because no rule has yet evolved as to the time required for its completion.

sums composing it . . .'). It is to be regretted that, the constant practice of States notwithstanding, some writers still continue to uphold their opposition against awarding interest. See Strupp, *Delikt*, p. 212, and Lapradelle-Politis in the *note doctrinale* to the *Alabama* arbitration. The author of the note speaks of '*analogie abusive*' and of '*artifice non seulement inutile mais dangereux*' (vol. ii. p. 981). He does not oppose the paying of an indemnity for the delay, and he does not even exclude the admissibility of awarding interest under this title, but he argues that the judge should be permitted to allow compensation for delay also in another form, not necessarily that of interest.

[1] For several cases illustrating this rule, see Ralston, No. 215. Compound interest is as a rule disallowed (see Ralston, No. 221; Lapradelle-Politis, *op. cit.*, ii. pp. 116, 117 (case of *Yuille, Shortridge & Co.*; see p. 269, *infra*). See also the award in French Claims against Peru, *A.J.*, xvii. (1923) p. 481, which summarises accurately the attitude adopted in this question by international tribunals. ('Whereas . . . it is not in order to admit the claim relative to the capitalisation of interest; whereas, in fact, the capitalisation of the interest can result only from a stipulation or from circumstances of fact making clear the consent of the debtor to assume such an onerous obligation. . . .') The same rule has been followed by the Permanent Court of Arbitration in the award of October 13, 1922 (*United States* v. *Norway*, *A.J.*, xvii. (1923) p. 396).

[2] *Montijo* case, Moore, p. 1445.

[3] So, for instance, Strupp, *Delikt*, p. 213; but see Ralston, Nos. 222-226. See also the award of May 1, 1924, in the *Lord Nelson*, Claim No. 20, British and American Claims Arbitral Tribunal, Nielsen, p. 435. ('It is a generally recognised rule of international law that interest is to be paid at the rate current in the place and at the time the principal is due.') It appears that with regard to the *dies a quo* arbitral decisions recognise, in the overwhelming majority of cases, that the date from which interest commences begins with the time at which the claim has first been presented. For a reasoned opinion, based on private law, on this subject, see the *Cervetti* case in Venezuelan Arbitrations, *Ralston's Report*, p. 658, and Russian Indemnity case, Scott's *Reports*, pp. 316, 317, and p. 258, *infra*.

§ 65. *The Problem of Analogy to Private Law with regard to the Measure of Damages. The Rejection of Compensation for* lucrum cessans.—A problem of a similar kind is involved in the question as to how far the general principle of private law, that in awarding damages *restitutio in integrum* should, as a rule, be aimed at, applies in cases when damages are to be awarded under international law. That principle means that the injured person is placed in the position he occupied before the occurrence of the injurious act or omission; it means that, to use the Roman law terminology, not only the *damnum emergens* but also *lucrum cessans* is taken into consideration. It may be safely stated that out of the practice of international tribunals the rule has gradually evolved that, in conformity with this principle of private law, loss of prospective profits is compensated if resulting directly from an international tort. This result has been achieved in the teeth of the usual arguments against following a rule of private law. For the prominence given to the much misunderstood *Alabama* award, and to some minor arbitral decisions, created the impression that international law does not recognise damages for prospective profits.[1] This impression was strengthened by the view put forward by some writers that an international law theory of damages should take into account the special and privileged position of States. At the London Naval Conference of 1909, when Article 52 of the Declaration was under discussion, it was taken for granted on the part of some delegates that in international law damages for lost profits are not awarded.[2]

[1] See pp. 219-221, *infra*.

[2] The London Conference is usually referred to in support of the contention that indirect damages are not recognised in international law (see, *e.g.*, Strupp, *Delikt*, p. 212). It appears that it was especially German and Austrian delegates who were under that impression. However, even they did not support this alleged exception; on the contrary, they

§ 66. *Indirect Damages and Compensation for Loss of Profits. The Practice of International Tribunals.* (Note: *Analysis of Cases in which Claims for Compensation for* lucrum cessans *have been rejected.*).—It is especially in international arbitration that recourse, as frequent as unavailing, is had to this argument. The parties usually fail here to distinguish between damages for prospective profits (which may be direct or indirect) and indirect damages. The principle of *restitutio in integrum* is, no doubt, an elastic one, inasmuch as it resolves itself ultimately into a question of fact. The border-line between direct and indirect damages, or between prospective and merely speculative profits, is seldom clear, and its determination is often dependent upon the subjective estimate of the arbitrator, who is, in fact, guided not so much by the technical distinctions between different kinds of damages,[1] as by the wish, perfectly justified in law, to afford full redress to the injured. But to maintain that international law disregards altogether compensation for *lucrum cessans* is as repellent to justice and common sense, as it is out of accord with the

maintained that 'there are no sufficient reasons for rejecting, in principle, the making good of loss of profit suffered by the owner of a ship wrongfully seized' (see Annex to the London Conference Blue Book, p. 262, quoted after Prof. Basdevant's speech before the Permanent Court of International Justice in the *Wimbledon* case; cf. p. 296, *infra*). Great Britain and the United States, who in the *Alabama* case and in the Behring Sea Arbitration advocated, in turn, the view that actual loss only, in the restricted meaning of *damnum emergens*, should be compensated, proposed at the Conference that full compensation should be paid in the case of illegal and unjustified seizure. For the views expressed in the official memoranda on this question, see *The Declaration of London, A Collection of Official Papers and Documents*, edited by J. B. Scott, 1919. Russia alone advocated compensation for direct losses only. Cf. also Bentwich, *Declaration of London*, 1911, p. 100. For the meaning of 'full compensation' in the practice of Prize Courts, see Moore, p. 2721.

[1] There is a tendency—see Yntema and Hauriou, quoted below, and the Opinion in the War Risk Insurance Premium Claims, *A.J.*, xviii. (1924) pp. 597, 598—to discard altogether these distinctions in favour of the general rule of full compensation. This seems to be pushing dissatisfaction too far. The terms 'direct' and 'indirect' are certainly very relative conceptions, and they do not provide an ever-ready formula for a solution, but they are nevertheless convenient stepping-stones and instruments of judicial reasoning.

practice of international tribunals.[1] An analysis of instances in which damages for loss of prospective profits have been rejected will show that these cases, far from establishing a special standard for international law, confirm the rule that in international law, as in private law, *restitutio in integrum* is regarded as the object of redress. The instances of rejection of claims are due either to special restrictive agreements, or to the lack of adequate proof and a reasonably reliable basis of compensation for the prospective profits, or to their uncertainty, their speculative character, or their

[1] The following is a (no doubt incomplete) survey of the more important cases where damages for loss of prospective profits have been awarded: In the *Betsey* (award of the Commission under Article 7 of the Treaty of November 19, 1794, Moore, p. 3207; opinion of Pinkney, Commissioner, *ibid.*, pp. 4205-4214); in the *Neptune* (by the same Commission, Moore, p. 3843; pp. 4217-4224, opinion of the Commissioner Gore); in the *Yuille, Shortridge & Co.* case between Great Britain and Portugal (judgment rendered by the Senate of Hamburg, October 21, 1861, Lapradelle-Politis, vol. ii. pp. 101-111; although the arbitrator rejected here the claim for indirect damages, he awarded damages for lost profits); in the *Colonel Lloyd Aspinwall* case between Spain and the United States (award of November 1870, Moore, p. 1015); in the case of the *Masonic*, between the United States and Spain (award of June, 1885, Moore, pp. 1062-1069); in the *Fabiana* case between Venezuela and France (award of December 30, 1896, Moore, pp. 4878-4915); in the *Lavarello* case between Italy and Portugal (award of March 12, 1893, La Fontaine, pp. 411-420); in the *Antiochia Railway* case between Great Britain and Colombia (award of October, 17, 1899, La Fontaine, pp. 545-554; the arbitrator admitted in principle the necessity of awarding damages for 'lucrum cessans'); in the case of the *Costa Rica Packet* between Great Britain and Holland (award of Prof. Martens of February 13, 1897, La Fontaine, p. 511, see p. 273, *infra*); in the Delagoa Railway arbitration between the United States, and Great Britain and Portugal (award of the President of the Swiss Confederation, May 30, 1890, *Sentence Finale*, 1900, pp. 154-188; see p. 271, *infra*); in the case of *The Hope On*, United States and Chilean Claims Commission of 1892, Moore, pp. 3264, 3265; in the arbitration between the United States and Russia (the *Cape Horn Pigeon* and other cases; award of 1902 by Prof. Asser, *United States For. Rel.*, 1902, Appendix I. p. 451; see p. 270, *infra*); as a rule, although subject to restrictions to be mentioned below (p. 150, n. 1, *infra*), in the Venezuelan Arbitrations of 1903 (see *Martini* case and *Roberts* case, *Ralston's Report*, pp. 843 and 145, respectively); as a clearly recognised rule, in several cases decided by the British - American Claims Arbitral Tribunal under the Convention of 1910 (see pp. 280, 281, *infra*); in the award of the Permanent Court of Arbitration of October 13, 1922, in the case of the United States and Norway (*A.J.*, xvii. (1923) pp. 392-395: 'Just compensation implies a complete restitution of the *status quo ante* based . . . upon the loss of profits of the Norwegian owners as compared with other owners of similar property').

remoteness.[1] The question of damages is thus yet another instance of an unsuccessful attempt to exclude

[1] It is proposed to analyse shortly, from this point of view, several cases in which claims for prospective damages were disallowed: In the case of the brig *William* (Moore, pp. 4226-4227; Lapradelle-Politis, vol. i. p. 470) the umpire rejected the claim for damages arising out of the fact that unlawful seizure deprived the brig of a complete cargo of passengers. He gave no reasons for the rejection of this claim, but it appears from his interlocutory decision 'that he demanded a proof whether the brig could count with safety on the passengers, or whether there was room for conjecture.' Such a proof was not forthcoming. He awarded, on the other hand, $2101 for the enforced employment of the vessel during the time of detention. It was, in fact, difficult to recognise *both* claims. In the *Lacaze* case between France and Argentine (award of March 19, 1864; Lapradelle - Politis, ii. 298) the arbitrators rejected an obviously exorbitant claim for consequential damages as arising merely out of 'espérances des bénéfices éventuels.' In the case of *The Canada* (Brazil v. United States, award of July 11, 1870, Moore, p. 1746) the arbitrator rejected the claim for prospective profits, 'for the ship might have been lost early in the voyage or the expedition might have been entirely unsuccessful and without profits'—a reason which it would be difficult to maintain as a general proposition. He explains, however, his refusal by the fact that in this particular case the objection is still stronger, because *The Canada* was commanded by a captain who, 'very little after sunset, when darkness could have hardly set in, ran his vessel upon a reef, with the existence and position of which he ought to have been well acquainted.' The prospects of a successful expedition were, in his case, very small indeed. In the *Rice* case (American-Mexican Commission under the Convention of July 4, 1868, Moore, p. 3248) an exorbitant claim of $50,000 for 'consular fees,' and similar damage, had been put forward on account of arrest and detention of the American Consul. The Commission awarded $4000, with interest, stating that awarding damages for consequential damages is conditioned by the proof '. . . of a fairly certain profit of the injured person, or the profit of an enterprise judiciously planned according to custom and business. A mere device of speculation, however probable its success would have been or may appear to the projector, cannot enter into the calculation of consequential damages.' In the *Hammaken* case (the same Commission, Moore, p. 3471), the umpire rejected the claim for consequential damages, because in this case '. . . it is impossible to measure them with any approach to justice; they are of an uncertain and imaginative nature, particularly in a country where the rate of interest is so high and where the chances of losing both capital and interest are quite as great as those of the realisation of an immense capital' (Moore, p. 3471). In the *Rudloff* case (Venezuelan Arbitrations, *Ralston's Report*, p. 198) the claim has been rejected because '. . . the case presented here is not that of the loss of the prospective profits of an established business, nor is it that of the loss of the ascertained profits derived from a contract unperformed. It is simply that of the loss of the expected profits of a business venture.' In the *Oliva* case before the same Commission (*op. cit.*, p. 781), a claim has been put forward based upon the calculation of the number of probable deaths and the probable profits arising from the sepulture. 'The number of interments in this Pantheon and the possible profits on each interment are so absolutely uncertain that they could not be accepted as a basis of calculation in an ordinary civil tribunal, much less in an international one,' says the umpire in rejecting the claim. As to the award in the *Alabama* arbitration, see pp. 219-221, *infra*. In this place it may be pointed out that although the tribunal rejected not only claims for indirect damages, but also claims for

a general principle of private law in deference to the special circumstances of international law.[1]

IX

OTHER INSTANCES OF ANALOGY

§ 67. *Quasi-contracts. Bankruptcy. Condominium. Self-help and Necessity. Equality of States. Conception of Sovereignty. The System of International Law.*—The problems discussed in this Chapter do not exhaust all the cases of analogy to private law occurring apart from treaties. The scope of this monograph allows the discussion of such questions only as have acquired actual importance in the practice of States and of international tribunals. There are, however, instances of analogy which, although they appear to be of theoretical value only, prove often of practical importance for the purpose of construction of legal relations between States. Some of them may be briefly mentioned here. Thus when Heffter gave place in his treatise to the notion of quasi-contracts, he met with but little response.[2] Nevertheless, repeated recourse has since

prospective profits, it appears that a lump sum has been allowed in lieu of prospective profits (see Protocol xix., *For. Rel.*, Geneva Arbitration). The *Alabama* Commissioners adjudicating upon claims based on the Geneva award were formally bound both by the award and by the Act of Congress, which excluded damages for prospective profits. The unjuridical character of considerations underlying some decisions in which damages of this kind have been disallowed may be gauged from a passage in the award of August 3, 1912, in an arbitration between Switzerland and France, in which the arbitrator states that 'friendly and cordial relations existing between the contesting parties make it desirable not to deduce rigorously all the juridical consequences' in the matter of damages (see *A.J.*, vi. (1912) p. 1002).

[1] In accordance with the view presented here are: Wise, in *A.J.*, xvii. (1923) pp. 245-251, where the practice of Great Britain in the course of the last war is discussed; Hauriou in *R.G.*, xxxi. (1924) pp. 203-231; Yntema in *Columbia Law Review*, xxiv. (1924) pp. 134-153, especially cf. p. 141; and Spiropulos in *N.Z.*, xxxv. (1925-26) pp. 59-134.

[2] § 100. The usual attitude of international writers is again expressed in Gemma, p. 232; but see Rivier, vol. ii. p. 41, and Despagnet, p. 731, who adopt the conception of

been had to this conception of private law.[1] Of other instances of analogy not discussed in this Chapter the following may be mentioned: the question of private law rules of bankruptcy as applied to the insolvency of States,[2] the influence of private law on the arrangement of the subject-matter of international law in treatises and text-books,[3] on the institute of *condominium*,[4] on the notions of self-help and necessity,[5] and on the conceptions of equality of States[6] and of sovereignty.[7]

§ 68. Justum bellum. *The Effectiveness of Blockade. The Nature and Extent of Military Occupation.* Transfers in transitu. *Lien on Belligerents' War Material. Article 55 of the Hague Regulations; International Usufruct.*—The question of recourse to private law occurs also in several branches of the law of war. Thus the Roman law conceptions of *iustus titulus* and *iusta causa* in relation to possession played a certain part in the develop-

quasi-contracts; cf. also Triepel, p. 222, n. 4. See now Kunz, in Strupp's *Wörterbuch*, vol. ii. p. 340, who merely repeats the argument on the inadmissibility of analogy to private law.

[1] See p. 252, *infra*. In the course of negotiations between Germany and Belgium with regard to the administration, pending the plebiscite, of Eupen and Malmédy, ceded to Belgium under Article 34 of the Treaty of Versailles, Germany is reported to have proposed that Belgium should act in the meantime as her *negotiorum gestor*. See Werveke, in *R.I.*, 3rd ser., vol. i. (1920) p. 243.

[2] Cf. Sir John Fischer Williams, *International Law and International Financial Obligations arising from Contract, Bibliotheca Visseriana*, vol. ii. pp. 52-55; Manes, *Staatsbankrotte*, 1922; and the same in Strupp's *Wörterbuch*, vol. ii. p. 597; cf. also p. 253 of this monograph (Venezuelan Preferential Claim arbitration).

[3] Cf. Bulmerincq, *Die Systematik des Völkerrechts*, 1858, *passim*, and Gorovtsev in *R.I.*, 3rd ser., vol. vi. (1925) pp. 176-178, 187-192.

[4] Cf. Nys, vol. i. p. 381; Fauchille, No. 556 (2); Politis in *R.G.*, xi. (1904) pp. 68-87.

[5] Cf. Liszt, p. 285; Cavaglieri, *Lo stato di necessità nel diritto internazionale*, 1918, pp. 16-20.

[6] Cf. Dickinson, *op. cit.*, pp. 86-88, 111-113; Vinogradoff, in *Bibliotheca Visseriana*, vol. i. (1923) p. 56; Creasy, *First Platform*, pp. 85, 86.

[7] It would be of interest to trace the influence of the conception of property upon the development of the theory of political sovereignty. 'Without the historical and juristic aid of the idea of property,' says Holtzendorff, vol. ii. p. 228, 'and its application to the territory of the State, it would not have been possible for the old theorists to discover the principle of political sovereignty.' See also Merriam, *History of the Theory of Sovereignty since Rousseau*, 1900, pp. 21-24.

ment of the conception of *iustum bellum*.[1] The principle of occupation and effective possession has been frequently resorted to in connection with the demand for the effectiveness of blockade,[2] and recourse has here been had to the conception of *possessio ad interdicta* in contradistinction to *possessio ad usucapionem*.[3] A similar question arises with regard to the nature and the extent of military occupation of enemy territory.[4] In prize law, the determination of the question when the property in goods passes in case of transfers *in transitu* is *prima facie* a question of private law.[5] Interesting problems of analogy to private law arise also in the law of neutrality in connection with the expenses of the neutral State caused by the internment of the belligerents' troops, and with its alleged right of lien on the belligerents' war material. Finally, Article 55 of the Hague Regulations concerning the laws and customs of war on land may be mentioned, which provides :

'The occupying State shall regard itself as being only administrator and usufructuary of the public buildings, immovable property, forests, and agricultural undertakings belonging to the hostile State, and situated in the occupied country. It must protect the substance of these

[1] See Lammasch in *A.J.*, x. (1916) p. 690, and in *Völkermord oder Völkerbund*, 1920, p. 43 ; Vanderpol, *La doctrine scolastique du droit de guerre*, 1919, p. 54.

[2] Cf. Hautefeuille, *Des droits et des devoirs des nations neutres en temps de guerre maritime*, 1858, vol. ii. p. 196 ; and also Ortolan, *op. cit.*, vol. ii. p. 295, who says : 'Sans une occupation véritable, résultant du fait d'un investissement actuel et complet, il n'y a donc pas de blocus réel.' Cf. also Pohl in *N.Z.*, xvii. (1907) pp. 24-33.

[3] Cf. Brocher in *R.I.*, v. (1873) p. 576. See, however, Rolin, *Le droit moderne de la guerre*, 1921, vol. iii. p. 300, who, like many others, rejects this theory on the ground that the high sea can never be the object of military occupation.

[4] Cf. the discussions at the Brussels Conference of 1874, quoted by Spaight, *War Rights on Land*, 1911, p. 326. Says Hall : 'The principle that occupation, in order to confer rights, must be effective, when once stated, is too plainly in accordance with common sense, and too strictly follows the law already established in the analogous case of blockade, to remain unfruitful' (p. 574).

[5] In Great Britain, however, municipal law is applied only when the sale takes place *bona fide* before the outbreak of war. See Oppenheim, vol. ii. § 92.

properties and administer them according to the rules of usufruct.' [1]

This, however, is an instance of a conception of private law being taken over in an international convention, and, as such, governed by the general considerations set forth in the next Chapter.

[1] For suggestive remarks on this question, see Holland on '*International Usufruct*' in *Letters to 'The Times' upon War and Neutrality* (1881-1909), 1st ed., 1909, p. 61. For the influence of Roman law on the theory of contraband in early international law, see Nys, *Études de droit international, Deuxième série*, 1901, p. 182.

CHAPTER IV

PRIVATE LAW ANALOGY IN APPLICATION TO TREATIES

I

TREATIES AS CONTRACTS

§ 69. *Treaties and the 'Special Character of International Law.'*—Before approaching the main subject of this Chapter, *i.e.* the problem of application and interpretation of terms of private law in international treaties, it is necessary to consider the question as to how far the conception of treaty itself is analogous to that of contract in private law. International law oscillates here, from its very inception, between two conflicting tendencies: one is to base the conception of treaties on the solid foundation of a consensual obligation as developed in private law; the other is to dispense, in deference to the special character of international law, with the two essential elements of the private law conception, namely, with the free consensus of the parties, and with the objectively binding character of the obligation. For it is generally accepted that the fundamental condition of the validity of contracts in private law, *i.e.* the free consensus of parties, is not essential in international law, and that, as a result of the predominant conception of the *clausula*, the binding force of international contracts is not only weaker in degree but also different in kind from that of their counterpart in private law. The classical writers were in the habit of stressing the elements common to both conceptions. Twentieth-century publicists emphasise the profound differences between them, and try to build up a theory of international treaties free from ingredients of private law. It is submitted that attempts at a new scientific formulation of the law of international treaties are doomed to failure so far as they start from the admissibility of duress and from the *clausula* as warranting and necessitating a totally independent treatment of the subject. For it is a mistake to assume that these exceptions are expressive of the special character of international law. What is true is that they are illustrative of the shortcomings of international law as a system of law. They are co-extensive, so far as they go, with the absence of law within the international community; and although they must not be disregarded by positive international law, the regard paid to them is one of recognition not as institutes of law, but as anomalies tolerated by law, the legal order not being powerful enough to subject them to its sway. They are incapable either of affecting the true nature of treaties, or of furnishing a basis for their legal construction.

§ 70. *The Legal Identity of Treaties and Contracts. The Relative Value of the Distinction between Law-making and other Treaties. The Origin of the Distinction.*—The legal nature of private law contracts and international law treaties is essentially the same. The autonomous will of the parties is, both in contract and in treaty, the constitutive condition of a legal relation which, from the moment of its creation, becomes independent of the discretionary will of one of the parties. It is the law of the State which gives objective force to a contract in private law, and it is the rule *pacta sunt servanda*, one of the fundamentals of international law, which imparts objective force to international treaties. It is, in law, not of the slightest importance that this objective validity, now independent of the will of one party, is in municipal law supported by external force, whereas in international law it is not. One must not be misled by the dogmatic statement that a treaty is an act of legislation in the sphere of international law, whereas a private law contract does not rise above individual interests. There are compacts of private law, for instance, the constitutions of corporations, which lay down abstract rules of conduct in a way very similar to that of legislation, and there are treaties between States, *e.g.* for the purchase of territory or the creation of a purely economic servitude, which do not materially differ from corresponding contracts between individuals. This view is compatible with the current division of international treaties in law-making and other treaties,[1] so long as it remains clear that that distinction, useful as it may be for the purpose of convenience and classification, does not entail any consequences so far as the juridical value of both kinds of treaties as source of international law is concerned. Every treaty contains rules governing the international conduct of the signatory States, and every treaty, law-making or not law-making, is a source of international law for the contracting parties —and for no one else. The above-mentioned distinction is useful if meant to emphasise the fact that some treaties are of more permanent and general application than others, and that they resemble therefore an act of legislation. Apart from this, however, it is obvious that its value is a relative one. For although every classification must needs be an artificial one and contain some element of fiction, in the classification based on the law-making character of treaties the element of fiction is represented in a marked degree. Nevertheless, that distinction does not cause much harm so long as it is

[1] Oppenheim, vol. i. p. 22; Hatschek, p. 9; Gemma, p. 212; Strupp, p. 8.

not being maintained that law-making treaties form the only kind of treaties which are sources of international law. Unfortunately, that is just what many writers are now doing.

The theory of law-making treaties and the abovementioned inference have been introduced into international law by Bergbohm and Triepel, and it was mainly through Oppenheim that the British-American publicists became familiar with them and incorporated them in their treatises.[1] According to Triepel and his followers, there is a fundamental difference between law-making treaties, which they call agreements (*Vereinbarungen*), and other treaties called contracts proper (*Verträge*). In the latter instance the will of one party is different from that of the other, the contract being here a means for achieving different and opposing ends. Thus, while the purchaser promises to pay the money, the seller undertakes to deliver the goods. On the other hand, the *agreement* serves the purpose of realising identical aims.[2] That is the reason why only 'agreements' may be regarded as sources of international law.

It is not necessary to pronounce here an opinion on the soundness of this distinction,[3] but it is submitted that a theory, which denies to some international treaties the quality of sources of international law, cannot be accepted. All international treaties are sources of law for the parties who conclude them, none is a source of

[1] But, ever since, there is a tendency to distinguish between treaties containing general rules and treaties dealing with a particular situation. This distinction lies at the basis of the division in treaties and pacts or conventions (Vattel, bk. ii. §§ 152, 153), transitory conventions and treaties (Wheaton-Dana, p. 340), executed and executory treaties (Westlake, vol. i. pp. 60, 61).

[2] See Triepel, *Völkerrecht und Landesrecht*, 1899, p. 53. For a criticism of the theory of agreement (*Vereinbarung*), see Kelsen, pp. 151-196; Kaufmann, *op. cit.* below, pp. 161 ff.; Verdross, in Strupp's *Wörterbuch*, vol. ii. p. 656.

[3] The distinction between *trattati-contratti* (ordinary treaties) and *trattati-accordi* (law-making) is put very clearly by Gemma; in fact, so clearly that its altogether relative value immediately comes to light (see pp. 212-213).

law for non-signatories. Both—when sufficiently uniform and general—may serve as evidence of the legal conviction of States which is at the basis of customary international law. That positive international law attaches no practical value to this distinction may be seen from Article 38 of the Statute of the Permanent Court of International Justice, which provides that the Court shall apply, *inter alia*, ' international conventions, whether general or particular, establishing rules expressly recognised by the contesting States.'[1] It is therefore impossible to agree with writers who complain that it is the conception of treaties as contracts which prevents publicists from recognising their legislative quality.[2] In fact, publicists treat both kinds of treaties as contracts so far as the conditions of their creation, their validity, and their dissolution are concerned.

§ 71. *The Identification of Treaties with Contracts, especially with regard to their Creation and Dissolution.*—Grotius' treatment of promises and contracts follows closely the lines of private law, although it is, as we have seen, obscured by the fact that he himself often stresses the differences between civil law and the law of nations.[3] It has become a commonplace to blame him for this strict adherence to the private law pattern. It is obvious, however, that almost all writers adopt a similar practice. The identification of the two conceptions is the starting-point; it is upon its foundations that authors elaborate distinctions which seem to them important. ' It is unnecessary here to enter into the general principles of the law of contract '—thus does Westlake begin the chapter on ' Treaties and other International Conventions.' And he proceeds: ' What is important for us is to notice the points in which

[1] Cf. here Fachiri, *The Permanent Court of International Justice*, 1925, p. 91.

[2] Cf. Hudson, quoted at p. 35, *supra*.

[3] See p. 13, *supra*.

contracts between States present any exception to those principles or any particular application of them.'[1] Pradier-Fodéré says: '*Les traités et les conventions sont les contrats des États; leur objet essentiel est de produire généralement des obligations réciproques et des droits corrélatifs.*'[2] This is the attitude of most writers.[3] It is remarkable how this identification of contracts and treaties finds uniform expression in the way in which modern authors deal with the creation and dissolution of treaties. The essential conditions of a private law contract, *i.e.* capacity of the parties, a permitted and possible object, and a proper declaration of will not vitiated by fraud, mistake, or duress, are as a rule the basis upon which publicists build their exposition of treaties. In this respect there is no difference of opinion between authors notoriously adhering to the private law pattern and extreme positivist writers.[4] And the general view on the dissolution of treaties may well be summarised by Liszt's statement to the effect that the dissolution of treaties takes place in accordance with 'principles belonging to general jurisprudence.'[5]

§ 72. *Contract as a Conception of General Jurisprudence.* —Some positivist writers, although acknowledging the contractual nature of treaties, emphatically deny the private law character of the institution of contract. It

[1] Vol. i. p. 290.

[2] § 888.

[3] Fiore, § 976; Phillimore, vol. ii. p. 69; Fenwick, p. 316; Taylor, p. 365. Cf. also Hyde, vol. ii. p. 2 ('an obligation of an essentially legal character, possessing the quality which the law familiarly attaches to contracts between individuals'); Hatschek, p. 297; Gemma, p. 208; Fauchille, No. 818. See, however, Niemeyer, pp. 126-130, and Hudson, *loc. cit.*

[4] Cf. Heffter (*Eine zulässige causa*, § 83; *Dispositionsfähigkeit der Contrahenten*, § 84; *Willensfreiheit*, § 85). De Louter, vol. i. p. 474 (*Pour avoir force obligatoire, un contrat politique doit répondre à certaines conditions. Elles se rapportent:* (a) *aux contractants*, (b) *à la déclaration de volonté*, (c) *au contenu*); Gemma (*La capacità della persona*, p. 207; *il consenso*, p. 208; *una prestazione possibile connessa con una causa lecita*, p. 210); similarly Hall, p. 380 (capacity to contract; freedom of consent: the object of the agreement must be in conformity with law).

[5] P. 263. See p. 35, *supra*.

belongs, they say, to the domain of general jurisprudence.[1] There would be no objection to basing both contracts and treaties on the wider basis of a universal conception if it were not the fact that the 'conception of general jurisprudence' is here frequently used for the purpose of explaining away an otherwise insurmountable difficulty, namely, how it can be that the free consensus of the parties is not essential in international treaties. It is simply being pointed out that the requirement of free will is nothing short of an inadmissible analogy to private law, and that contract being a 'universal conception' it may be looked upon as dispensing, in international law, with the free declaration of the parties as an essential condition of the validity of the compact.[2] The construction of treaties as 'concepts of universal jurisprudence' should therefore as a rule be received with appropriate caution.

§ 73. *Disregard of the Vitiating Influence of Duress. The General Opinion and its Modifications.*—There are few questions in international law in which there is such a measure of common agreement as this, that duress, so far as States are concerned, does not invalidate a contract; nevertheless, it is submitted that this exception does not affect the view presented here of the fundamental identity of contracts and treaties. It has already been pointed out that analogy fails here so far as international law is an undeveloped law; it may safely be said that with the development of international law to a system of *law* without qualifications and limitations the analogy will hold with

[1] See p. 35, *supra*, and Rapisardi-Mirabelli in *R.I.*, 3rd ser., vol. iv. (1923) pp. 652-667.

[2] But it is most instructive to note how, for instance, Nippold (*op. cit.*, p. 176), a champion of 'general jurisprudence,' denounces the prevalent opinion on the admissibility of duress as running counter to a clear principle of universal jurisprudence. The meaningless fallacy of this term, when detached from the mother-soil of private law, cannot be better illustrated.

undisputed force. In addition, it seems that the acquiescence of writers in the rule that the use of force in order to obtain consent does not vitiate a treaty, is more apparent than real. Their support is certainly not a whole-hearted one. While laying down this widely accepted rule of positive international law, they deem it their duty to explain and to justify it. They regard it as a *malum necessarium*, the absence of which would tend to perpetuate the state of war within the unorganised society of nations. Moreover, a large body of publicists recognise the binding force of treaties concluded under duress only in those cases in which the State exercising compulsion does it in the name of law and in accordance with it—as the arm of the law, as it were. The number of these writers is certainly greater than the general acquiescence in the admissibility of duress seems to suggest.

§ 74. *Grotius. Vattel. Modern Publicists.*—That Grotius, in an age of wars, was apt to sacrifice a legal principle for the sake of peace, should cause no surprise. *Expedit rei publicae ut sit finis litium*:

> "As by the consent of nations a rule has been introduced that all wars, conducted on both sides by authority of the sovereign power, are to be held just wars; so this has also been established, that the fear of such a war is held a justly imposed fear, so that what is obtained by such means cannot be demanded back.'[1]

This is a bold statement on the part of the great jurist who took pains to distinguish between *bellum iustum* and *iniustum*. It is not made clearer by the argument that 'he who gave cause why he should suffer force, or be compelled by fear, has himself to blame for what happens: for an involuntary act arising from a voluntary one is

[1] L. ii. c. 17, s. 19.

held morally for a voluntary one.'[1] Then what about the attacked who did not give cause 'that he should suffer force'? And yet, although in the chapter on 'Promises' he is entirely of the opinion of those who think that, setting aside the civil law, he who has promised anything under fear is bound, he is cautious enough to add the following proviso: 'But I also think that this is certainly true: that if the promisee has produced a fear not just, but unjust, even though slight, and if the promise was occasioned by this, he is bound to liberate the promiser if the promiser desires it.'[2] This cannot be regarded as a refutation of his view in the main question, but it is certainly illustrative of the difficulties with which he had to cope.

Even more instructive is Vattel. He lays down the rule that a sovereign cannot repudiate a treaty of peace by alleging that it was extorted from him by fear or constraint, and sets forth the reasons usually given in support of this proposition.[3] However, he qualifies it by the following important limitation: 'If ever the plea of constraint may be admitted, it is against an agreement which does not merit the name of a treaty of peace, against a forced submission to terms which are equally contrary to justice and to all duties of humanity.'[4] And he proceeds, after having given some historical instances, with the following impassioned argument:

'Although the natural law prescribes fidelity to promises as a means of securing the welfare and the peace of nations, it does not favour oppressors. All of its principles are directed to procuring the greatest good of mankind; that

[1] L. ii. c. 17, s. 18.
[2] L. ii. c. 11, s. 7.
[3] Bk. iv. ch. 4, § 37.
[4] *Loc. cit.*; cf. also Ayala, *De Jure et Officiis bellicis*, 1582, newly edited by Scott in the *Classics of International Law*, with a translation by Bate, 1912, vol. ii. p. 60, and Pufendorf, viii. 8, 1 (Barbeyrac, who is usually at pains to pay due regard to the practice of States, admits here, in a note, of exceptions in cases 'where the injustice is plainly notorious').

is the great end of all laws, written and unwritten. Shall he who himself violates all these principles which bind society together be allowed to invoke the aid of them? If it happens that the plea of constraint is abused, and is offered by a nation as a pretext for revolting without just cause and renewing the war, it is better to risk that ill than to furnish usurpers with an easy means of perpetuating their injustice and establishing their usurpation upon a solid foundation. But when it is sought to preach a doctrine which is contrary to all the instincts of human nature, where shall hearers be found?'

G. F. de Martens is quite explicit in stating that force illegitimately used confers no right, although, there being no judge above sovereign States, it is to be assumed in case of doubt that the use of force was legitimate; this presumption, however, does not apply when flagrant injustice is perpetrated by the use of force.[1] Klüber also expresses the opinion that a free declaration of will is essential for the validity of the treaty, and that it is void if brought about by unjust compulsion. As just compulsion he defines such an exercise of force as is necessary for the defence of an attacked right.[2] Heffter adheres literally to the rule of private law, and declares that force applied in such a manner that it puts into jeopardy the very existence or self-preservation of the State, vitiates a treaty.[3] Pradier-Fodéré denies, after a lengthy discussion, the binding force of treaties concluded under the influence of force.[4] Hall says:

'. . . Consent . . . is conceived to be freely given in international contracts, notwithstanding that it may have been obtained by force, so long as nothing more is exacted than it may be supposed that a state would consent to give, if it were willing to afford compensation for past wrongs and

[1] Vol. i. § 50 (p. 165 of the French edition of 1858; the first edition appeared in 1788).

[2] § 143.

[3] § 85. He does not, however, consider as concluded under duress a treaty entered into for the purpose of liberating a province occupied by the enemy.

[4] § 1076.

security against the future commission of wrongful acts. . . . When this point however is passed, constraint vitiates the agreement. . . .' [1]

And it is indicative of the present position of the question that a thoroughly positivist writer expresses, in 1924, the following opinion:

'When, therefore, it is said that "in international law force and intimidation are permitted means of obtaining redress for wrongs, and it is impossible to look upon permitted means as violating the agreement made in consequence of their use," the statement can be accepted only as expressing a rule of law in so far as the recognition of the agreement by third States is concerned, not as implying that the agreement creates the obligation of good faith.' [2]

It is not intended, by putting forward the views of these publicists, to call into doubt the well-established rule of international law as to the admissibility of duress. What is intended is to stress the fact that the recognition of compulsion is qualified, with a strong and authoritative body of publicists, by the postulate that it should be lawful and just. Compulsion thus conceived does not fall under the category of duress, but of enforcement of law. In addition, the recent practice of States affords instances of governments repudiating the time-honoured principle that duress does not in international law vitiate a treaty, and invoking the fact of compulsion as invalidating the provisions of an international compact.[3]

[1] P. 381.

[2] Fenwick, p. 328; cf. especially Fleischmann in Liszt, p. 246, and Verdross, *Die Verfassung der Völkerrechtsgemeinschaft*, 1926, p. 50. See also Manning, *International Law*, 2nd ed., by Amos (1875), p. 124: 'Nevertheless, though this act [a treaty of peace imposed by force] really qualifies the actual cogency of such treaties, it does not qualify their legal cogency in the minutest degree.' Cf. also the '*note doctrinale*' in the *Croft* case, in Lapradelle-Politis, vol. ii. pp. 36, 37, and Hyde, vol. ii. p. 9. See Grosch, *Der Zwang im Völkerrecht*, 1912, especially pp. 99 ff., and Raventos y Noguer in *R.I.* (*Geneva*), iv. (1926) pp. 20-32.

[3] The following recent instances may be useful for the appreciation of some of the aspects of the question: (1) In May 1915, China, acting under the threat of an ultimatum by Japan,

It is believed that the lack of analogy of treaties and contracts so far as it is occasioned by the admissibility of duress cannot survive in an organised community of nations. The development of international law towards a true system of law is to a considerable degree co-extensive with the restoration of the missing link of analogy of contracts and treaties, *i.e.* of the freedom of will as a requirement for the validity of treaties, and with the relegation of force to the category of sanctions. The Covenant of the League of Nations, which, in its Article 10, safeguards the political independence and territorial integrity of the Members of

accepted the so-called twenty-one demands, impairing seriously her rights as an independent State. The Chinese Government, immediately after signing the treaty, published a formal statement protesting against the agreements which it had been compelled to sign (Willoughby, *China at the Conference*, 1922, p. 255). The Chinese delegation, at the Conference at Washington, 1921, raised the question, and demanded the cancellation of the treaty. It stated that 'the Chinese people had always regarded these agreements as peculiar in themselves by reason of the circumstances under which they had been negotiated, and that the conditions arising from them were only *de facto* and without any legal recognition upon the part of China' (*ibid.*, p. 253). (2) In the course of the Tacna-Arica arbitration of 1925-1926 (see pp. 290-292, *infra*), Peru frequently referred to the fact that she had been unlawfully compelled to sign the Treaty of 1884. See *Tacna-Arica Arbitration, Arbitration between Peru and Chile, The Counter Case of Peru*, 1924, pp. 34-38 ('We assail most confidently the claim that Chile lawfully occupied the provinces of Tacna and Arica at the time when the Treaty of Ancon was made. No nation has a right to make war upon an inoffensive neighbor, for the sole purpose of taking from that neighbor his territory.') In 1920, Bolivia and Peru addressed communications to the Assembly of the League of Nations asking for revision of their treaties with Chile (see p. 174, n. 2, *infra*), one of the grounds of the request being that the treaties were imposed by force. (3) No expression of opinion is intended on the juridical merits of the German declaration at the time of the signing of the Treaty of Versailles that, 'yielding to overwhelming force' and without abandoning her view 'on the unheard-of injustice of conditions of peace,' Germany is prepared to sign the Treaty. It is of interest to note, however, that in the exchange of Notes preceding the Treaty with China of 1921, Germany refused to recognise generally the Treaty of Versailles because such voluntary recognition would prejudice her right of asking for revision of the Treaty (cf. Verdross, *op. cit.*, p. 51). (4) Attention may also be drawn to Article 293 of the Treaty of Versailles, which provides: 'Should an Allied or Associated Power, Russia, or a State or Government of which the territory formerly constituted a part of Russia, have been forced since August 1, 1914, by reason of military occupation, or by any other means or for any other cause, to grant . . . concessions, privileges and favours of any kind to Germany or to a German national, such concessions, privileges and favours are *ipso facto* annulled by the present Treaty.'

the League from acts of external aggression, may be regarded as containing, *in gremio*, the elements of this development.

§ 75. *How far is the* clausula rebus sic stantibus *a generally recognised Principle of Law?*—The 'special structure of international law' deprives the conception of a treaty of one of the essential elements of contract, namely, of the requirement of a free declaration of will. But it deprives it also of another equally essential element, namely, the binding force of the obligation as independent of the discretionary will of one of the parties. This it does through the doctrine of the *clausula rebus sic stantibus*, the doctrine that a State may lawfully rescind a valid treaty if there has taken place such a change of circumstances that, in its opinion, the fulfilment of the treaty would dangerously affect its vital interests.

There are only few problems of international law which have caused more embarrassment to international publicists, or which are more unsettled, than the doctrine in question. The *clausula* is, on one hand, commonly styled as 'mischievous' and 'notorious,' and as revealing in a striking manner the absence of law within the international community. It is, on the other hand, almost universally conceded that some aspects of the doctrine are just and necessary, and that it would be unreasonable to reject it lock, stock, and barrel. These two opposing opinions are, as a rule, held by the same writers, who try to bridge the gulf between the two points of view by advising the utmost caution and conscientious self-restraint in the resort had to the *clausula*. It may be doubted, however, whether such a method is conducive to the realisation and solution of the difficulties inherent in the doctrine.

For it will be observed that there are two distinct

aspects to the *clausula.* One is perfectly recognised in private law and is expressive of the principle that there are grounds other than *mutuus dissensus* for dissolving an unfulfilled treaty. The rule *pacta sunt servanda* is also, in private law, of relative validity. There are promises which the law forbids and which it will not enforce; there are promises which the law does not forbid, but which, nevertheless, it will not enforce; there are, finally, promises which the law will not enforce after certain events have taken place. The reasons for this are mainly of two kinds. They emanate either from the necessity of giving effect to the real will (express or implied) of the parties, or of safeguarding certain social values relating either to the public good in general or to the freedom and development of human personality in particular. Both sets of ideas are general principles of law, and they are both inherent in the *clausula.*

With this perfectly legitimate and salutary principle embodying a universal rule of law, international publicists try to reconcile that aspect of the *clausula* which must be regarded as the very negation of law. Whether it be Oppenheim, a positivist writer with moderate and idealistic views, who defends it on the ground that 'self-preservation and development, in accordance with the growth and the vital requirements of the nation, are the primary duties of every State,' [1] or Kaufmann, an exponent of the extreme Hegelian doctrine of sovereignty, whose argument closes with the plea that 'the ultimate social ideal is not a community of free men, but the victorious war,' [2]—all these views are tantamount to saying that in so far as one party claims to possess the right to free itself from a more or less inconvenient obligation according to its own appreciation of facts, to that extent law is absent. It

[1] Vol. i. p. 690.

[2] *Das Wesen des Völkerrechts und die* clausula rebus sic stantibus, 1911, p. 146.

is true that in the interests of propriety of speech and for other good reasons we seldom use the expression 'absence of law'; we prefer to call it 'the special character (or imperfect development) of international law,' or 'the specific structure of a law of co-ordination as represented by international law,' but such praiseworthy euphemisms ought not to be allowed to conceal facts.

§ 76. *The Condition of its Recognition. Why the* clausula *has never been a Rule of Positive International Law.*—It may be said that there being in international law no compulsory judicial authority to judge whether an express or implied condition has been fulfilled, or to what degree the performance of an obligation has been rendered impossible, the application of the *clausula* must needs be different from the application of any similar conception in municipal law. In fact, however, the existence of this judicial authority is such an essential condition for the working of the juridical principle of the *clausula* that in its absence the principle itself, however just and salutary, becomes inoperative, or, when operative, ceases to be a rule of law and becomes a maxim of politics.[1, 2] Because and so far as the

[1] That even such authors as do not reject the *clausula* regard the recourse to it as an act standing outside the law may be seen from the writings of publicists who devote special attention to this aspect of the problem. One of the three classes of cases in which, according to Westlake (vol. i. p. 301), political action is justifiable, is that 'in which opinion is felt to be outgrowing the rule, so that a change in law may be asserted in good conscience to be necessary, and yet, from the want of an international legislature, it is difficult to effect such change otherwise than by setting the example to it.' Oppenheim says that if the request for the abrogation of a treaty is refused, 'a conflict arises between the treaty obligations and the right to be released from them, which, in the absence of an international court that could give judgment in the matter, cannot be settled juridically' (vol. i. p. 692). And Schmidt, who has done most to shatter the current view that the *clausula* is a rule of positive international law, approves of it so far as it is expressive of the ultimate law-creating influence of facts (*op. cit.*, below).

[2] That, on the other hand, the existence of a competent judicial authority renders quite possible a strictly legal application of the doctrine may be seen from the decision of the Swiss Federal Court of 1882 in a dispute between the cantons Luzern and Aargau. The Court held that 'there is no doubt that treaties may be denounced

international society is legally unorganised, it is prevented from having recourse to a rule whose application is essentially dependent upon the existence of a competent judicial authority.

The two above-mentioned aspects of the *clausula* are by their very nature irreconcilable, and international publicists have rendered a bad service to the cause of international law in attempting to show that the doctrine has become a rule of positive international law. The opinion may be ventured that if the doctrine has become notorious, it has become so certainly not because States had frequent recourse to it, but because international lawyers were using it as yet another argument in support of the ultimate independence of sovereign States of the rule of law.

The doctrine has *not* become a rule of positive international law; not only because the instances of its application are highly infrequent, but also because in those rare cases in which it has been invoked it has been rejected by the other contracting party against whose interests the denunciation of the treaty was directed.[1]

unilaterally by the party under obligation, if their continuance is incompatible with its vital interests as an independent commonwealth or with its fundamental purposes, or if there has taken place such a change of circumstances as, according to the apparent intention of the parties, constituted, at the time of its creation, an implied condition of its continued existence' (see Decisions of the Swiss Federal Court, 1882, vol. viii. p. 57, and Kaufmann, *op. cit.*, p. 34). Similar in principle is a recent decision of the Supreme German State Court (Staatsgerichtshof) in a suit between Prussia and Bremen (June 26, 1925; *Bulletin de l'Institut Interméd. Internat.*, xiv. (1926) p. 289).

[1] This has been shown with convincing clearness by Schmidt (*Die völkerrechtliche clausula rebus sic stantibus*, 1907, pp. 43-53) with regard to the three main cases in which in the last hundred years recourse has been had to the *clausula* (the denunciation by Russia, in 1870 and 1886 respectively, of the obligations imposed upon her by the Treaty of Paris of 1856 with regard to the neutralisation of the Black Sea, and by the Treaty of Berlin of 1878 with regard to the freedom of the Port of Batoum; and by Austria-Hungary, in 1908, of the clauses of the Treaty of Berlin relating to Bosnia and Herzegovina), as well as to two minor instances (the demand by Saxony at the beginning of the nineteenth century to be relieved from some territorial restrictions in favour of Austria dating so far back as the seventeenth century; and the denunciation, in 1852, by Germany and Austria-Hungary of the Protocol of 1852 in which the European Powers bound themselves to maintain the Danish

The recourse to it has been, in the majority of cases, described as a gross violation of international law by those very publicists who assign to the *clausula* an important place in their text-books.[1] Even more instructive are those historical instances in which governments refused to avail themselves of the benefits of the doctrine although an obvious opportunity of invoking it presented itself.[2] So far as conventional

monarchy). Hatschek (p. 239) mentions the case of denunciation by Austria, in 1870, of the *concordat* with the Papal State after the adoption by the Vatican Council of the dogma of infallibility. Lammasch (*Das Völkerrecht nach dem Kriege*, 1917, pp. 143-150), who fully concurs in Schmidt's conclusions, quotes yet another instance referred to by Zouche, in which the Netherlands, against whom Queen Elizabeth invoked the *clausula*, rejected as unsound in law the argument put forward by the Queen's advisers and containing a classical exposition of the doctrine; however, 'afraid to anger so mighty a princess,' they relieved her from the obligation. These cases complete, so far as the author is aware, the enumeration of instances of modern recourse to the *clausula*. It will be observed that their number is quite out of proportion to the place assigned to them in text-books of international law. In all of them the recourse to the *clausula* met with a protest by the other contracting party or parties. Kaufmann (*op. cit.*, p. 8) alleges that the last-mentioned fact did not prevent the *clausula* from becoming a part of the positive law because the other party did not, as a rule, protest against the doctrine itself, but against its application in the particular case, and, secondly, that it is only natural that it should have protested. It is submitted that while the second part of this argument is only ingenious, the first is not in accordance with facts. The protests were in almost every case directed against the principle which —to use Lord Granville's expression —'tends to bring the entire authority and efficacy of treaties under the discretionary control of each one of the Powers who have signed them; the result of which would be the entire destruction of treaties in their essence.' It was as a general principle that the States forming the Concert of Europe rejected it, in 1871, in an outspoken declaration (see Martens, *N.R.G.*, xviii. p. 278).—It seems that the doctrine was recently invoked by France in the dispute with Great Britain before the Permanent Court of International Justice (see Advisory Opinion, No. 4, p. 29). The Court, however, expressed no opinion on this question.

[1] Unless, indeed, they are citizens of the offending State—in which case the science of international law is frequently put to shame. Lammasch, for instance, passes lightly over the Bosnia-Herzegovina incident, because, as he says, the annexation did not change anything in the existing state of affairs (*op. cit.*, p. 148).

[2] The negotiations between Great Britain and the United States which preceded the substitution of the Clayton-Bulwer Treaty for the Hay-Pauncefote Treaty may be specially mentioned in this connection (see here Hyde, vol. ii. p. 81, n. 4, and also Mowat, *The Diplomatic Relations of Great Britain and the United States*, 1925, pp. 150 ff., 225 ff., 285 ff.). The United States demanded originally the abrogation of the treaty because of changed circumstances, but met repeatedly with resistance on the part of Great Britain. Eventually the inapplicability of the *clausula* was recognised by the Government of the United States itself. In 1896, Mr. Olney, the then Secretary of State, addressed to the President a

international law is concerned, the habit practised in the seventeenth and eighteenth centuries of inserting in treaties a proviso containing the *clausula* has since been discarded.[1]

§ 77. *The Application of the Doctrine by the Permanent Court of International Justice. Article 19 of the Covenant of the League of Nations.*—It has been shown that it is the unorganised character of the international society which renders a general principle of law inapplicable in international law, and which causes, in this respect, the lack of analogy to private law. The new international order as represented by the League of Nations and by the Permanent Court of International

memorandum in which, after having expressed his disapproval of the attitude assumed by his predecessors, he said: 'Upon every principle which governs the relations to each other either of States or individuals, the United States is completely estopped from denying that the treaty is in full force and vigour. If changed conditions now make stipulations, which were deemed advantageous, either inapplicable or injurious, the true remedy is not in ingenious attempts to deny the existence of the treaty or to explain away its provisions, but in a direct and straightforward application to Great Britain for a reconsideration of the whole matter.' This condemnation of the *clausula* by the statesman of a nation which originally invoked it is highly instructive. So also is the fact that in the whole course of the prolonged dispute between Great Britain and the United States centring round the North Atlantic Fisheries, the *clausula* was never invoked by Great Britain, although the right of fishery had been granted to the United States so far back as 1818. The same may be said of the analogous dispute between France and Great Britain relative to fishery rights in Newfoundland. Cf. here Baker, in *B.Y.* (1925) p. 99, who mentions this case in support of the *clausula*. What the author actually shows, however, is that Great Britain did not plead the doctrine, although 'it was plainly open to Great Britain to plead it.'—It is to be regretted that distinguished international publicists, otherwise rejecting the *clausula* as a means of unilateral liberation from a treaty obligation, succumb to the habit of indiscriminately constructing cases of application of the *clausula* where in fact no official action or declaration justifying such a construction has taken place. Quite recently Fauchille (Nos. 853 (4) and 853 (8)) quotes cases where one 'could maintain that by the application of the *clausula rebus sic stantibus* the stipulations have become void.' The same author quotes here as instances of the application of the *clausula* Articles 31 and 435 of the Treaty of Versailles, and—what is even more strange—the denunciation, in 1924, by Norway of the Treaty of guarantee of 1907 with Germany, France, Great Britain, and Russia, although the treaty in question expressly reserved to Norway the right of denunciation (see *R.G.*, xxxi. (1924) p. 299).

[1] See Schmidt, *op. cit.*, p. 71, and Wharton, *A Digest of International Law*, 1886, vol. ii. p. 59.

Justice supplies, in the same way as in the case of duress, to a large extent a solution of this crux of the law of treaties. For it seems that the Permanent Court will be competent to deal with the purely legal aspect of the *clausula*, namely, with those cases in which a State will claim the right to be relieved from an obligation on account of supervening impossibility of performance, or of frustration of the object of the treaty as a result of the fulfilment of an express or implied condition. The Court will be in a position to entertain requests of this kind notwithstanding the fact that the *clausula*, even in its purely legal aspect, is neither a customary nor a conventional rule of international law. For international law applicable by the Court does not consist solely and exclusively of rules expressly recognised by States; also, 'the general principles of law recognised by civilised nations' are, according to Article 38 (3) of the Statute, applicable as binding rules of international law when there are no conventional or customary rules at hand. It is as a generally recognised rule of law that the Court is competent to apply that part of the doctrine which is juridical in its essence.[1] The fact that international publicists have incorporated it in their writings will to a certain extent—although by no means to a large extent [2]—assist the Court in the application of this universal principle of law.

[1] See p. 68, *supra*.

[2] Beyond a quite general acceptance of the *clausula* by international lawyers, there is no kind of agreement between them as to the essentials of the application of the doctrine. Different and opposing answers are, for instance, given to such questions as: Does the 'implied condition' relate only to such circumstances as induced the parties to conclude the treaty and as were present in their minds at the time of its conclusion, or does it relate to the welfare and development of the State in general? If the implied condition covers cases not only of physical but also of moral impossibility of performance, what is meant by the latter: compatibility with self-preservation, or with vital interests, or with some political advantage? Is it a condition implied by both parties, or only by one? Does a vital change of circumstances render the treaty void, or voidable at the option of one of the parties, or does it merely result in imposing upon one party the moral obligation to release the other from the contractual obligation? See here Brierly, in *Transactions of the Grotius Society*, vol. xi. (1926), pp. 11-20.

The Court will have to determine especially to what extent the danger to the existence, independence, or development comes within the purview of impossibility of performance or frustration of the implied object of an international transaction. It ought to be clear, however, that it will not be in a position to give a very wide interpretation to those conceptions, and thus to supply a remedy for the unavoidable obsolescence of some treaties, unless, indeed, it will exercise a function of an international legislature—which it cannot properly do. A treaty may become obsolete, oppressive, and out of accord either with postulates of justice or with political and economic conditions, and yet it need not necessarily come within the scope of the legal application of the *clausula*.[1] The remedy is here obviously a political one, and it lies within the competence of the international legislature, but not of the international judiciary.

It is this political process of international legislation which is envisaged in Article 19 of the Covenant of the League of Nations: 'The Assembly may from time to time advise the reconsideration by Members of the League of treaties which have become inapplicable, and the consideration of international conditions whose continuance might endanger the peace of the world.' The Assembly of the League will thus assume those legislative functions which cannot properly be exercised by an international court. It may be hoped that the effectiveness and the importance of that legislative function will in future become more real than they are now,[2] the procedure of a unanimous recommendation

[1] Such cases will and must happen even if statesmen will pay more consideration than they do now to the necessity of concluding treaties for limited, and possibly short, periods. Executed treaties, like cessions of territory, must needs remain outside the purview of the *clausula*. They cannot be limited in time, and, legally, no question can here ever arise as to the possibility of their continued performance.

[2] On the attempt, in 1920, by Bolivia and Peru to effect the revision, under Article 19, of the treaties of 1904 and 1883, respectively, between those countries and Chile, and on the adverse report on

being obviously insufficient to prevent undesirable stereotyping and stabilising of the international political order. Such a development will leave the Permanent Court to apply free and unhampered the strictly legal aspect of the doctrine of the *clausula rebus sic stantibus*, which will thus become a bulwark of international conventional law instead of being one of its chief weaknesses. This will definitely restore the missing link of analogy to private law with regard also to the binding force of treaties. As, however, the law stands now, there is not yet in existence any effective machinery to adjust and alter politically obsolete treaties. It is not accurate to maintain that such a remedy is already provided for in international law, or that it can be applied, without express authorisation, by an international Court.[1]

§ 78. *The Question of Error and Fraud.*—Apart from the exceptions involved in the admissibility of duress and the recognition of the *clausula*, the fundamental identity of contracts and treaties is the usual basis of the exposition of the law of treaties. This may be seen from the fact that fraud and error are generally regarded as vitiating a treaty.[2] And yet there is no doubt that, from the juristic point of view, duress, error, and fraud all stand on the same footing: whenever they occur, real and free consent is lacking.[3]

Moreover, an examination of the leading text-books and treatises shows that, with one or two insignificant exceptions, there are no historical instances of fraud or

this question by the commission of jurists appointed by the Assembly, see *Acts of the Second Assembly*, pp. 45, 50, 261, 446; Goellner, *La revision des traités sous le régime de la Société des Nations*, 1925, pp. 46-57; and Scott in *A.J.*, xvii. (1923) p. 84.

[1] See, however, Baker, *op. cit.*, p. 98, and his reference to Prof. Higgins' suggestions in the 8th ed. of Hall (p. 407).

[2] Nippold, *Der völkerrechtliche Vertrag, etc.*, p. 176; Heffter, p. 190; Westlake, vol. i. p. 290; Klüber, § 143.

[3] See on this point, Taylor, p. 386.

error in the conclusion of treaties.[1] What writers say on this point is nothing else than theoretical reasoning based on analogy to private law. The elaborate manner in which negotiations are conducted, and the time which lapses between the signature of a treaty and its ratification, exclude any reasonable possibility of fraud and error. It is, however, the conception of the treaty as a contract in which real consent is an essential element, which induces international publicists, and justly so, to assign to fraud and error a place in the system of international law.[2] It is impossible to proceed differently without destroying the very conception of contract and treaty.

§ 79. *The Limits of Analogy. Roman Law.*—From the fact that, according to the general opinion of writers, treaties are legally contracts and that the essential requirements of the validity of the latter apply also to treaties, the false inference is frequently drawn that every rule of a particular system of private law may be resorted to for the purpose of construction and interpretation of treaties. Nothing is more likely to obscure the identity of contracts and treaties, or to bring into disrepute the recourse to analogy based on recognition of such identity, than the indiscriminate appeal to rules belonging exclusively to one system of private law and owing their origin to special reasons of time and place. It is only general principles of the private law of contracts, following with logical necessity from the very conception of that institute of law, which

[1] Phillimore, vol. ii. pp. 75-76; Rivier, vol. ii. p. 55; Diena, p. 372; Liszt, p. 246. The monotony with which they revert to the instance of forged maps is both pathetic and significant.

[2] But there are writers who deny the vitiating influence of fraud and error. They explain this attitude by pointing to the improbability of cases of serious error and fraud ever arising, and to the impossibility, owing to the lack of adequate tribunals, of determining whether they have occurred. See, for instance, Cruchaga-Tocornal, *Nociones de derecho internacional*, 3rd ed., 1923, vol. i. p. 434.

may, and must, be applied.[1] No doubt, the proof of logical necessity of this kind will be found *prima facie* in scientific analysis guided by considerations of legal justice, but the ultimate practical test must be sought in the inquiry whether the rule or principle in question has been universally adopted. If it has not become a general principle of law through recognition by all or by the main systems of private jurisprudence, then it can hardly be resorted to as a suitable basis for the process of analogy. The application of the rules relating to lesion (*laesio enormis*) and to *pacta in favorem tertii* may be mentioned as examples of such unwarranted recourse to private law.

According to Roman law, a contract of sale could be rescinded when a thing was sold for less than half of its actual value. This rule has been included in the law of some modern countries. It is unknown to others. To claim it as a rule of international law, as was done by many early publicists, is obviously inadmissible, and writers are therefore quite justified in rejecting this instance of analogy.[2] The same applies to the question of conventions in favour of third States. The various systems of jurisprudence differ so largely in this respect that any straining of inferences based on analogy must be misleading.[3] There is no good reason for asserting the superiority of one system of private law over the other, especially in view of the fact that in this particular question international law can and does develop its own devices, *i.e.* accession and adhesion, for extending to third parties the possible advantages of a treaty.[4] Finally, to mention yet another instance, there is, in international law, no warrant for testing

[1] See p. 85, *supra*.

[2] Phillimore, vol. i. p. 176; Klüber, § 143.

[3] Roxburgh, *International Conventions and Third States*, 1917, pp. 6-18; see also Diena in *N.Z.*, xxv. (1915) p. 19, who construes Article 1, s. 1, of the Hay-Pauncefote Treaty of 1901 as a *pactum in favorem tertii*.

[4] Roxburgh, *op. cit.*, p. 45.

the validity of a treaty from the point of view of the English-American doctrine of consideration.[1]

Neither is there any cogent reason for maintaining that Roman private law constitutes an exception to the principle that rules and technicalities of particular systems of private law must not be advanced for the purpose of interpretation and construction of treaties. There is undoubtedly a marked tendency, notably in the English and American international jurisprudence, to attribute to Roman law the quality of general principles of law.[2] In addition, international arbitration is rich in examples showing that the conception of Roman law as the *ratio scripta* is by no means a totally abandoned habit of mind.[3] This may be justifiable to a certain extent, namely, so far as Roman law has become a part of the positive law of nations (and it has become so to a large extent), or so far as it gives, in the absence of an international legal language, a convenient expression to general principles of law proper. But beyond this its authority does not go. To attribute to one system of a particular time and space the qualities of a universal law, and to see in it a vehicle of development of international law, may easily result in checking that development.[4]

§ 79*a*. *The Alleged Principle of Restrictive Interpretation of Treaty Obligations.*—With regard to interpretation, both publicists and international tribunals incline to the view that the universally accepted principles of

[1] See *Hooper* v. *United States*, Scott's *Cases on International Law*, 1922, p. 470. The recourse to this doctrine played an important part in the development of the specific American interpretation of the most-favoured-nation clause. Cf., on the other hand, *The Amiable Isabella* (6 Wheaton 1), where the Court refused to apply the doctrine of *cy-près* to the interpretation of treaties.

[2] The subject is treated in another part of this monograph, where an attempt has been made to explain these tendencies. See pp. 25-30, *supra*.

[3] See Venezuelan Preferential Claim arbitration, p. 251, *infra*.

[4] Cf. here Geny, *Méthode d'interprétation et sources en droit privé positif*, 1919, vol. i., 2nd ed., pp. 171-186. See especially Neumeyer, *Ein Beitrag zum internationalen Wasserrecht*, in *Festschrift für G. Cohn*, 1915, pp. 159-163.

interpretation of private law contracts and statutes may be applied to the interpretation of treaties.[1] But the great majority of writers are not content with enunciating a general statement of this kind, and there are but few publicists who have not succumbed to the temptation of formulating a more or less lengthy list of rules of interpretation. Not much harm is caused by this habit of filling several pages with rules calculated to ease the task of getting at the real intention of the parties, although the experience of international litigation shows that such rules tend rather to swell the bulk of written and oral arguments than to help the arbitrators. However, they are innocuous so long as they are no more than statements of general principles of interpretation, and not of such as belong to one particular system of jurisprudence. But they become, on the other hand, definitely misleading when they purport to be derived from the special character of international law. Thus it is frequently maintained that a treaty being a restriction of sovereignty, such of its provisions as impose obligations upon either of the contracting parties must be interpreted restrictively. It is pointed out that the very fact of concluding a treaty constitutes a limitation of sovereignty, and that restrictive interpretation should therefore be a general rule governing the construction of treaty obligations. Now, the maxim *in dubio mitius* is certainly a well-founded rule of private law, but it is only a subsidiary means of interpretation, subject to the dominant principle which says that effect is to be given to the declared will of the parties and that the compact is to be effective rather than ineffective. But among international lawyers 'restrictive interpretation' has become almost a catchword, and the attempts to make it a governing

[1] Wharton, *A Digest of International Law of the United States*, 1886, vol. ii. § 133; Pradier-Fodéré, vol. ii. § 1174.

consideration in the interpretation of treaties in deference to the principle of sovereignty are very frequent. It is obvious that neither the science of international law nor international tribunals can, in the long run, act upon such doctrine without seriously jeopardising the work of interpretation. Thus the Permanent Court of International Justice said in the Advisory Opinion concerning the Polish Postal Service in Dantzig:

'In the opinion of the Court, the rules as to a strict or liberal construction of treaty stipulations can be applied only in cases where ordinary methods of interpretation have failed.' [1]

The Court stated the same principle in even plainer terms in its first judgment, in the case of the *Wimbledon*:

'The Court declines to see in the conclusion of any treaty by which a State undertakes to perform or refrain from performing a particular act an abandonment of its sovereignty. No doubt any convention creating an obligation of this kind places a restriction upon the exercise of the sovereign rights in the State, in the sense that it requires them to be exercised in a certain way. But the right of entering into international engagements is an attribute of State sovereignty.' [2]

Expression has been given to the same view in the Court's Advisory Opinion concerning the Exchange of Greek and Turkish Populations [3] and the Competence of the International Labour Organisation. [4]

[1] Publications of the Court, Series B, No. 11, p. 39.

[2] Publications of the Court, Series A, No. 1, p. 25.

[3] Publications of the Court, Series B, No. 10, p. 21.

[4] See Advisory Opinions, Nos. 2 and 3. At its first ordinary session, the Court was called upon to give an Advisory Opinion on the following question: 'Does the competence of the International Labour Organisation extend to international regulation of the conditions of labour of persons employed in agriculture?' The question was obviously one of interpretation of the clauses of the Treaty of Versailles (Part 13 of the Treaty). Counsel for the French Government, who asked that the question should be answered in the negative, urged the necessity of restrictive interpreta-

II

INTERNATIONAL LEASES

§ 80. *The Legitimate Occasion for Application of Private Law in the Interpretation of Treaties.*—The proposition has been put forward in the preceding section that the recourse to analogy for the purpose of interpretation of treaties is unwarranted when the rules to be applied are not common to modern private law as a whole, but only to particular systems of municipal jurisprudence. When, however, a legitimate occasion arises to apply a private law principle common to all systems of private jurisprudence, it is useless and misleading to oppose, in deference to certain positivist formulas, the recourse to a corresponding rule of private law. When does such a legitimate occasion arise? It arises, apart from the cases discussed in the preceding Chapter,[1] and apart from the consequences flowing from the fundamental identity of treaties and contracts, mainly and ostensibly in all cases in which the parties to a treaty have themselves deliberately made use of a conception of private law; for instance, when they employ *expressis verbis* such technical terms of private jurisprudence as lease, mandate, prescription,[2] purchase,[3]

tion. He pointed to a rule of private law according to which, in case of doubt, liberty cannot be presumed to have been restricted, and he proceeded: '*A fortiori*, when important legal personalities such as States are concerned, it is a principle that, in case of doubt, their special attributes, which include not merely liberty but sovereignty, cannot be considered as having been in any way restricted' (speech of Prof. Lapradelle, *Acts and Documents*, p. 174. See, however, *Additional Observations* to the Declaration by M. Thomas, pp. 275 ff.). The Court, however, refused to act on the basis of this argument. It said: '. . . the question in every case must resolve itself into what the terms of the Treaty actually mean, and it is from this point of view that the Court purposes to examine the question' (Advisory Opinions, Nos. 2 and 3, p. 23). The same contention was—with an equal lack of success—put forward by Bulgaria in the case concerning the interpretation of Article 179, Annex, paragraph 4 of the Treaty of Neuilly (see *Acts and Documents* relating to this case, pp. 15, 33-35).

[1] See p. 145, *supra*.

[2] See p. 229, *infra*.

[3] See p. 97, *supra*.

servitude,[1] usufruct,[2] trust,[3] due diligence.[4] In all these cases the jurist has been relieved by the signatories of the treaty themselves from the task of putting forward a construction of the legal relation in question. However, so strong is the influence of the adverse criticism of the recourse to private law that even positivist writers are apt to neglect the declared intention of the parties. Clear conceptions of private law are being deprived of the meaning usually accorded to them, and publicists, instead of describing what the law is according to the declared intention of the parties, indulge in political conjectures drawn from their interpretation of international politics. It is proposed to devote the following pages to an examination of this method.

The problem is here a different one from that discussed in the preceding Chapter. There the question at issue was how far, taking into consideration the practice of States, the decisions of international tribunals, and the opinions of writers, international law has drawn from or been influenced by analogies of private law, and, consequently, how far and in what cases the shaping of relations between States according to the pattern of private law is permissible. Accordingly, the answer will be also found there to the question how far the international jurist is justified in applying a private law construction or classification to the provisions of a treaty in which no express reference is made to a term of private law.[5] But now the question to be considered is how far, if at all, he is at liberty to disregard a conception of private law if States themselves as contracting parties have express recourse to it. Of all the above-mentioned instances, international leases and mandates seem to be best suited for the purpose of illustrating the problem.

[1] See p. 123, *supra*.
[2] See p. 153, *supra*.
[3] See p. 202, *infra*.
[4] See p. 217, *infra*.
[5] See especially p. 145, *supra*.

§ 81. *International Leases of a Purely Private Law Type.*—There are two categories or leases in international law. The first, generally overlooked in the literature, furnishes no difficulties, as will be seen in the following instance: In an agreement concluded in January 1905 with the Italian Government, Great Britain agreed to lease to Italy an area of land on the east side of Kismayu, in the British East Africa Potectorate, not exceeding one hundred and fifty yards square, for the erection of a bonded warehouse or other necessary building. According to Articles 3, 4, and 5 of the Agreement, the Italian Government have to pay for the land leased an annual rent of £1, the lease to be in force for 33 years (or subject to the fulfilment of certain conditions for 66 or 99 years), and on its termination the buildings erected on the land are to become the property of the British Government. Article 6 provides that no Italian troops shall be landed at Kismayu without the previous consent of British authorities, with the important exception of expeditionary forces, which are permitted to land after previous notification. According to Article 8, both the land leased and the persons residing thereon remain under the authority of the laws and regulations in force in the British East Africa Protectorate.[1] Essentially the same are the provisions of Annex 4 of the Convention between Great Britain and France (June 1898) concerning the delimitation of the possessions and spheres of influence of both countries east of the Niger, in which a portion of land was leased to France on the Niger for the purposes of landing, storage, and transhipment of goods,[2] and of Article 8 of the Convention between Germany and France of November 1911 concerning their possessions in equatorial Africa.[3] In Articles 363 and

[1] Hertslet's *Treaties*, vol. xxiv. p. 689.

[2] Martens, *N.R.G.*, 2nd ser., xxix. pp. 126-130.

[3] Martens, *N.R.G.*, 3rd ser., v. p. 656.

364 of the Treaty of Versailles, Germany leased to the Czechoslovak State, for a period of 99 years, areas in the ports of Stettin and Hamburg to be placed under the general régime of free zones, and used for the direct transit of goods coming from or going to that State.[1] There are other recent instances of agreements of this kind.[2] It seems that, owing partly to the clear and detailed provisions of the treaties in question, and partly to the fact that their relative unimportance attracted to them little attention from international lawyers, the legal character of leases of this type remained unobscured by political interpretations. In all these leases the lessor retains the sovereignty over the leased territory, and the legal relation between him and the lessor remains the same as in private law. At the same time, it is obvious that these agreements belong to the domain of international public law.[3]

§ 82. *Political Leases. The Theory of 'Disguised Cessions' and the Practice of States.*—With regard to 'political' leases, like those granted by China in the years 1898 and 1899 to Germany,[4] Russia,[5]

[1] Leases of this kind may prove of special importance for States which have no natural approach to the sea. Cf. Spiropulos, in *Z.V.*, xiii. (1924) p. 11.

[2] Two recent conventions afford further examples of the variety of these agreements. By a convention between the Government of India and the French Government concerning the French Loge at Balasore, of April 26, 1920 (Hertslet's *Treaties*, xxx. p. 227), the Government of Bihar and Orissa, on behalf of the Government of India, took a lease of the French loge of Balasore for a period of three years subject to the payment of a sum of Rs. 4000 per annum (Article 1). The lease includes the right to levy taxes upon the lands appertaining to the French loge. Article 6 contains elaborate provisions relating to the prosecution for crimes committed within the lease, the British administration being as a rule under the obligation to hand over the criminal to French authorities outside the leased territory. The French sovereignty over the leased territory is expressly reserved (Article 7).—A purely private law lease has been brought into existence by the treaty between Italy and Czechoslovakia, of March 23, 1921 (*League of Nations Treaty Series*, xxxii. p. 251), as one of the concessions and facilities granted to Czechoslovakian traffic in the port of Trieste.

[3] For a good discussion of these leases, see Schönborn, in *Z.V.*, vii. (1913) pp. 438-445.

[4] Martens, *N.R.G.*, 2nd ser., xxx. p. 326.

[5] McMurray, *Treaties and Agreements concerning China*, 1921, vol. i. p. 119.

England,[1] and France,[2] or to some of the rights acquired by the United States in Central America,[3] most authors agree that they are cessions disguised in order to spare the susceptibilities of the lessor State,[4] and enumerate them as one of the modes of acquisition of territorial sovereignty.[5] It is submitted that this view is neither sound in law nor in accordance with the provisions of the treaties in question as interpreted by the actual practice of the interested States. For the purpose of illustration, a short analysis of the Chinese leases may be ventured.

According to the above-mentioned treaties, China retained the sovereignty over the leased territories, and parted, 'in order to avoid conflicts,' with the exercise of her sovereign rights for a limited number of years (25 years in the case of Port Arthur, 99 years in two other cases). The lessees were either prohibited from sub-letting the leased territories to another Power, or bound to obtain for this purpose the permission of the lessor. In Port Arthur and Talienwan, China retained the jurisdiction over her subjects in regard to crimes committed in leased territories, and within the walled city of Wei-hai-wei the jurisdiction of Chinese officers was to continue. In a

[1] Martens, *N.R.G.*, 2nd ser., xxxii. p. 90.

[2] McMurray, *op. cit.*, p. 124.

[3] See, for instance, the agreement between the United States of America and the Republic of Cuba for the lease to the United States of lands in Cuba for coaling and naval stations, July 1903 (Martens, *N.R.G.*, 2nd ser., xxxiv. p. 338); as to the grant in perpetuity (not lease) by Panama to the United States of a zone of territory for the purpose of constructing a canal across the Isthmus of Panama, cf. Martens, *N.R.G.*, 2nd ser., xxxi. p. 599, and *infra*, p. 190, n. 1.

[4] Westlake, vol. i. p. 136. Leases of the kind granted from 1886 to 1892 by the Sultan of Zanzibar to the British East Africa Company and to the German East Africa Company (see Lindley, *op. cit.*, p. 237), as well as those granted to each other by Great Britain and the Independent State of Congo over territories not yet occupied by them (Agreement of May 12, 1894; Hertslet's *Treaties*, xix. p. 179), may be safely left out of account.

[5] Cf. Strupp, p. 53; Lawrence, p. 177 ('The attempt to separate property or sovereignty on the one hand from possession on the other, by the use of phrases taken from the law of usufruct, is in its very nature deceptive. The terms in question are mere diplomatic devices for veiling in decent words the hard fact of territorial cession'); Despagnet, § 385.

treaty with Japan, of December 1905, China exercised her right of sovereignty by giving consent to the handing over of the leased territory from Russia to Japan,[1] and again, in Article 1 of the treaty of May 1915, to the extension of the term of the lease from 25 to 99 years.[2] In the same treaty she gave consent to the rights of Germany over Kiaochow being transferred to Japan.[3] After her declaration of war against Germany, she consulted a number of international lawyers as to whether, by this act, her agreement to transfer the German rights to Japan had not become inoperative, and obtained advice to the effect that her declaration of war against Germany, notwithstanding the contract which had been made with Japan in 1915, of itself vitiated not only the German lease, but also the treaty with Japan.[4] In the course of the Washington Conference, in December 1921, the leader of the Chinese Delegation declared :

> 'While the measure and extent of control by the lessee powers over the leased territories varied in different cases, the leases themselves were all limited to a fixed period of years. Expressly or impliedly they were not transferable to a third power without the consent of China. Though the exercise of administrative rights over the territories leased was relinquished by China to the lessee power during the period of the lease, the sovereignty of China over them had been reserved in all cases. The leases were all creatures of compact, different from cessions both in fact and in law.' [5]

Recognition has, in part, been given to this legal position, as interpreted by the Chinese Delegation, by the fact that, with the exception of the Liaotung Peninsula

[1] Martens, *N.R.G.*, 2nd ser., xxxiv. p. 748 ; this right has been expressly recognised in Article 5 of the Peace Treaty between Japan and Russia.

[2] McMurray, *op. cit.*, vol. ii. p. 1221.

[3] McMurray, *op. cit.*, vol. ii. p. 1216.

[4] Willoughby, *Foreign Rights and Interests in China*, 1920, p. 392.

[5] See also Willoughby, *China at the Conference*, 1922, p. 182; *A History of the Peace Conference in Paris*, ed. by H. W. V. Temperley, 1924, vol. vi. p. 377; Godshall, *The International Aspects of the Shantung Question*, 1923, pp. 121, 140-142.

held by Japan, the Powers declared their readiness to agree, under certain conditions, to the termination of the leases contracted in 1898 and 1899.

§ 83. *The Task of Interpretation. Legal and Political Interpretation.*—These facts do not seem to warrant the contention that the leases referred to in the preceding paragraph are nothing else than instances of acquisition of territorial sovereignty by cession. Publicists construe these transactions as disguised cessions, with the avowed object of grasping the real facts of international life, and not merely their legal appearance; not the declared, but the real intention of the parties. This is, no doubt, a right course for the international jurist or judge to take, so long as the determination of getting at the will of the parties at all costs does not degenerate into a political interpretation of facts as a result of attention being paid to the intention of one contracting party only. The ultimate object of the work of interpretation is to explain and classify legal transactions according to the declared will of both parties. The *reservatio mentalis* of one of them is not a proper basis upon which the work of interpretation can be built. A recent American authority expresses this view with all requisite clearness:

> 'It is the contract which is the subject of interpretation, rather than the volition of the parties. It may be that while certain expressions are used in a particular sense, a contracting State has in fact given its consent with the design of accomplishing a purpose hostile thereto. Proof of such an intention is not decisive of the rights of the parties under the agreement.' [1]

The usual construction of international leases offers an instructive instance of such misdirected emphasis

[1] Hyde, vol. ii. p. 63.

laid on the intention or exclusive interests of one party to the contract. States use here in a treaty a conception, obviously taken from private law, the broad meaning of which is generally accepted and without ambiguities. In the many systems of private law there exist differences of opinion as to the right of the hirer to sub-let,[1] as to the effect of the accidental destruction of the object of the lease during the term of the lease, as to the rights and duties of both parties with regard to improvements effected by the tenant,[2] or as to the limits of the duration of the lease; and different systems of private law give different answers to the question whether the right of the lessee is a real or a contractual one.[3] No one will, however, seriously challenge the statement that 'the lessee of the land is he who rightfully possesses it, but does not own it, and that the lessor of the land is he who owns it, but who has transferred the possession of it to another';[4] nor would any one shrink from the logical conclusion that, the essence of the relation between the lessor and the lessee being the separation of the rightful possession of a thing from the legal ownership of it, although this separation is usually temporary, there is no difficulty in conceiving of it as a permanent one. Whatever

[1] According to Roman, English, and French law, sub-letting is not prohibited unless there is a provision to the contrary in the contract of lease; according to the German and Japanese codes the lessee is, in the absence of an express provision to the contrary, not entitled to sub-let.

[2] Holland, *The Elements of Jurisprudence*, 12th ed., 1916, p. 294.

[3] Pollock, *The Land Laws*, 1896, p. 144; Salmond, *Jurisprudence*, 6th ed., 1920, pp. 397-400. In Roman law the right of the lessee was a purely contractual one. The purchaser of an estate encumbered with a lease could eject the lessee, who, in turn, was free to claim damages from the lessor. In English law the contract of lease confers a real right, at least in the meaning that the lease 'runs with the land.' It seems that this fact induced continental, and especially German, writers to regard international leases as modelled on a specifically English institute of law (see Jellinek, *Deutsche Juristen Zeitung*, iii. (1898) p. 305, and Schönborn, *op. cit.*). However, the new German code abandoned the old rule of the German common law and of Roman law ('*Kauf bricht Miete*'), and the lease remains now unaffected by subsequent changes of ownership. Similar is the position in French law.

[4] Salmond, *loc. cit.*

the attitude of individual systems of jurisprudence with regard to the above-mentioned points of difference may be, this fundamental relation between the lessor and the lessee is universally recognised. To this extent the term 'lease' is a general conception of law and a *terminus technicus*. It is entirely unwarranted to assume that when used in a public treaty it becomes entirely meaningless, and that it admits of the international ownership, *i.e.* sovereignty, being vested in the lessee State. To adopt such an interpretation is to do violence to the generally accepted meaning of a word in deference either to the interests of the lessee or to the wish to explain 'facts' as they really are. This latter consideration has been disproved by events; the first need not be discussed except for the purpose of stating that while it is only natural for the lessee to regard the lease as approaching cession, the intention of the lessor will usually go in an opposite direction.

It is sometimes said that such leases are merely stepping-stones to cession pure and simple. It may well be doubted whether this be so. But even if it is so, it is by no means clear why it should be left to international lawyers to confound the transitory stage with the ultimate result. The jurist called upon to interpret and to construe the treaty cannot act upon either of the conflicting reservations. His starting-point must be the declared intention of the parties embodied in a term of law with a clearly accepted meaning. International lawyers should experience no difficulty in distinguishing between legal sovereignty and the actual exercise of rights of jurisdiction, as well as in correctly construing legal relations between States in which not only rights of property *stricto sensu* but also their counterpart in international relations, namely, the rights pertaining to territorial sovereignty, are made the object of a contract of lease. It appears now that publicists are beginning to discard the theory of disguised cessions.[1]

The practical consequences of the theory of disguised cessions are obvious. The treaty is regarded as an executed one;[2] the legal obligation to restore the leased territory to the owner after the expiration of the term of the lease becomes abortive; in case of war the validity of the treaty continues; the grantee is entitled to dispose of the leased territory; his sovereignty is supreme. The consequences would be, of course, different when the rule suggested in this Section to be the correct one is applied. This rule states that whenever in a treaty a generally accepted term of private law is being used, the interpretation and construction of the treaty must, unless otherwise provided, follow the principles generally recognised as implied in this particular term.[3]

[1] Oppenheim is clearly of the opinion that the lessor State remains in law owner of the territory leased, and that the lessee has only the exercise of sovereignty. He gives examples of the termination of lease by expiration of time or by rescission (vol. i. p. 301). It is difficult to see, however, why he classifies them as cessions. Cf. now Hatschek, p. 26, who accepts without reservation the application to 'political' leases of the rules relating to lease in private law; Heilborn in Strupp's *Wörterbuch*, vol. i. p. 634 and vol. ii. p. 220; Guggenheim, quoted above, p. 49, n. 107; Donati, quoted above, p. 41; Cavaglieri, *Corso di diritto internazionale*, 1925, p. 317; Verdross, *Verfassung der Völkerrechtsgemeinschaft*, 1926, pp. 192, 193. For an impartial statement of the question of sovereignty over the Panama Canal Zone, see Woolsey in *A.J.*, xx. (1926) pp. 117-124, who is of the opinion that the treaty in question does not convey an absolute title upon the United States, that 'she (the United States) could not sell or transfer the zone or any part of it, because she has not complete title in fee' (p. 122), and that 'a reversionary sovereignty' is still vested in the Republic of Panama. See also Rutherford, *ibid.*, pp. 321, 322.

[2] On the analogy of transitory or disposive treaties to 'conveyance,' and on the dangers of constructing international law by analogy to municipal law, see Roxburgh, quoted above, p. 108.

[3] The results of this desire for uniformity which finds in the notion of cession, open or disguised, an ever-ready instrument for grasping the different ways of territorial adjustment, are clearly illustrated by the case of Bosnia and Herzegovina. Many writers treated this right of occupation and administration as an instance of a disguised cession (Liszt, p. 161; for ample references, see *ibid.*, p. 45, n. 65). It is not possible to go here into the details of this question and to investigate whether the right left to the Sultan amounted to something more than a *nudum ius*. But be that as it may, Article 25 of the Treaty of Berlin was not, in law, a cession. Only the unjuridical tendency to grasp the political significance

III

INTERNATIONAL MANDATES

§ 84. *The Current Interpretations of Article 22 of the Covenant. The Task of Juristic Interpretation.*—Three main tendencies may be ascertained in the vast literature dealing with the subject of international mandates.[1] There are writers who regard the expressions 'mandate' and 'mandatory' occurring in several sections of Article 22 of the Covenant as euphemisms used in order to conceal the fact of real annexation lying at the bottom of the whole system. Any recourse to the analogy of the private law institute of mandate leads, according to them, to untenable consequences and runs counter to actual facts. They point out that the alleged mandant, namely, the League of Nations, neither chooses the mandatory nor fixes the terms of the mandate agreement; that it has no right to terminate the mandate, or to exercise any attributes of sovereignty over the mandated territory. The expression that the mandate is exercised 'on behalf of the League' means, according to this view, no more than that the League has the right of supervision and of demanding annual reports from the mandatory. The League is, as Lord Balfour said, not the author of

of the treaty made it appear so. Nevertheless, when in 1908 Austria-Hungary annexed the two provinces, there was an almost unanimous consensus of opinion that a clear provision of the Treaty had been broken. However, if Article 25 was, in international law, a cession, then the annexation was, in international law, lawful. Thus Oppenheim (vol. i. p. 379) regards the transaction as a cession, but asserts at the same time (p. 395, n. 1) that 'such annexations are certainly unlawful in time of peace and of doubtful legality in war.'

[1] It is intended to discuss here the question of mandates only so far as the general proposition put forward in this monograph is concerned. A comprehensive bibliography will be found in Schücking-Wehberg, quoted below, p. 688, and Redslob in *Bulletin de l'Institut Interméd. Internat.*, xv. (2) (1926) pp. 284, 285.

the policy, but its instrument. The mandatory power is the sovereign over the mandated territories.[1]

This interpretation of the Covenant is strongly opposed by those publicists who see in the term 'mandate' and in its implications embodied in the general principles of law a conclusive expression of the declared intention of the parties. The League is, according to them, the lawful sovereign over the territories subjected to mandate, and it has the undoubted right to revoke it in all cases in which, in its opinion, the provisions of the mandate are consistently disregarded by the mandatory.[2]

The third group tends to reconcile the conflicting views by assuming that sovereignty over the mandated territories is divided between the League and the mandatory, or, what amounts to the same thing, that sovereignty belongs 'to the mandatory acting with the consent of the Council of the League.'[3]

Since mandates afford a clear illustration of the application by treaty of a private law conception to an international transaction, the question of the ultimate sovereignty over mandated territories is from

[1] Rolin, *R.I.*, 3rd ser., vol. i. (1920) pp. 329-363; see also Baty, *B.Y.* (1921-1922), p. 116; and especially Diena in *Recueil des Cours, Académie de Droit International*, 1923 (iv.), pp. 239-245. Vallini, *I mandati internazionali della Società delle Nazioni*, 1923, p. 80, attributes sovereignty to the Principal Allied and Associated Powers subject to supervision by the League. This also seems to be the opinion of Fauchille, No. 588 (1).

[2] A statement of this point of view will be found in Schücking-Wehberg, *Kommentar zur Völkerbundsatzung*, 2nd ed., 1924, pp. 688-711; Bileski in *Z.V.*, xii. (1923) pp. 65-85: Cioriceanu, *Les mandats internationaux*, 1921, p. 84; Redslob, *op. cit.*, pp. 284-329. See also Verdross, *op. cit.*, pp. 212-215, who defines the mandated territories as territories belonging to the community of nations (*Staatengemein-schaftsgebiete*). Schneider, *Das völkerrechtliche Mandat*, 1926, puts forward the theory of a *co-imperium* between the Allied and Associated Powers and the League of Nations.

[3] Wright, *A.J.*, xvii. (1923) p. 698, and *ibid.*, xviii. (1924) pp. 301-315; Higgins in Hall, p. 162. Cf. also Stoyanovsky, *La théorie générale des mandats internationaux*, 1925, who adopts the Roman law conception of *tutela* (guardianship) as the basis of his construction of international mandates, and attributes 'virtual sovereignty' to the inhabitants of the mandated territories. This is also the view of Pic in *R.G.*, xxx. (1923) pp. 321-371, especially at pp. 330-334, and Millot, *Les mandats internationaux*, 1924, pp. 91, 115.

the point of view of legal analysis and interpretation both interesting and of paramount importance. It may therefore be regarded as unfortunate from the jurist's point of view that it has become a political problem, offering, as it does in the opinion of many, a test of the possibilities of the new international order envisaged by the League of Nations, and of the sincerity of States which, at and before the Peace Conference of 1919, disclaimed any intention of annexing the colonies and possessions of the defeated enemies. If an opinion may be ventured on the course of events up to date, it appears that the fears of the pessimists and the claims of annexationists have not been borne out by facts. Owing partly to the cautious but vigilant activity of the Permanent Mandates Commission appointed by the Council of the League, as well as to the growing prestige of the League itself, and partly to the circumstance that, morally and psychologically, the claims of the mandatories, so far as they are based on conquest, become less impressive with the passage of years, it appears that the ultimate authority of the League over the mandated territories is becoming generally recognised. When, for instance, in 1926 the manner in which the French mandate over Syria was carried out became a matter of widespread criticism, there was a general consensus of opinion that the revocation of the mandate might well be within the province of the League.

But be that as it may, the framers of the existing law relating to mandates, notably the Council of the League and the Mandates Commission, have repeatedly expressed the opinion that it is for the science of international law to supply a correct construction of Article 22 of the Covenant. It is submitted that international jurists, while discarding all attempts at the interpretation of mandates in terms of the wishes or the expectations of one group of the signatories of the Covenant, will have to base their construction: (*a*) on the provisions of Article 22, on the Mandate Agreements concluded between the Mandatories and the Council of the League, and on the relevant pronouncements of the Mandates Commission, of the Council and the Assembly of the League: (*b*) on a juristic analysis of the controversial term 'mandate' used in the Covenant. It is from these two main sources that the answer must be drawn to the question, In whom does sovereignty over the mandated territories reside?

§ 85. *The Powers of the Mandatory.*—If the provisions of the Covenant and of the individual mandates are taken into consideration, it is difficult to see how, putting aside questions of legal theory, the sovereignty over the mandated territory can be attributed to the mandatory. The sovereignty of a State over its territory usually finds expression in the fact that the inhabitants assume the nationality of the sovereign; that he has the right of disposal over his territory; that he is free in utilising its revenue in any manner he thinks proper; that he has the right of levying troops and of conscription; that he is free to institute such fiscal policy as he may choose, and that restrictions, if any, are conditioned by reciprocity; that the right of interference by other States in the internal administration is, as a rule, excluded. One or two of these requirements may, it is true, be absent without materially affecting the sovereignty of a State. But, in the absence of all of them, can it be maintained that the administering power is sovereign?

The inhabitants of the mandated territories, even those of the 'C' mandates, do not *ipso facto* acquire the nationality of the mandatory;[1] he has no right,

[1] See the resolution of the Council of April 23, 1923 (*Official Journal*, June 1923, p. 568).

without the consent of the Council, to assign the mandate to another power, let alone to part with it in the way of cession, or to annex it;[1] he cannot use the revenue of the mandated territory for purposes outside its borders; he has no right, in the 'A' mandates, to organise military forces except on a voluntary basis, and, in the 'B' and 'C' mandates, the military training of the natives, otherwise than for purposes of internal police and the local defence of territory, is prohibited;[2] the establishment of military or naval bases or fortifications is prohibited in 'C' mandates, and allowed in 'B' mandates only so far as required by reasons of defence of territory; the most favoured nation clause—without reciprocity and in most comprehensive terms, no distinction being made between the nationals of the mandatory and those of other countries—forms part of the 'A' and 'B' mandates; the mandatory is under the obligation to supply the Mandates Commission with annual reports and to submit himself to an examination by the members of the Commission; finally, any member of the League has the right to demand a decision by the Permanent Court of International Justice in any question relating to the application of the terms of the mandate which cannot

[1] The Mandates Commission expressed, in its Report on the Second Session, its disapproval of the fact that a part of the Belgian mandated territory of Ruanda had been ceded to Great Britain. And although the British member denied at the Commission's meeting of August 1, 1923, the right of the Mandates Commission to interfere, he recognised that it is within the competence of the Council to ratify or to reject the agreement thus reached between the two States. The Council, after the modifications proposed by it had been adopted, confirmed the agreement (*Official Journal*, 1923, November, p. 1273). When at the meeting of the Mandates Commission in June 1925 certain statements by South African politicians and in the press concerning the incorporation of South-West Africa in the Union were discussed, it was the unanimous opinion of the Commission that such a step would be against the letter and the spirit of the mandate. Sir F. Lugard said that 'as long as the country remained under the mandate there could be no incorporation. If incorporation took place, it would be subject to the grant of complete self-government and the surrender of the mandate, with the consent of the League' (Mandates Commission, *Minutes of the Sixth Session*, p. 59).

[2] To French mandates this rule does not apply.

be settled by negotiation.[1] It is submitted that the cumulative effect of these limitations is hardly such as to justify the contention that the mandatory is, in international law, the sovereign of the mandated territories.

The crux of the question lies in the interpretation of the terms 'mandate' and 'mandatory' used in Article 22. If these words are taken in their usual meaning, then it is clear that alongside of the 'mandatory' there exists a corresponding 'mandant,' who is logically and legally the 'principal,' and from whom the authority of the mandatory is derived, no matter how nominal the authority of the mandant may be. In this case the ultimate sovereignty of the League of Nations over the mandated territories is a necessary inference. It has been submitted in connection with international leases that 'whenever in a treaty a generally accepted term of private law is being used, the interpretation and construction of the treaty must, unless otherwise provided, follow the rules generally recognised as implied in this particular conception.'[2] The same principle applies to the law of mandates. Individual systems of private law may differ as to particular rules regulating the relations between the mandant and the mandatory or between the principal and the agent, as, for instance, with regard to the remuneration of or the care to be exhibited by the mandatory, but they all agree as to the ultimate authority resting with the mandant and as to the fundamental relation of delegation of powers existing between the principal and the agent. Commercial law may adapt the conception of mandate to special requirements of business and commercial intercourse. So, also, constitutional law may adapt it for

[1] See the judgment and dissenting opinions in the *Mavrommatis Palestine Concession* case between Great Britain and Greece before the Permanent Court of International Justice, August 30, 1924, and March 26, 1925.

[2] See p. 190, *supra*.

its special purposes. In no case, however, can it be seriously alleged that the basic relation of derivation of authority has become obliterated. The legal relation in which the mandatory acts on behalf of the mandant can never be reduced to a relationship in which the mandant is an instrument of the policy of the mandatory.

It is an excess of caution to say that 'if the term mandate had an accepted meaning in international law, doubtless there would be a strong presumption that the treaty nations accepted that meaning, but it apparently has not.'[1] For if 'mandate' has no accepted meaning in international law—how could it? —it certainly has a meaning in this branch of law from which it is derived. Mandate is a legal *terminus technicus*. To assume that conceptions of private law adopted in a public treaty have no meaning, or, to put it more clearly, lose their usual meaning, amounts to saying that States are debarred from taking over, with any useful effect, conceptions of private or any other law, and that they must employ in treaties such terms only as have a well-defined meaning in international law.

It is submitted that it is no more than a habit inculcated by the current rejection of private law to assert that a conception of private law taken over in a treaty means nothing or next to nothing because international law has not yet evolved a definite meaning of that conception. When in a treaty a *terminus technicus* is taken from a particular branch of science—for instance, from the field of economics and geography—is it necessary to leave it to time and to events to determine what this particular term means? Surely not. There is no reason why a *terminus technicus* belonging in the first instance to private law should be treated

[1] Wright, *op. cit.*, p. 694.

differently? We shall see in the course of the discussion of the relevant cases of international arbitration that many disputes would have to be left undecided if only such legal terms as have a well-established meaning in international law were to be allowed to serve as a basis for decision. Positive international law is at liberty to modify individual rules of an institute of private law which it takes over in a treaty and to adapt them to its specific needs and requirements, but in the absence of such modification the general principles of that source of law from which the particular conception has been derived must prevail.

§ 86. *The League of Nations as the Sovereign. Limitations of Analogy.*—The ultimate sovereignty of the League of Nations over the mandated territories, and, indeed, the admissibility of analogy to private law mandates, are often contested because the League of Nations neither selected the mandatories nor fixed the terms of the individual mandate. This fact, however, in no way precludes the sovereignty of the League or its position as mandant. The League became mandant and sovereign over the mandated territories at the moment the Council approved the draft mandates laid before it, and the Powers agreed to administer the mandates 'on behalf of the League.' By and through this fact the mandate agreement between the two parties, the League and the mandatory, has been concluded. The circumstance that the former's influence on the choice of the mandatories has been small, or none, is not decisive. In a contract of sale and purchase the price is usually fixed by the parties to the contract, but this task may lawfully and validly be entrusted by the parties to a third person, to a *bonus vir*. The argument originally propounded that the League cannot legally fulfil the function of a mandant because it lacks distinct juridical personality, is now being abandoned even by those writers who still adhere to the view that the sovereignty rests with the mandatory.[1] The main difficulty lies in the fact that the writers and statesmen do not always take the trouble to distinguish between legal sovereignty proper and the exercise of sovereignty.[2] The first rests with the League, the second with the mandatory, subject to supervision on the part of the League.[3] That is why even those who question the ultimate sovereignty of the League do not deny that in case of the mandate having been terminated for reasons other than the completion of the mandatory's task, the right of appointing a new mandatory devolves upon the League.[4]

It may well be asked whether the above interpretation of Article 22 of the Covenant takes sufficiently into

[1] See Diena, *op. cit.*, p. 232.

[2] See p. 189, *supra*.

[3] The test of *exercise* of sovereignty should be quite sufficient to cover such cases as *Jacobus Christian* v. *Rex*, Supreme Court of South Africa, November 1923, reported in *B.Y.* (1925), pp. 211-219. Although in this case the Court refused to accept the view that the relation between the mandatory and the League can be likened to that between principal and agent, it arrived nevertheless at the definite conclusion that 'the Government of South Africa is not possessed of *majestas* in the full sense of the term; in other words, it is not a sovereign and independent State.' Even more explicit was the Palestine Supreme Court *in re Ezra Goralshvi*: 'To hold that the petitioners are British subjects would involve holding that the Crown having accepted the responsibility of governing Palestine as a mandatory, has thereby acquired sovereignty, a view for which no authority has been cited' (reported in *A.J.*, xx. (1926) p. 771). In the Report of the Mandates Commission on Syria (March 1926, C. 174, M. 65, 1926, vi. p. 208) the mandatory is described as provisionally exercising a political guardianship over the inhabitants of the mandated territories. An authoritative and clear, although indirect, definition of the status of the mandatory Power will be found in the following resolution adopted by the Mandates Commission and the Council: 'The Council of the League of Nations . . . declares that obligations assumed by a mandatory Power in a mandated territory and rights of every kind regularly acquired under its administration shall have under all circumstances the same validity as if the mandatory Power were sovereign' (*Minutes of the Sixth Session*, p. 117). It may be useful to recall here the opinion expressed on March 5, 1919, by Mr. Schanzer, Italian Minister of Foreign Affairs in the Italian Senate: 'I mandati sono temporanei e revocabili, ma non sono limitati nel tempo. Saranno limitati e revocabili come erano certe concessioni papali di territori o certe concessioni feudali, o quelle amministrazioni, di territori altrui affidate in tempi recenti ad alcuni Stati europei' (Schanzer, *Sulla Società delle Nazioni*, 1925, p. 41).

[4] Wright, *op. cit.*, p. 702.

account both the wide differences between the three kinds of mandates and the practical requirements of stability and efficiency of the mandatory's administration. This question may be answered in the affirmative if we consider that the basic principle upon which stress has been laid here in connection with the construction of treaties and international leases, namely, that only such rules of private law are applicable as enjoy universal or almost universal recognition, applies with no less force to mandates. Rules of that kind are, with regard to mandates, few and simple; indeed, so simple that, so far as the practical consequences of a particular interpretation are concerned, there is no difference between the construction proffered on these pages and based on the private law mandate, and those based either on the English law institute of trust, which is regarded by some as the proper basis of a legal construction of international mandates,[1] or on the conception of guardianship. These general and fundamental principles are the relation of derivation of powers or delegation on one hand, and of trust, duty, and confidence on the other. The technicalities, exceptions, and historical peculiarities of any given system of private law have no application in the interpretation of mandates.

The applicability of the principle here set forth may be tested on the paramount question as to the termination of mandates. It is common to all systems of private law that either party has as a rule the right to terminate the mandate at any time.[2] This right is the expression both of the permanent authority of the mandant and of the element of confidence and trust involved in the mutual relation. However, although there is no

[1] Lee, *The Mandate for Mesopotamia and the Principle of Trusteeship in English Law*, 1920.

[2] German Code, Article 671; French Code, Article 2004; Japanese Code, Article 651.

way of escaping, in the international law of mandates, from the consequences of this general rule, the latter is here, as in private law, capable of modifications by virtue of an agreement, tacit or express, of the parties. Thus in Article 22 of the Covenant, and in the mandates approved by the Council, the mandate agreement has been concluded for a definite purpose and, impliedly, for a definite period. This is especially clear in the 'A' mandates, where the advice and assistance rendered to the mandated peoples are limited 'until such time as they are able to stand alone.' It would seem therefore that, until the completion of the task entrusted to the mandatory, the right of the League to revoke the mandate is limited to cases of breach of the provisions of the mandate on the part of the mandatory, either through voluntary default or through his incapacity to carry out the mandate. The permanency of the administration seems thus to be assured. Similarly, owing to the same reason, the right of the mandatory to withdraw before completing his task is restricted to those cases in which the continuation of the mandate is fraught with danger to his vital interests.[1] In both cases it would be for the Permanent Court of International Justice to state whether the alleged facts are objectively existent or not.

In many respects this construction of mandates reaches, in close analogy to the corresponding conception of private law, the same results as those flowing from the theories which oppose this method of interpretation. It differs from them in the fact that, in recognition of the fundamental legal relation between the mandant and the mandatory, it places the ultimate sovereignty in the League of Nations. Thus it avoids the necessity

[1] Cf., for instance, Article 671 of the German Civil Code, which provides that if a grave reason exists the mandatory is entitled to give notice even though he has waived the right to do so.

of ignoring the declared intention of the parties and of reducing the *termini technici* used by them to a mere form of speech.[1]

[1] A very similar problem, which, however, cannot be discussed in this monograph, is presented by Article 49 of the Treaty of Versailles, in which Germany renounces the government of the Saar territory in favour of the League of Nations, acting as a trustee, the ultimate sovereignty over the territory to be decided by a plebiscite after a period of fifteen years. The question is discussed with great lucidity by Bisschop, the *Saar Controversy, The Grotius Society Publications*, No. 2, 1924, pp. 22-28, who deals with the legal position of the German and French Governments, as well as with that of the inhabitants of the Saar territory in their capacity as the *cestui qui trust*. Schücking and Wehberg, *op. cit.*, simply regard the League of Nations as the trustee of the German Government (p. 120), whereas Fauchille (vol. i. pt. i. p. 685) discusses the problem under *droit de superficie*.

CHAPTER V

PRIVATE LAW RULES OF EVIDENCE AND PROCEDURE

§ 87. *Estoppel and Preclusion. The Universal Application of the Doctrine of Estoppel.*—States are, in their mutual relations, subject to rules either expressly recognised by them, or flowing from the very nature of these relations and from the legal character of the international community. An attempt has been made in the preceding chapters to establish that, in the absence of rules expressly provided by custom and treaty, it is, on the whole, private law as generally accepted by civilised communities which supplies the formulation of this necessary complement of international law. The same applies to private law rules of evidence and procedure, of which it is proposed to discuss some typical instances illustrating this general proposition. Of them, in turn, the most instructive and best illustrated by cases taken from the practice of States is that of estoppel.

The doctrine of estoppel is *prima facie* a private law doctrine forming a part of the law of evidence. 'Where one by his word or conduct wilfully causes another to believe in the existence of a certain state of things, and induces him to act on that belief so as to alter his previous position, the former is concluded from averring against the latter a different state of things as existing at the same time'—this is the classical formulation of the English doctrine of estoppel *in pais* (estoppel by conduct).[1] It might seem that this is a doctrine exclusively confined to English law, and that it cannot therefore be regarded as a general principle of private jurisprudence. But this is so only in form. In substance, the principle underlying estoppel is recognised by all systems of private law, not only with regard to estoppel by record (estoppel by judgment, *res iudicata*), but also, under different names, with regard to estoppel by conduct and by deed.[2] Where the Anglo-American lawyer refers to estoppel, the continental jurist will usually say that the party is 'precluded' from asserting a fact or putting forward a demand.[3] But apart from the differences in terminology and from the fact that in the common law countries the doctrine has received a more thorough and systematic treatment, there is nothing that would justify us in asserting that the position is radically different in various systems of law. 'The doctrine of estoppel "*in pais*,"' says Sir Frederick Pollock, 'is perhaps the most powerful and flexible instrument to be found in any system of civil jurisprudence.'[4] It is of interest to see how strongly English judges believe in the universality of this rule. Says Baron Cleasby in *Halifax Union* v. *Wheelwright*:

'It is perhaps only an application of one of those general principles which do not belong to municipal law of any particular country, but which we cannot help giving effect to in the administration of justice, viz. that a man cannot take advantage of his own wrong, a man cannot complain

[1] Lord Denman, C.J., in *Pickard* v. *Sears* (1837), 6 A. and E. at p. 474.

[2] Cf. Articles 122, 307-309 of the German Code; Articles 1341, 1350, 1351, 1352, 1356 of the French Code; and Riezler, quoted below, pp. 114, 121, 122, 144, 166; see also Schuster, *Principles of German Civil Law*, 1907, pp. 361-362; and Sherman, *Roman Law in the Modern World*, 2nd ed., 1922, vol. ii. p. 417. It cannot be investigated in this connection how far estoppel originated from an equivalent Roman doctrine (*Inst.*, 3, 21); cf. here Riezler (*Studien im römischen, englischen und deutschen Civilrecht*), *Venire contra factum proprium*, 1912.

[3] Cf. Sir Arthur Cohen's Argument before the Hague Tribunal in the Venezuelan Preferential Claim, p. 254, *infra*.

[4] *The Expansion of the Common Law*, 1904, p. 108.

of the consequence of his own default against a person who was misled by that default without any fault of his own.' [1]

It is not easy to adduce reasons why those general principles underlying estoppel should be disregarded in the relations between States.[2] As a matter of fact, in no less than seven important arbitration cases was the doctrine of estoppel or preclusion put forward by the parties or made the basis of the award.

§ 88. *Instances from International Arbitration.*—In the judgment of the Senate of Hamburg in the *Croft* case between Great Britain and Portugal the plea of preclusion was dealt with *in extenso* and recognised in principle by the tribunal.[3] In the Behring Sea arbitration, Lord Hannen admitted the possibility of basing the claim of the United States on estoppel, and it appears that the terms of reference to the tribunal were in part based on a virtual recognition of that doctrine.[4] In the British Guiana arbitration, where it was claimed by Venezuela that the acceptance by Great Britain of the so-called Palmerston line of 1850 estopped her from claiming any territory beyond that line, neither Great Britain nor the members of the tribunal denied the admissibility of estoppel as between States.[5]

In the Pious Fund case it was maintained by the United States that, quite apart from the plea of *res iudicata*, Mexico was estopped by its conduct from questioning the jurisdiction of a previous joint commission, and this assertion was accepted by the tribunal.[6] In the Venezuelan Preferential Claim case both sides availed themselves of the argument of estoppel,[7] and the tribunal

[1] (1875), L.R. 10 Exch. 183. Cf. also Lord Campbell in *Cairncross* v. *Lorimer* (1860), L.T. 130.

[2] On the question of estoppel in international law, cf. McNair, *B. Y.* (1924), p. 34.

[3] See p. 268, *infra*.

[4] See p. 224, *infra*, and n. 1, *ibid.*

[5] See p. 232, *infra*.

[6] See p. 248, *infra*.

[7] See p. 254, *infra*.

took the fact that the Government of Venezuela itself recognised in principle the justice of claims presented to it by the blockading Powers as one of the grounds of its decision.[1] The award in the Russian Indemnity case of 1912, which states that the Russian Government was by its conduct estopped from demanding moratory interest from Turkey, is, in its decisive point, based on preclusion.[2]

In the Agreement between the United Kingdom and the United States, of August 1910, constituting the American and British Claims Arbitral Tribunal, great latitude was given to the tribunal to treat as conclusive any admission of liability by the Government against whom a claim is put forward.[3] Apart from this, in a number of cases decided by this tribunal, estoppel proper was pleaded by the parties, and in some cases recognised by the arbitrator.[4] Finally, when in the arbitration between Great Britain and Costa Rica (award of October 18, 1923) estoppel was pleaded by the latter, the arbitrator, far from denying the applicability of that doctrine in international law, proceeded to inquire whether the argument put forward by Costa Rica contains the elements of equitable estoppel as understood in municipal law.[5] These examples show how a private law rule of evidence, never expressly recognised by positive international law, may now be regarded as a working rule of international arbitral law.

§ 89. *Res iudicata.*—The same applies to the doctrine of *res iudicata*, which, while forming a part of the English doctrine of estoppel, is at the same time a fundamental

[1] In the Corvaia case (Venezuelan arbitrations of 1903) it was held that estoppel operates against a claimant State, a national of which has forfeited his citizenship by accepting foreign diplomatic employment abroad. *Ralston's Report*, p. 782.

[2] See p. 259, *infra*.

[3] See p. 278, *infra*.

[4] See pp. 277-281, *infra*.

[5] See *A.J.*, xviii. (1924) p. 155, and the arbitrator's references to other instances of alleged estoppel.

principle of municipal law in general. Is an express recognition by sovereign States necessary in order to make it binding between nations ? A strictly positivist theory would answer this question in the affirmative. But the practice of States cannot and does not follow such a course. In the Pious Fund arbitration, where the question of *res iudicata* formed the central problem confronting the tribunal, the principle itself was recognised by both parties. It will be seen from the analysis of that case that the actual dispute turned upon the question whether the force of *res iudicata* extends to the award only, or whether it embraces also other elements of the judgment. In answering this latter question, the Court followed what may be fairly called a general principle of private jurisprudence.[1] There was no need to have recourse to 'general jurisprudence,' because, as Professor Scott rightly points out, *res iudicata* is so generally recognised that it may be regarded as a rule of national jurisprudence of such recognised standing that it need not be justified as a principle of general jurisprudence in order to be applied by an international tribunal.[2] Few private law rules of evidence and procedure have since enjoyed more authority in international arbitration than that of *res iudicata.*[3]

§ 90. *The Scope of Competence.*—It is a broad rule of private arbitral law that the arbitrators possess the power to determine their jurisdiction and to give an interpretation to the instrument constituting the reference to

[1] See p. 246, *infra.* For two other cases illustrating the principle of *res iudicata*, cf. Wehberg, *op. cit.* (at p. 65, *supra*, p. 22 (the Phare case), and Lapradelle-Politis, vol. i. p. 266 (the case of the Duchy of Bouillon).

[2] J. B. Scott, *Der kalifornische Kirchengüterstreit zwischen den Vereinigten Staaten von America und Mexico*, in Schücking's *Das Werk von Haag*, vol. i. pt. i. p. 167.

[3] See the case of the *Newchwang* before the British American Claims Arbitral Tribunal of 1910 (p. 283, *infra*), and the Advisory Opinion of the Permanent Court of International Justice concerning the Polish Postal Service in Dantzig (Publications of the Court, Series B, No. 11, pp. 19, 30).

them. The same rule applies to ordinary courts of justice. It is a rule grounded in principles of logic and expedience upon which it is not necessary to expatiate. But it was only after prolonged discussion, lasting over a century, that the competence of an international tribunal to determine its own jurisdiction became a recognised principle.[1] The question arose during the deliberations of the Mixed Commission formed under Article 7 of the Treaty between the United States and Great Britain of November 1794, when the British Commissioner denied the power of the Court to determine its jurisdiction.[2] It also occupied the tribunals in the *Alabama* arbitration and in the Pious Fund case.[3] It would be an idle task to inquire whether it is due to a conscious application of a private law rule, or to the intrinsic merits of the matter, that there is now a consensus of opinion and of practice in giving an affirmative answer to this question.[4] Both views are probably right in the sense that it is primarily private law which provides in most cases a clear formulation of the 'reason of the thing.'

§ 91. *Appeal and Revision.*—The same can be said with regard to the question of appeal in international arbitration. It flows from the conception and the purpose of arbitration that the finding of the arbitrators should be final. This was a clear rule of Roman law followed

[1] As recently as in the Samoa Claims arbitration under the Convention of November 7, 1899, this principle was hotly contested by Germany. Cf. p. 14 of the *Case* of the United States, and p. 4 of the *Second Supplement* of the German *Case*.

[2] Moore, p. 2277 (*The Betsey*).

[3] Cf. pp. 220, 247, *infra*.

[4] Cf. Lammasch, *Die Rechtskraft*, pp. 67-70; *Lehre*, p. 166; Higgins, *Hague Peace Conferences*, 1909, p. 176; Article 73 of the Convention for Pacific Settlement of International Disputes, and Article 36 of the *Statute* ('In the event of a dispute as to whether the Court has jurisdiction, the matter shall be settled by the decision of the Court'). See also the Judgments of August 30, 1924, in the *Mavrommatis Palestine Concession*, and of August 25, 1925, in the case concerning German interests in Polish Upper Silesia. (Cf. especially 57-60 of the award in the *Mavrommatis* case, Dissenting Opinion of Judge Moore, Publications of the Court, Series A, No. 2.)

closely by Grotius [1] and the first classical writers, and it is now accepted, on the whole, as a principle of modern private jurisprudence. On the other hand, while regarding the arbitral award as final, modern systems provide a safeguard against abuses either by demanding a formal authorisation for the execution of the award by the State courts [2] or by granting relief in cases of obvious miscarriage of justice.[3] It may now be said that, after a long battle in books and at conferences, internationa law has followed, so far as the finality of the award is concerned, the generally accepted principle of private law. The Hague Convention provides: 'The Award, duly pronounced and notified to the agents of the parties, settles the dispute definitely and without appeal.'[4]

It is significant how frequently even recent writers support their views on this question by references to private law. Lammasch's treatment of appeal bristles no less than that of Grotius with citations from the *Digest*; he also has recourse to modern writers on private law and to modern codes.[5] But the analogy has not been carried so far as to provide a remedy 'in case of invalid compromise, or in case of excess of authority, or of proved corruption of one of the arbitrators or of essential error.' [6] The respective proposals at the second Hague Conference proved abortive because of Germany's opposition to the establishment of a permanent court of arbitral justice which could decide in cases of alleged nullity of the award. [7] But there is no reason why now,

[1] L. iii. c. 20, s. 46.

[2] Halsbury, *The Laws of England*, vol. i. pp. 473-481.

[3] Austrian Civil Procedure, § 595; German Civil Procedure, § 1041.

[4] Hague Convention for the Pacific Settlement of International Disputes, Article 81; see also Article 60 of the *Statute*; and Salvioli, quoted below, pp. 288-292.

[5] See *Rechtskraft*, pp. 129-134.

[6] *Resolutions of the Institute of International Law*, Scott's edition, 1916, p. 7.

[7] The 'Revision' of Article 83, which *may be* provided for in the arbitration treaty, and which can be demanded only 'on the ground of discovery of some new fact which is calculated to exercise decisive influence upon the award, and which at the time of the discussion was unknown to the tribunal and to the party demanding revision,' is obviously inadequate.

with the Permanent Court of International Justice in existence, the analogy should not be completed. This would substantially strengthen the judicial settlement of disputes so far as it takes place outside the Permanent Court of International Justice.[1]

§ 92. *Various Rules of Procedure and Evidence.*—It is impossible, in a monograph dealing only with the broad outlines of the question of private law, to investigate in detail how far particular rules of procedure and evidence applied by international tribunals have developed on the basis of recourse had to corresponding rules of private law. International arbitration, although its name and origin point to the analogous institution of private law, fulfils on the whole the function of judicial settlement of disputes. This statement, as pointed out above, is none the less true because some writers, acting under the praiseworthy impulse to promote the substitution of casual and isolated tribunals by a regularly working international court, attempt to show that the strictly judicial element in modern international arbitration is comparatively small.[2] It is in their capacity as courts of justice that international tribunals have taken over and adapted for their purposes private law rules of evidence and procedure. Intervention,[3] exceptions (demurrers),[4] the rules of evidence, the burden of

[1] The Statute of the Permanent Court of International Justice (referred to as *Statute*) contains provisions relating to the revision of its own judgments, when the application for revision 'is based upon the discovery of some fact of such a nature as to be a decisive factor, which fact was, when the judgment was given, unknown to the Court and also to the party claiming revision, always provided that such ignorance was not due to negligence' (Article 61). Cf. here the Orinoco Steamship Company case before the Permanent Court of Arbitration, p. 265, n. 1, *infra*.

[2] Cf. p. 64, n. 4, *supra*.

[3] See Article 84 of the Hague Convention for the Pacific Settlement of International Disputes; Articles 62 of the *Statute* and 58 of the Rules of the Permanent Court of International Justice, and *Proceedings* of the Committee of Jurists, p. 592; cf. also the case of the *Wimbledon* before the Permanent Court, and Salvioli, quoted below, pp. 129-138.

[4] Cf. here Lammasch, *Lehre*, p. 165; cf. also p. 320 of the *Proceedings* of the Committee of Jurists

proof [1]—all these questions touch upon the subject under discussion. A study of the development of these rules, beginning with disputes between sovereign American States decided by the Supreme Court, which treated a boundary dispute between States exactly as one between two private landowners,[2] and ending with the procedure of the Permanent Court of International Justice, would no doubt show that in this respect also the work of international courts was and is impossible without a large measure of recourse to general principles of private law. It is especially with regard to the relative authority of common and civil law rules of evidence, and to the beneficial influence which the clash and the subsequent mutual adjustment of these two systems of rules exercised upon the work of international tribunals, that such a study is bound to prove most fruitful.[3]

(according to Lord Phillimore, Mr. Root's argument on the Jurisdiction of the Court was partly based on the 'demurrers' of the Anglo-American practice).

[1] See on the question of the burden of proof in the *Alabama* arbitration, p. 223, n. 2, *infra*; in the Behring Sea arbitration, p. 227, n. 2, *infra*; in the Alaskan Boundary arbitration, p. 237, n. 3, *infra*; in the Venezuelan Preferential Claim case, p. 255, n. 2, *infra*.

[2] See *Rhode Islands* v. *Massachusetts* (1846), 4 Howard 591; and Smith, *The American Supreme Court as an International Tribunal*, 1920, p. 16.

[3] Cf. here Ralston in the *Commonwealth* (California), 1925, pp. 300, 301, and No. 365; see also p. 237, *infra*.

PART III

INTERNATIONAL ARBITRATION

CHAPTER VI

RECOURSE TO PRIVATE LAW IN INTERNATIONAL ARBITRATION

(*The Five British-American Arbitrations*)

§ 93. *The British-American Arbitrations.*—While the positivist theory was engaged in banishing from international law all that threatened its postulated independence of other sources of law, British and American practice was laying strong foundations for the building of modern arbitration, which, in the long run, was bound to prove the futility of that widespread iconoclasm. The five great British-American arbitrations—the *Alabama*, Behring Sea, British Guiana,[1] Alaskan Boundary, and North Atlantic Fisheries arbitrations—while constituting politically the most instructive instances of international arbitration, are at the same time of paramount importance from the legal point of view. The written pleadings in these arbitrations were carefully prepared, and the forensic discussions, conducted as a rule by the most able representatives of the legal profession of the two countries with an incomparable thoroughness and love of legal argument, afford classical instances of a living and powerful international jurisprudence. We shall see how, one after another, these arbitrations shatter the fiction of an international law totally independent of conceptions and rules of private law.[2]

[1] See p. 227, n. 3, *infra*.

[2] It will be noted that the discussion of these and following arbitration cases is by no means meant as an exhaustive analysis of the individual cases; it deals with them so far only as they are believed to illustrate the problem of application

I

THE 'ALABAMA' ARBITRATION

§ 94. *The Three Private Law Questions.*—The *Alabama* arbitration stands on the threshold of modern international arbitration, not only owing to the importance of the legal questions which it had to answer, and to the application, on an unprecedented scale, of a well-ordered arbitral procedure, but also owing to its political importance as the first instance of settling a dispute which raised high national feeling on both sides, and which, if unsettled, would have proved a real hindrance to peaceful relations between the two nations. Previous instances of arbitration are either restricted to cases of minor importance, or fulfil the task of settlement of questions decided in principle by a peace treaty.

At the first sight it might seem that the object of this arbitration, as concerned chiefly with certain duties of neutrals, does not leave much scope for the examination of the problem of recourse to private law. However, it was the application of private law, both by the parties and the members of the tribunal, that had a large share in deciding the main issues of the arbitration. The legal battle in Geneva centred upon three questions: (*a*) What constitutes 'due diligence' required from a neutral in the discharge of the obligation as defined in Article 6 of the Arbitration Treaty of Washington? (*b*) In the event of Great Britain being

of private law. — The reader is referred, for an excellent analysis of the juridical aspects of the *Alabama* arbitration, to the *note doctrinale* in Lapradelle-Politis, vol. ii. pp. 902-983. Cf. also Bluntschli, in *R.I.*, ii. (1870) pp. 453 ff.; Calvo, *ibid.*, vi. (1874) pp. 466-488. See also Cushing, *The Treaty of Washington*, 1873, and Bernard, *A Historical Account of the Neutrality of Great Britain during the American Civil War*, 1870, pp. 385 ff.

found negligent in the fulfilment of her duties of neutrality, what is the measure of damages to be awarded to the United States? (*c*) In the event of damages being awarded, should interest be allowed? It would have been in vain to rely, for the purpose of answering these questions, upon settled rules of international law. There were no such rules.

§ 95. *Due Diligence.*—The contention of the United States that 'the extent of the diligence required to escape responsibility is gauged by the character and magnitude of the matter which it may affect, by the relative condition of the parties, by the ability of the parties incurring the liability to exercise the diligence required by the exigencies of the case, and by the extent of the injury which may follow negligence,'[1] was supported to a large extent by references to common law, to Roman and continental law, to the Pandects, and to judgments of municipal courts.[2] The question before the tribunal was: Are the criterions of due diligence as applied between individuals applicable to States and their mutual relations, or has the duty to show due care a different and special meaning so far as States are concerned? The much debated and much misunderstood answer was: 'The due diligence . . . ought to be exercised by neutral Governments in exact proportion to the risks to which either of the belligerents may be exposed from a failure to fulfil the obligations of neutrality on their part.'

This part of the Geneva award has been subjected to much criticism not only on account of its alleged obscurity, but also on the ground that it amounts to an adoption of a standard different from that obtaining

[1] *The Case of the United States*, Government's Printing Office, 1871, p. 152.

[2] *Op. cit.*, pp. 153-157. In the printed *Argument* they relied on analogies to the rules relating to collisions at sea (see *The Argument at Geneva*, quoted below, p. 156).

in private law.[1] This last objection, however, seems to be based on a misunderstanding. It is true that, as pointed out by Hall[2] and Lawrence,[3] the United States originally insisted on 'due diligence' being 'commensurate with the . . . magnitude of the results of negligence,' but it will be seen from the above quotation from their *Case* that they modified their attitude in the course of the arbitration. They spoke of the extent of injury which 'may follow negligence,' not which actually followed. In so far as they insisted on a reasonable estimate on the part of the defaulting State of the possible consequences of its negligence, their contention was in accordance with a general principle of private law. So also was the award. It did not refer to risks to which the belligerent has become exposed, but to which it may be exposed.[4] What it refused to admit was the principle of the *diligentia quam in suis rebus* embodied in the British contention that '. . . it would not be reasonable to exact, as of right, from the Government a measure of care exceeding that which Governments are accustomed to exert in matters affecting their own security or that of their own citizens.'[5] It is a well-settled principle of private law that although the degree of diligence required by law varies from case to case, it has nevertheless an objective criterion, namely, that the amount of caution required of a citizen in his conduct is proportionate to the 'magnitude and the apparent imminence of the risk.'[6] The diligence of 'an average prudent man'

[1] See Oppenheim, vol. ii. p. 501.

[2] P. 271.

[3] P. 633.

[4] Neither does the award amount to an adoption of *culpa levissima*, as is frequently maintained. Strupp's *Wörterbuch* (vol. i. p. 257) commits a similar mistake. The award does not speak of the dangers '*die dem kriegführenden Staat durch die Verletzung der Neutralitätspflichten erwachsen*'; the correct translation is '*erwachsen können.*'

[5] *The Argument at Geneva, A Complete Collection of the Forensic Discussions on the part of the United States and of Great Britain before the Tribunal of Arbitration under the Treaty of Washington*, 1873, p. 156; also Moore, pp. 573, 612.

[6] Pollock, *The Law of Torts*, 12th ed., 1923, p. 440.

constitutes an objective test independent of the idiosyncrasies of the individual citizen. It is evident from the opinion of Count Sclopis how great a part the Roman law distinctions of *culpa lata* and *levis* played in the formulation of the award.[1] On the whole, the adoption by the tribunal of what may be called a private law interpretation of 'due diligence' remains unshaken by the criticism waged against it. And it may well be doubted whether the framers of Article 25 of the XIII. Hague Convention, who shared in the expressions of criticism of the term 'due diligence' and of its interpretation adopted at Geneva, succeeded in substituting a better one in its place.[2]

§ 96. *Measure of Damages.*—With regard to the measure of damages to be awarded for an international tort, this arbitration is generally referred to as rejecting a well-recognised principle of private law in favour of the rule that indirect losses cannot be compensated for, and that damages for the loss of prospective profits cannot be allowed by an international arbitral award. The first was formulated by the tribunal in a preliminary decision which declared that indirect losses 'do not constitute, upon the principles of international law applicable to such cases, good foundation for award of compensation or computation of damages between nations';[3] the second, obviously running counter to the general principle of private law which takes the *restitutio in integrum* as a basis for compensation, was embodied in the final award.[4]

There was nothing in previous cases of arbitration that could, as a precedent, justify the tribunal in indiscriminately rejecting all claims for prospective

[1] Moore, p. 4069; see also the Opinion of Sir Alexander Cockburn, *Papers relating to the Treaty of Washington*, Washington, 1872, vol. iv. pp. 261-265.

[2] See p. 139, n. 1, *supra*.

[3] Moore, p. 646.

[4] *Ibid.*, p. 658.

damages. Subsequent arbitrations do not follow its lead,[1] and recent arbitral awards quite clearly recognise the right to damages for the loss of prospective profits.[2] In fact, never was a decision of a competent international tribunal more consistently disregarded by subsequent arbitral awards.[3] It found some, although by no means a great, following amongst writers, and was as a rule appealed to in international arbitrations by States called upon to pay damages. Thus, the next forensic contest showed Great Britain claiming damages for the loss of prospective profits and the United States opposing the claim and appealing to the Geneva award. The doctrine propounded by the tribunal is now generally rejected by publicists.[4] But, erroneous and misleading as this decision has been, it was not altogether without good effects. It showed that in those rare cases in which an arbitral tribunal sacrifices a juridical principle for the sake of a political compromise, its influence upon arbitral jurisprudence is conspicuously small.

There are no doubt circumstances explaining this unsuccessful attempt to introduce a rule which, while opposed to a general principle of private law, is at the same time contrary to justice and equity. Firstly, the history of this arbitration must be considered, especially the fact that the formal right of the tribunal to award compensation for this kind of damages was challenged by the British Government, and that the arbitration itself was put in danger because of this question.[5]

[1] See pp. 149, 150, *supra.*

[2] See pp. 280, 281, *infra.*

[3] For a recent criticism of this part of the *Alabama* award, see Opinion of Umpire Parker, of November 1923, Mixed Claims Commission, United States *v.* Germany; Opinion in War-Risk Insurance Premium Claims, *A.J.*, xviii. (1924) p. 598.

[4] See p. 151, n. 1, *supra.* See also for a good discussion of this aspect of the Geneva award, Yntema in *Columbia Law Review*, xxiv. (1924) pp. 149-151. The author, however, seems to oscillate between two desires: one, to show that the arbitrators did not in fact reject indirect damages; the other, to explain why they did reject them.

[5] See the Opinion of the Mixed Claims Commission of November 1, 1923, quoted above, *loc. cit.*, and Lapradelle-Politis, vol. ii. pp. 828-841.

Secondly, in the course of the proceedings before the tribunal 'indirect damages' were constantly being confused with 'prospective damages,' and the latter had thus been made to suffer the fate of the former. Now, the rejection of the demand for indirect damages may be justified by the character of the American claims, which extended to losses caused by the transfer of the American commercial marine to the British flag, the enhanced payments of insurance, the prolongation of the war, the addition of a large sum to the cost of the war, and the suppression of rebellion.

The rejection of claims of this character cannot seriously affect the general rule. Even so, however, the decision of the tribunal could hardly serve as a precedent; for although it is a recognised principle of private law that *causa proxima non remota spectatur*, the 'directness' of the damage remains nevertheless a question of degree, and the difficulty cannot be solved by a sweeping general statement of the kind propounded by the tribunal.[1]

The argument of Great Britain in the question of damages, coupled with the plea of contributory negligence on the part of the United States, was based to a large extent on decisions of American and English Courts.[2] So was that of the United States, who supported their claim by reference to the unanimous opinion of jurists 'both of the common law, as in Great Britain and the United States, and of the civil law, as in the countries of the Roman law in Europe and in America.'[3]

[1] It will also be observed that in the lump sum awarded by the tribunal prospective profits have, it seems, been included. See Moore, p. 647. Cf. also British *Counter Case*, pp. 131-134, 137-140 (Geneva edition).

[2] *Counter Case*, p. 35. Says the British national judge in his dissenting opinion (*Papers relating to the Treaty of Washington*, vol. iv. p. 537): 'Where damage to property arises not directly from a wilful injury—but indirectly only, from want of due care—an indemnity against actual loss is all that by the law of England and America, or by any principles of general jurisprudence, can possibly be awarded.'

[3] *Argument* of the United States, p. 213.

§ 97. *The Question of Interest.*—The question of interest on the sums awarded for losses was of considerable importance, as the interest claimed by the United States amounted to about 75 per cent. of the principal.[1] The Treaty of Washington contained no mention of interest to be awarded in addition to the gross sum, but the United States demanded that it should be allowed as an element of damage within the gross sum, and quoted historical instances in which interest has been awarded.[2] The accuracy of those instances, as having any bearing on the case under consideration, and the demand itself, were strongly contested by Great Britain.[3] Both sides based their arguments on private law. Great Britain[4] contended that according to settled rules of civil jurisprudence interest can be allowed only where there is a principal debt of liquidated and ascertained amount, the fault of the delay in payment resting with the debtor.[5] Pandects, French, English, and American authorities, were cited. However, she had to concede that private law 'admits interest when given as damages,'[6] although, pleading absence of gross negligence on her part and contributory negligence on the part of the United States, which, it was alleged, were responsible for the delay in the settlement of those claims, she thought the allowance of interest inadmissible.

But it is significant that, while availing herself to the full of the rules of private jurisprudence, Great Britain recurred time and again to the plea that it is a claim 'between nation and nation,' and quoted Sir Christopher Robinson to the effect that sovereign powers do not usually pay interest.[7] The

[1] See Summary of American Claims, *Argument* of the United States, p. 573.

[2] *Argument* of the United States, p. 220.

[3] *Counter Case* of Great Britain, p. 141 (Geneva ed.).

[4] *Argument of Sir Roundell Palmer on the claim of the United States for interest by way of damages: The Argument at Geneva*, pp. 551-567.

[5] *Ibid.*, p. 551.

[6] *Ibid.*, p. 553.

[7] *Ibid.*, p. 565; see also *Counter Case*, pp. 140, 141. Cf. also *Reply on the part of the United States to the*

tribunal decided not to disclose the manner in which it arrived at the gross sum of 15,500,000 dollars awarded to the United States, but Sir Alexander Cockburn revealed in his dissenting opinion that the arbitrators took 6 per cent. interest as the basis of assessment.[1, 2]

II

THE BEHRING SEA ARBITRATION

§ 98. *The Plea of Prescription.*—Among the five questions submitted to the tribunal in Paris in 1893,[3] the following two were of decisive importance : (*a*) 'How far were Russia's claims to exclusive jurisdiction in the Behring Sea and to exclusive rights in the fisheries therein recognised and conceded by Great Britain ?'[4] (*b*) 'Has the United States any right, and if so, what right, of protection of property in the fur seals frequenting the islands of the United States in Behring Sea when such seals are found outside the ordinary three-mile limit ?'[5] In both questions recourse was had to private law, namely, to the doctrine of prescription with regard to the first, to rules of property and possession with

Argument of H.B.M. Counsel on the Allowance of Interest in Computation of Indemnity: The Argument at Geneva, pp. 568-573.

[1] See Moore, p. 651. For an adverse criticism of this decision, see Lapradelle-Politis, vol. ii. p. 981.

[2] With regard to the burden of proof, the tribunal adhered to the well-established principle of private law that, as a rule, it is upon the claimant to supply the proof. But it was asserted by the United States that as a State is responsible for all offences against international law arising within its jurisdiction, by which a foreign State suffers injury, unless the former can clear itself of the responsibility by demonstrating its freedom from fault in premises, after proof of hostile acts on neutral territory the *onus probandi* of due diligence rests upon the neutrals (*Argument* of the United States, p. 154). This contention was vigorously opposed by Great Britain (*Argument* of Great Britain, p. 423).

[3] On the Behring Sea arbitration, see Moore, pp. 755-961 ; Calvo, vol. vi. pp. 370-447; Barclay in *R.I.*, xxv. (1893) pp. 417 ff. ; Engelhardt, *ibid.*, xxvi. (1894) pp. 386-400 ; for further bibliography, see Fauchille, vol. i. pt. ii. p. 245, n. 1.

[4] Cf. question 2 of Article 6 of the Arbitration Treaty of Washington of February 1892, Moore, p. 801.

[5] Question 5.

regard to the second. The first question was implicitly related to estoppel in so far as it could be maintained that the United States had been induced by the conduct of Great Britain to acquire a territory with which they believed certain exceptional jurisdictional rights to be connected.[1] However, neither the term nor the doctrine is mentioned in the written and oral arguments of the parties, or in the pronouncements of the arbitrators—with the exception of a casual remark on the part of Lord Hannen, who, while denying the existence of prescription in international law, suggested the possibility of arguing the case on the ground of estoppel.

On the other hand, it appears clearly, both from the opinions of the American arbitrators and from the oral argument, that it was on the basis of prescription that the United States originally founded one of their main contentions. They urged that after acquiescence for a period of more than sixty years in the Russian assertions of an exclusive right over the sealing industries on the Pribilof Islands, it is not competent for Great Britain to deny now the existence of this right.[2] Senator Morgan, one of the arbitrators, after quoting authorities in favour of prescription, asked while delivering his opinion : ' Will this tribunal shrink from the recognition of this doctrine now that an opportunity, distinctly given, calls for a firm declaration ? '[3] In the course of the oral argument, in a lengthy discussion with Sir Richard Webster, he urged the same view.[4] But the United States failed to prove acquiescence on the part of Great

[1] Cf. here the similar provision in the Alaska Boundary arbitration convention, p. 234, *infra*; and the suggestive remarks on this point in Pitt Cobbett, *Leading Cases*, 4th ed., 1922, vol. i. p. 108.

[2] *Oral Argument*, *Report of the Proceedings of the Tribunal of Arbitration convened at Paris*, 1893, pp. 361, 725-729; Opinion of Senator Morgan, *Proceedings*, Sen. Doc. 53rd Congress, 2nd Session, Ex. Doc. 177, vol. i. pp. 30-54.

[3] *Op. cit.*, p. 46.

[4] *Oral Argument*, pp. 1271-1280.

Britain, and the proceedings established the very opposite of the American contention.[1] It is admitted by the agent of the United States in his final report that early in the preparation of the case the conclusion was reached that it would be difficult to sustain the plea of prescription, and that the decision of the tribunal on this point was not unexpected.[2]

§ 99. *Property and Possession in Animals* Ferae Naturae.—Anticipating defeat *qua* prescription, counsel for the United States put their whole strength in proving the United States' right of property in seals. The question presented a double aspect. The first was whether, assuming that international property in animals is possible, there is in private law any basis for applying to seals the same rules determining the acquisition of property as those applied to bees, pigeons, deer, etc. For both parties agreed that they must look to private law for a decisive answer on this point. The second problem was whether, in the absence of a rule of international law on the subject of State property in animals on the high seas, the claim of the United States, which, in addition, clashed with the principle of the freedom of the sea, could in any event be entertained. It was only natural that in this last respect Great Britain adopted what may be called a decidedly positivist attitude; on the other hand, in no modern arbitration did a State profess greater faith in the law of nature as a source of international law than the United States in the Behring Sea arbitration.[3] But Great Britain subsequently abandoned the positivist attitude, and, once this obstacle was removed, the

[1] See the impartial opinion on this question of Justice Harlan, *Proceedings*, vol. i. pp. 74-83.

[2] *Proceedings*, vol. i. p. 9.

[3] See *Argument* of the United States, in *Proceedings*, vol. v. pp. 1-26; *Oral Argument*, pp. 365, 367, 1883-1902; Opinion of Justice Harlan, *Proceedings*, vol. i. pp. 143 *et seq.* For a summary of the Argument, cf. Moore, pp. 830-839, 845-849, 850-857, 877-895.

question whether according to private law property in seals is admissible became the central issue of the arbitration. The United States claimed to have established the following facts: that the fur seals were begotten, born, and reared on the Pribilof Islands, owned by the United States; that they made these islands their home and spent there a large part of each year; that while absent from them they possessed the *animus revertendi* and never resorted to any other land; and that the existence of the race depended upon the care and industry of the United States. They put forward, as a general proposition of private law and the law of nature, that whenever any useful thing is dependent for its existence upon the exertions of men, the men who exercise such care and industry have a right of property in it.

The arbitration thus turned into a theoretical discussion of common and Roman law on the subject of animals *ferae naturae* and the meaning of *animus revertendi*. Great Britain adhered throughout the arbitration to the proposition that, the seals being strictly animals *ferae naturae*, the property in them depends on actual physical possession.[1] The tribunal held that 'the United States has no right of protection or property in the fur seals frequenting the island of the United States in Behring Sea when such seals are found outside the ordinary three-miles limit.'[2] It is difficult to say what part the arguments based on private law played in bringing about this decision. There is reason to believe, however, that the majority of the arbitrators regarded the principle of the freedom of the sea as warranting the exclusion of other juridical considerations. Nevertheless, this aspect of the Behring

[1] British *Argument*, in *Proceedings*, vol. x. pp. 31, 32; *Oral Argument*, Sir Charles Russell's speech, pp. 7, 8.

[2] The Award, *Proceedings*, vol. i. p. 78.

Sea arbitration remains one of the most instructive instances of recourse to private law.[1] [2]

III

THE BRITISH GUIANA ARBITRATION [3]

§ 100. *The Questions at Issue.*—Article 3 of the Arbitration Treaty of Washington, of February 1897, between Great Britain and Venezuela, instructed the tribunal to ascertain the extent of the territories that might lawfully be claimed by the United Netherlands or by the kingdom of Spain, respectively, at the time of

[1] This arbitration furnishes an instructive example how both parties did not hesitate to assume, in the question of damages for lost profits, an attitude directly opposed to that assumed in the Alabama arbitration. Great Britain, basing herself on decisions of her courts, demanded now damages for prospective profits, and pointed out that 'the refusal of the Geneva arbitrators to award damages to the United States for the loss of prospective earnings must be understood with reference to the actual conditions of the case before them' (*Argument* of Great Britain, p. 64). The United States invoked private law authorities and, with more justification, the award of the Geneva Tribunal (*Argument* of the United States, pp. 217-227). The tribunal did not pronounce upon this question.

[2] The attempt was made by the United States to throw upon Great Britain the burden of proving that Russia had lost her alleged jurisdiction in the Behring Sea (*Case* of the United States, p. 57), but Great Britain objected, pointing out that when a nation is contending for a jurisdiction in excess of that which is admitted by international consent, the *onus* must rest with that nation of proving the existence of such jurisdiction (*Counter Case* of Great Britain, p. 54). It seems that the principle that the *onus probandi* rests upon the party alleging an exception to a general rule was adopted, in practice, by the United States in the course of the arbitration.

[3] There is a certain continuity, so far as the parties to the dispute are concerned, between the two arbitrations mentioned above and the British Guiana arbitration. The United States, basing their intervention on the Monroe doctrine, were instrumental in bringing about this arbitration; they also provided both counsel and the national arbitrators. (On this arbitration, see Hall, pp. 136-137; Hyde, vol. i. pp. 143-147; Moore, *Digest*, vi. § 966; Cleveland, *The Venezuelan Boundary Controversy*, 1913). The abridged references in this section relate to the following printed documents: *British Guiana Boundary Arbitration with the United States of Venezuela: Case, Countercase, and Argument, with Appendices and Maps* (9 vols.; printed at the Foreign Office, London, 1898); *Venezuela-British Guiana Boundary Arbitration: the Case of the United States of Venezuela* (3 vols.), the *Counter Case* (3 vols.) and the printed *Argument* (2 vols.), New York, 1898; *British Guiana-Venezuelan Boundary Arbitration, etc.* (11 vols.), Paris, 1899 (*Oral Argument*).

the acquisition by Great Britain of the colony of British Guiana, and to determine the boundary line between the colony of British Guiana and the United States of Venezuela. The latter based their claim to the whole land between the Orinoco and the Essequibo on Spain's discovery of America, which gave her the right to reduce to possession the countries there discovered; on her actual possession thereof from early in the sixteenth century, and her actual control over the Orinoco and Essequibo rivers and the adjacent territory during the seventeenth, eighteenth, and the first part of the nineteenth century; on the fact that the Dutch rights acquired against the established title of Spain and the Treaty of Münster must be limited only to such land as was actually reduced by them into possession; on the fact that the disputed region being a geographical and political unit, Venezuela had during this period acquired constructive possession of the whole region; and, finally, on the circumstance that the occupation by Great Britain of portions of this region, being in violation of the Treaty of Münster and of the agreement of 1850 between Great Britain and Venezuela, could not be regarded as a valid basis of a title.[1]

Great Britain denied that either Spain or Venezuela, after her declaration of independence, had at any time real possession of the disputed territory; that long prior to and at the date of the Treaty of Münster, the Dutch had founded settlements in the various parts of the territory of British Guiana; that they gradually extended their possessions between 1648 and 1796, when Great Britain first occupied a part of the Dutch settlements, or in 1814, when she acquired by formal cession the territories originally claimed by the Dutch.[2] The dispute was, no doubt, to a large extent a dispute over

[1] *Case* of Venezuela, pp. 229-236.
[2] See *Case* of Great Britain, pp. 159-164.

facts of actual possession, occupation, and exercise of jurisdiction, but it was necessarily coupled with questions of law, the two most prominent being those in which rules of private law were freely invoked by the parties.

§ 101. *The Requirements of Prescription in International Law.*—There was, firstly, the question of prescription, which was of decisive importance with regard to British settlements established after 1796. Rule A of Article 4 of the terms of submission of the treaty of 1897 provided : 'Adverse holding or prescription during a period of 50 years shall make a good title. The arbitrators may deem exclusive political control of a district, as well as actual settlement thereof, sufficient to constitute adverse holding or to make title by prescription.' This provision of the treaty is rightly quoted as an instance of recognition of the notion of prescription in international law. However, it did not settle the whole problem. For it was contended by Venezuela that possession during a period of fifty years is not enough ; that time is but one of many elements essential to create title by prescription ; and that prescription between nations, as between individuals, must be *bona fide,* public, notorious, adverse, exclusive, peaceful, continuous, uncontested, and maintained under a claim of right.[1] It was pointed out that although the treaty fixed fifty years as the period of prescription, it left its other elements unimpaired. Counsel for Venezuela urged that, a concept of private law having been expressly incorporated into a treaty, it is incumbent upon the tribunal to follow all the implications of this term : [2]

'Whenever in a legal document a word occurs which in the law bears a technical meaning, that technical meaning

[1] Venezuelan *Case,* p. 229 ; Venezuelan *Argument,* pp. 353-392. Cf. here especially the award in the Chamizal arbitration, p. 277, *infra.*

[2] See especially Oral Argument, Speech of General Tracy, *Proceedings,* Paris edition, 1899, vol. ix. pp. 2690-2707.

is the primary meaning for the purpose ; thus words having a well-known legal meaning, whether they occur in statutes, deeds, will, or contracts, are given their legal meaning unless the context clearly indicates the contrary. . . . No terms are better known or have a more precise and exact meaning than the terms 'adverse holding' and 'prescription.' Effect must be given to that meaning when ascertained, unless there is something in the context of the treaty which indicates the intention to use the terms in a different sense.' [1]

They proceeded to apply to the British settlements the common law and Roman law requirements of prescription, and attempted to show that those specific requirements have not been fulfilled either by the Dutch or by the British occupation.[2] It is not possible to go here into the merits of this argument. The Venezuelan contention seems to be sound in principle—with the exception, perhaps, of the requirement of *bona fides.* An impartial reading, however, of the arbitration treaty in question conveys the impression that it was the intention of the parties to constitute the element of time as the only essential requirement of adverse holding.[3]

§ 102. *Occupation and Possession.*—The questions of discovery, occupation, possession, and abandonment were throughout the arbitration in the centre of the argument. It was Venezuela who, as a successor of Spain, put forward extensive claims resting on the fact of discovery. She contended that discovery gave to Spain an inchoate title by occupation, that the Dutch could not therefore rightfully occupy, as *terra nullius*, any part of the disputed territory, and that any title acquired by them must consequently rest upon

[1] General Tracy, *op. cit.*, p. 2690.

[2] *Op. cit.*, pp. 2710-2722; vol. x. p. 3094.

[3] Cf., on the British Guiana arbitration of 1904, p. 276, *infra*. See also p. 117, n. 4, *supra*.

conquest, cession, or prescription.[1] In opposition to this claim, Great Britain put forward the contention that discovery merely confers the right of effective occupation within a reasonable period of time, and that failing such occupation the first Power which subsequently occupies the territory obtains an absolute title.[2] Great Britain also invoked other modifications of the absolute title conferred by discovery and formulated with great clearness in the Oregon and Louisiana disputes, namely (*a*) that when a nation takes possession of any extent of the sea-coast, that possession extends not from sea to sea but only to the country covered by the rivers emptying within that coast and their branches; (*b*) when a European nation makes a discovery, and takes possession of any portion of that continent, and another afterwards does the same at some distance from it where the boundary between them is not otherwise determined, the middle distance becomes the boundary between the two territories.[3, 4] It was further denied by Great Britain that there had been such an extent of practical control and possession on the part of either Holland or Spain as to create a presumption of perfect title.

The influence of private law rules of possession upon the respective doctrines showed itself clearly in the course of the argument. Venezuela demanded that the requirements of *corpus* and *animus* should be strictly applied to the claims of the Netherlands and Great Britain as conflicting with their good and original title;[5] private law was resorted to by Great Britain, who resisted the Venezuelan claims founded on first discovery.[6]

[1] Venezuelan *Case*, p. 230.

[2] See British *Case*, pp. 149 *et seq.*

[3] Twiss, *The Oregon Question Examined*, 1846, especially pp. 271 ff.

[4] *Proceedings*, vol. viii. pp. 2189-2219. Speech of Sir Robert Reid, and especially the discussion between the latter and the President of the Tribunal on the *animus habendi* and the *animus possidendi*, pp. 2196, 2197; Speech of Sir Richard Webster, vol. iii. pp. 823-842.

[5] *Proceedings*, vol. ix. pp. 2599, 2603.

[6] *Proceedings*, vol. iii. pp. 819-849.

§ 103. *The Argument of Estoppel.*—It is impossible, in the absence of a reasoned award, to state how far the argument of estoppel raised by Venezuela affected the decision of the arbitrators, but the circumstances of the case, the force of the plea and the attention paid to it by the arbitrators, make it one of the most illustrative instances of the application of the doctrine of estoppel in international law.

In 1850, in the course of protracted negotiations, Lord Palmerston adopted and handed to Venezuela a map, the so-called Schomburgk sketch-map, which was regarded by Venezuela as the extreme claim of Great Britain. It was now contended by counsel for Venezuela that this was an admission on the part of Great Britain that her claim would not extend beyond the area defined in the map, that it was acted upon by Venezuela when she made the subsequent agreement in 1850, that she would never have entered this agreement but for the representations made that the extreme claim of Great Britain would not extend beyond the line of 1840, and that, accordingly, Great Britain was estopped from putting forward claims going beyond that line. We quote some parts of the argument dealing with this question:

'Lord Russell (*arbitrator*): Is your point, then, that Great Britain is estopped from saying anything outside the Palmerston line ?

'Mr. Soley : Absolutely, my lord.

'Lord Russell : Estoppel ?

'Mr. Soley : Absolute and complete estoppel.

'Lord Russell : So that, if he made a mistake and was wrong, any different right cannot be asserted ?

'Mr. Soley : Yes.'

'Lord Russell : Is that agreement really anything more than a *modus vivendi* till the respective rights are ascertained ?

'MR. SOLEY: It was vastly more. . . . There are consequences that arise from the agreement. The very fact of a statement by Great Britain of the territory that she claimed was one of the most important elements for Venezuela to consider in entering into this agreement not to occupy or encroach. . . .'

'LORD RUSSELL: It depends if you can show that either party acted to their prejudice.

'MR. SOLEY: They agreed not to occupy this territory. It says that they conceded something. They made some promise, and I say that there was a consideration. . . .' [1]

The discussion was continued in the course of the subsequent stages of the oral argument.[2] There was no suggestion that the doctrine, being a rule of private law, had no application between States.[3] But it was pointed out on the British side that Schomburgk's letter was an unauthorised communication not followed by any official action, and that admissions of this kind, unless deliberate and authorised, are not matters to which an international tribunal ought to attach importance.[4]

IV

THE ALASKA BOUNDARY DISPUTE

§ 104. *The Subsidiary Character of Recourse to Private Law. Prescription and Interpretation.*—The application of private law is, and should be, of a subsidiary character. Where there are available other sources, as international

[1] *Proceedings*, vol. vii. pp. 2024-2029.

[2] Vol. vii. pp. 2039-2043 (Speech of Mr. Soley). He said: 'There is no question there was a mutual consideration by the two parties . . . whereby, as they extended their claim to a certain point, they also limited their claim to that point. . . . That is the meaning of the agreement, and that is sufficient in itself to constitute estoppel; the admission constitutes an executed consideration which makes an estoppel.'

[3] Cf. vol. viii. p. 2339 (Speech of Sir Robert Reid).

[4] See pp. 268, 269, 279, *infra*.

custom or rights arising out of a treaty, it is to those sources that States prefer to have recourse. This is seen clearly in the case of the Alaska Boundary arbitration of 1903, constituted under the convention signed at Washington in January 1903.[1] The judicial task of the tribunal was that of interpretation. It had to decide what was the meaning of Articles 3, 4, and 5 of the Treaty of 1825 between Great Britain and Russia, which, *inter alia*, defined a line separating the Russian from the British possession in South-Eastern Alaska, the rights of Russia having been subsequently acquired by the United States through the purchase of all Russian possessions upon the North-West Coast of America, to which was given the name of Alaska. The arbitrators had to decide, in the answer to the fifth question, whether, in the intention of the parties to the Treaty of 1825, the eastern boundary was to run round the heads of the bays, ports, havens, and waters of the ocean, or to cross them. If running round the inlets, the line granted to Russia included a substantial strip or *lisière* of territory upon the mainland extending so far south as the Portland Channel.

The United States based their claim to the *lisière* on the Treaty of 1825, on the intention of the parties to it, and on the evidence of this intention as revealed both in the negotiations preceding the treaty and in the subsequent actions of the interested parties. The arbitration treaty provided that the tribunal 'should also take into consideration any action of the several governments or of their respective representatives preliminary to the conclusion of the said treaties, so far as the same tended to show the original and effective understanding

[1] On this arbitration, see Balch, *The Alaska Frontier*, 1903, and Pitt Cobbett, *Cases*, 4th ed., 1924, i. 99-108. The printed Cases, Counter Cases, and Arguments of both parties, as well as the oral proceedings, are printed in *Proceedings of the Alaskan Boundary Tribunal*, U.S. Sen. Doc., No. 162, 58th Congress, 2nd Session, 7 vols., 1904.

of the parties.' It was as an element of interpretation of the intention of the interested parties that the United States put forward their main argument, namely, acquiescence for over seventy years, on the part of Great Britain, in the exercise of jurisdiction by Russia and the United States over the waters and coasts in dispute.

The United States, placing themselves on the strong ground of treaties in question and of the arbitration treaty, expressly disclaimed the intention of availing themselves of the plea of prescription or of estoppel, although both were implicitly contained in their argument.[1]

> 'If I shall be able to show'—counsel of the United States urged [2]—'that there was a concurrent view between Russia and Great Britain which gave an interpretation which was in effect at the time the United States bought, then the United States would succeed to the rights of Russia under that interpretation. I do not mean by way of estoppel, and I do not mean to predicate anything upon that or upon the doctrine of prescription, or upon the doctrine of acquiescence, so far as acquiescence may set up an adverse claim . . . and the only point upon which I shall insist upon acquiescence is that acquiescence may be looked to as indicating an understanding and interpretation.' [3]

The Canadian arbitrator and the British counsel tried to construe the United States argument as a plea of prescription,[4] which they promptly proceeded to reject, in this case, as a rule of international law. In the course of this stage of the argument, the President, Lord Alverstone, associated himself with the view expressed by Lord Hannen in the course of the Behring Sea arbitration,

[1] Cf. here p. 224, *supra*, and n. 1, *ibid.*

[2] Argument of Mr. Dickinson, *Proceedings*, vol. vii. p. 813, *op. cit.*, and of Taylor, vol. vii. p. 622.

[3] The same argument is repeated in *Proceedings*, vol. vii. pp. 878, 880. See also *Case* of the United States, p. 102: *Counter Case*, *Proceedings*, vol. iv. p. 91; *Opinion of the American Arbitrators*, vol. i. p. 49.

[4] *Proceedings*, vol. vi. p. 344.

that while prescription properly so called was not recognised in international law, estoppel and acquiescence might be of considerable importance.[1] But counsel for the United States, being in possession of what they thought a clear treaty right, were quite unwilling to exchange it for a contested analogy. Although they quoted in their argument the *loci classici* of the international doctrine of prescription,[2] they were careful not to invoke the doctrine itself.[3] And it appears from the opinion of Lord Alverstone that they were well advised to adopt this course.[4]

§ 105. *The Authority of Roman and Common Law. Merger. Rules of Evidence.*—This arbitration gave also occasion for some interesting discussion on the relative authority of Roman and common law in international arbitration. Counsel for Great Britain did not hesitate to apply the common law rule of merger in order to rebut some of the evidence adduced by the United States. They pointed to the rule of common law according to which a contract supersedes the previous negotiations,[5] and urged that although the rule is not generally recognised in other systems of law, it should be followed when both parties are governed, in their municipal law, by the common law of England.[6] However, it appears that the arbitrators did not regard themselves as bound by this common law rule.[7] But it is interesting to note

[1] *Ibid.*, pp. 344, 346.

[2] Cf. *Argument* of the United States, vol. v. pp. 201-204. They referred to *Indiana* v. *Kentucky*, 136, *U.S. Reports*, 509, 510, and the *Passamaquoddy Bay Commission under the Treaty of Ghent*; see Taylor's *Argument*, vol. vii. pp. 619 ff. Hyde, vol. i. p. 193, n. 1, is here likely to be misunderstood. Prescription was *not* pleaded by the United States.

[3] Cf. also the opinions of the American arbitrators, *Proceedings*, vol. i. pp. 49, 63, 64.

[4] *Ibid.*, p. 42.

[5] Argument of Mr. Christopher Robinson, *Proceedings*, vol. vii. pp. 502, 503.

[6] For an interesting case of the application of the doctrine of merger, see the award in the arbitration between Chile and Peru, 1875 (Moore, p. 2092).

[7] See opinion of Lord Alverstone. *Proceedings*, vol. i. p. 41; of the American arbitrators, *ibid.*, p. 49.

how this contention led to an opposite, and no less extreme, assertion on the part of the United States[1] to the effect that the common law rules of evidence have no validity in international disputes because 'the substructure of the whole international system is the Roman law as developed and embodied in the codes of continental nations,' and that an international tribunal being governed by the rules of procedure and the rules of evidence which prevail in Roman law tribunals, every evidence is admissible which, in the opinion of the arbitrators, is pertinent to the issue.[2, 3]

V

THE NORTH ATLANTIC COAST FISHERIES ARBITRATION

§ 106. *The Adoption of Strict Analogy by the Tribunal.*—It is often asserted that the juridical value of the award in the North Atlantic Coast Fisheries arbitration is marred by the element of compromise contained in it. However, a careful reading of the award shows that the juridical aspect of the finding of the arbitrators is unaffected by the wish of the tribunal to arrive at a solution satisfactory to both parties. The compromise lies rather in the use made by the tribunal of Article 4 of the Arbitration Treaty of January 1909, in which the arbitrators were empowered to recommend rules and methods of procedure for determination of all questions which may arise in the future regarding the exercise

[1] *Proceedings*, vol. vii. p. 557.

[2] *Loc. cit.*, and p. 578.

[3] Also in this case the question of the burden of proof formed a disputed issue. The United States contended that it was upon Great Britain to prove that the unnavigable Portland Channel was meant as a boundary and not the *thalweg*, because the burden of proof lies upon him who asserts that a special and conventional rule has been substituted by the parties in the place of a general principle (Argument of Mr. Taylor, *Proceedings*, vol. vii. p. 595).

of the right of fisheries. But it seems that in the principal question of the arbitration, *i.e.* in that of international servitudes, the attitude of the tribunal was determined by a strictly juridical reasoning, and by a meticulous, perhaps too meticulous, adhering to the consequences of a private law conception.[1]

The United States contended that the liberty of fishery granted to them constituted an international servitude, that is, a derogation from the sovereignty of Great Britain, the servient State, and a limitation of her independent right to regulate the fishery. This part of the American argument the tribunal adopted almost in its entirety. It recognised that a servitude in international law predicates a grant of a sovereign right, and that it involves an analogy of a *praedium dominans* and a *praedium serviens*.[2] But the victory of the American theoretical contention caused its practical defeat. It proved too much. For it was owing to the real and extended rights conferred by an international servitude that the tribunal was prepared to affirm it only on the 'express evidence of an international contract.'[3] It did not reject the conception of servitudes, but it demanded a strict proof that a servitude has been created. Such a proof could not be supplied by the United States.

It was in the last days of the arbitration that counsel for the United States apprehended where the danger lay, and began, very wisely, to secure the way of retreat. They were helped in this endeavour by the American arbitrator, Judge Gray. He asked in the course of the closing argument of Senator Root:

'. . . This right does not depend upon its classification as technical servitude ?

[1] For an analysis of this case, see Scott, in Schücking, vol. i., pt. ii., pp. 143-519, especially on the question of servitudes, pp. 248-312; Basdevant, in *R.G.*, vol. xix. (1912) pp. 421-582; Sir Erle Richards, in *Journal of Comparative Legislation and International Law*, vol. xi. (1910) pp. 18-27; and Lansing in *A.J.*, vol. v. (1911) pp. 11-19.

[2] Award on question 1 (3).

[3] *Loc. cit.*

'SENATOR ROOT: Certainly not.

'JUDGE GRAY: You do not suppose Lord Salisbury had that in mind, or that any of the negotiators . . . had in mind any relation to this definition by the writers up to that time?

'SENATOR ROOT: I suppose the negotiators understood the way in which rights of that character are generally regarded. . . . I do not suppose that they considered that they were acting under a technical rule of servitude.'[1]

He was cautious enough to express the same opinion on a previous occasion:

'. . . The rights are not made to depend upon analogy; they are explained by analogy. . . . We are not here and we never have been claiming that we are entitled to have our treaty right here held inviolable because it is a right founded upon an analogy to the Roman law of servitudes. We are here saying that this is a right which may be understood under a treaty which must be interpreted in the light of explanations of this and similar rights during a long series of years and explanations accepted by the nations of the world. . . .'[2]

But it was too late. He had already succeeded in impressing upon the tribunal the necessity of applying the principles of the Roman and private law of servitudes with all the implications of their real character.

§ 107. *The Question of Analogy in the Pleadings of the Parties. The Consequences of a Real Right.*—That part of the written and oral argument of the United States which dealt with the construction and interpretation of the Treaty of 1818 as an international servitude may rightly be regarded as a classical instance of a full and determined application of analogy. As the main contention of the United States in this respect, namely, the

[1] *Argument of the Hon. Elihu Root on behalf of the United States*, The World Peace Foundation edition, 1912, p. 250.

[2] *Ibid.*

question as to the nature and the extent of the real right conferred by an international servitude, has been accepted by the tribunal, it may be useful to recall here the relevant passage of Senator Root's speech on this subject. He said :

'There is a difference between the results which would follow from treating this right that passed to the United States by the ratification of the Treaty of 1818 as a real right, on the one hand, and treating it as an obligation in terms perpetual on the part of Great Britain, on the other hand. The first difference in the nature of the right is that in the first view the treaty would be deemed to take out from Great Britain a fragment of her sovereignty itself, and from that it would follow as a logical conclusion that Great Britain could not order, regulate, control, limit, or restrict the right that has passed to us, because it was not hers. . . . On the other hand, if this is to be regarded as not creating a real right, but as creating an obligation, Great Britain is prevented from exercising control, limitation, or restriction over the right which passed by her obligation, and therefore the obligation is such that it excludes her from doing that thing. . . .[1]

'There is a second difference—this one as to the result. If this be a real right, as we think it is, the United States would have a right of control over the conduct of its citizens in the exercise of the real right in this territory, and laws made to govern the time and the manner in which they exercise that right would be laws which, for their validity, required the assent of the United States. They would be invalid, as affecting its citizens, but for the assent of the United States. . . . On the other hand, if the treaty creates an obligatory limit upon Great Britain, if the limitation of her sovereignty is a limitation created by perpetual obligation, and if in the exercise of the sovereign power Great Britain in that territory makes a law which oversteps the limits of her obligation which she was bound in the contract not to make, that is a wrongful exercise of her

[1] P. 227.

sovereignty, from which this tribunal is bound, if it can see it, to restrain her. . . .'[1]

It does not appear that counsel for Great Britain made any attempt to shatter this part of Senator Root's argument. No doubt the insistence on a thorough analogy between a private proprietor and the sovereign of a State presented many difficulties, and the British lawyers did not fail to take full advantage of the weak links of the comparison, much to the embarrassment of their opponents, who were forced to admit that it is not possible to square international servitudes in every respect with the servitudes of Roman law. They also had to concede that the *praedium dominans* is not the territory of the United States, but the sovereignty of the United States, and thus exposed themselves to the objection that the right in question does not constitute a real, but only a personal servitude.[2] But the American assertions as to the consequences of the real character of a servitude were not seriously challenged. The main effort of the British counsel was directed towards showing the inapplicability, without an express grant, of the doctrine of servitudes to relations between States. Much of what has been said in this connection in the course of the oral argument may be put to the account of the forensic atmosphere,[3] but the gist of the British plea on this aspect of the question did not fail to influence the tribunal. Counsel for Great Britain admitted that arrangements in which one State grants to another certain rights over its territory, for instance, for the purpose of building a railway, may be necessary and of advantage for both contracting parties, but they urged that States should not be discouraged from entering such

[1] *Op. cit.*, p. 229.

[2] See *North Atlantic Coast Fisheries Arbitration at the Hague, Oral Argument*, Foreign Office edition, London, 1910, pp. 351 *et seq.* and 1025 *et seq.*

[3] Cf. especially those relating to the offended pride of the servient State, pp. 1024 ff. of the *Oral Argument*.

agreements by having the doctrine and the name of servitudes forced upon them, and by being subsequently confronted with the assertion that, quite independently of their original intentions, they have contracted out of a part of their sovereignty.[1] The American argument was conspicuously weak in combating this part of the British objections. Thus, there was not much force in the contention that the recognition of rights which are independent of the control of the grantor and of his successors is even more necessary in international law than in civil law, because there is no rule of international law under which a nation can be made to respond in damages for breaches of its treaty obligations.[2] It is a clear rule of international law that the breach of a treaty obligation constitutes an international delinquency imposing the duty of reparation.

§ 108. *The Award and the Future of the Doctrine of Servitudes.*—The North Atlantic Fisheries arbitration was undoubtedly instrumental in revealing the great difficulties of analogy with regard to this particular conception. But it cannot be maintained that it gave a final or a clear verdict. This task has been left to the science of international law, whose function in this connection is commented upon elsewhere in this book. The award did not pronounce a ban upon servitudes in international law, although it demanded a strict proof of an express contract creating such a restriction of territorial sovereignty. This provision does not render the acceptance valueless. For should States avail themselves in the future, in a public treaty, of this institute of law, then the decision of the tribunal may be invoked as one of the most authoritative formulations of the consequences flowing from such a treaty. Finally,

[1] See Speech of Sir William Robson, *Oral Argument*, pp. 1012 *et seq.*

[2] See *Oral Argument*, p. 335.

it must not be forgotten that although the ingenuity and the success of the American argument with regard to servitudes in general caused its defeat with regard to that particular servitude which it was alleged had been created by the Treaty of 1818, the final recommendations of the tribunal very dangerously approached the creation of a new servitude.[1]

[1] The award says with regard to Article 4:

'1. . . . All future municipal laws, ordinances or rules for the regulation of the fishery by Great Britain . . . shall be published in the *London Gazette* two months before going into operation. Similar regulations by Canada or Newfoundland shall be similarly published in the *Canada Gazette* and the *Newfoundland Gazette* respectively.

'2. If the Government of the United States considers any such laws or regulations inconsistent with the Treaty of 1818, it is entitled to so notify the Government of Great Britain within the two months referred to in Rule No. 1.

'3. Any law or regulation so notified shall not come into effect with respect to inhabitants of the United States until the Permanent Mixed Fishery Commission has decided that the regulation is reasonable within the meaning of this award.' The entire recommendation relating to Article 4 of Question 1 has been embodied in the Agreement of July 20, 1912 (see Hertslet's *Treaties*, vol. xxvii. p. 1095), between Great Britain and the United States; and Prof. Scott says after having quoted the provisions of this Agreement: 'If the grant of 1818 did not constitute a servitude in 1910, the Agreement of July 20, 1912, to all appearances did so, concluded as it was for the purpose of giving effect to the real intention and meaning of the Treaty of 1818' (*op. cit.*, p. 303). See also the Report of the Agent of the United States to the Secretary of State, vol. i. of the *Proceedings*, Sen. Doc., 61st Congress, 3rd Session, Doc. No. 870, p. 16.

CHAPTER VII

RECOURSE TO PRIVATE LAW IN INTERNATIONAL ARBITRATION

(The Permanent Court of Arbitration)

I

THE PIOUS FUND OF CALIFORNIA CASE

§ 109. *The Principle of* res iudicata *recognised by both Parties.*—The Pious Fund of California case of 1902, the first case before the Permanent Court of Arbitration under the Hague Convention of 1899, gained prominence by the fact that it vindicated the validity, in international law, of the principle of *res iudicata.* The text-books simply characterise it as *the* arbitration which affirmed the applicability of that principle in international law.[1] It may, however, be doubted whether such a statement is accurate. For neither party to this arbitration disputed the applicability of the principle itself, and it was conceded by Mexico throughout the whole dispute that *res iudicata* applies to international arbitral awards. 'That *res iudicata pro veritate habetur* is a principle, admitted in all legislation and belonging to the Roman law, certainly no one will deny. Nor is it denied that a tribunal or a judge established by international arbitration gives to its

[1] Hyde, vol. ii. pp. 115-117. For an analysis of this case, see Scott, in Schücking, vol. i., pt. i., pp. 45-247; Descamps, *Le premier arbitrage de la Cour de la Haye*, 1902. See also p. 207, *supra*.

decisions pronounced within its limits of jurisdiction the force of *res iudicata* '—that was the official declaration of the Minister of Foreign Affairs of Mexico addressed in 1900 to the American Minister.[1] This attitude was invariably maintained by Mexico in the course of the proceedings before the Hague Tribunal,[2] although counsel for the United States deemed it necessary to expatiate upon this point and to defend the rule of *res iudicata* as a fundamental principle of every jural society.[3] It is significant how a rule never before expressly recognised as binding between States received recognition even on the part of the State whose interests seemed to demand its rejection.[4]

§ 110. *The Scope of* res iudicata.—It was, however, contended by Mexico that *res iudicata* is limited in its application to the condemnatory parts of the judgment, and does not embrace the considerations and premises upon which the judgment is founded; that only the *dispositif* (the decisory part) of the judgment comes under the scope of *res iudicata*, and that therefore the award of the umpire, Sir Edward Thornton, of 1875, to the effect that Mexico should pay to the United States $904,700 as representing 21 annuities due on the Pious Fund, has no binding effect upon the future.[5] On the other hand, it was insisted upon by the United States that whatever was of necessity implied or flowed as a necessary consequence from the judgment is to be considered as an integral part of it.[6] Both sides

[1] Cited in the *Supplemental Brief on the part of the United States*, p. 43, in *United States* v. *Mexico*, *Report of J. H. Ralston*, Washington, 1902 (this Report includes also other acts and documents cited in this section).

[2] Cf. p. 250 of the *Record of the Proceedings*, The Hague, 1902, Speech of M. Bernaert.

[3] U.S. *Brief*, p. 29.

[4] Cf. here Scott, in Schücking, *op. cit.*, pp. 167-173. On the recognition of the doctrine in previous and subsequent arbitrations, see p. 207, *infra*.

[5] *Mexican Answer to the Memorial of the United States, Exhibit 'A' of the Replication of the United States*, p. 23.

[6] Speech of Mr. Penfield, *Record of Proceedings*, p. 331; also speech of Mr. Ralston, p. 127.

quoted amply private law rules, cases, and authorities as the main source of the decision of the tribunal.

This was the first occasion on which an important international tribunal had been confronted with this problem. There was, however, no doubt that, in the absence of an express rule of international law, the generally recognised rules of private law may be and should be applied.[1] But is there a general rule of private law governing this question? The fact that both parties quoted private law in upholding their contention would indicate that there was no generally accepted rule of private law upon which the judges could rely. But it seems that the authorities cited by Mexico referred to considerations of an explanatory character, and not to those forming logically an essential part of the judgment proper.[2] No doubt it is frequently difficult to draw the line between the two kinds of reasons. In such cases it is for the tribunal to decide as a question of fact what is the nature of the considerations in question, the decision to be governed by the broad principle adopted in all systems of law that what is logically an essential part of the judgment falls under the scope of *res iudicata.* In this light should be read that part of the award which affirms ' that all the parts of the judgment or the decree concerning the litigation enlighten and mutually supplement each other, and they all serve to render precise the meaning and the bearing of the *dispositif* (decisory part of the judgment) and to determine the points upon which there is *res iudicata* and which thereafter cannot be put in question,' and that this principle of private law

[1] Cf. the large number of cases and private law authorities in the *Mexican Answer to the Memorial of the United States, op. cit.*, pp. 23-29, and, on the part of the United States, *Brief and Statement*, pp. 45-55 ; *Supplemental Brief*, pp. 52-53.

[2] See Speech of M. Descamps, *Record of Proceedings*, p. 297 ; see also Speech of M. Bernaert, *ibid.*, p. 231.

'should for a still stronger reason be applied to international arbitration.'[1]

§ 111. *The Right of the Tribunal to Determine its Jurisdiction.*—But should the tribunal come to the conclusion that the question of future annuities falls within the scope of *res iudicata,* in this case—so ran the further contention of Mexico—the umpire had given a decision lying outside the scope of the authority conferred upon him by the compromise.[2] Thus arose the second 'private law question': Has an arbitral court the inherent power to determine its jurisdiction? The United States pointed to the analogy existing between international and private arbitration, and asserted that if private arbitrators possess the power to determine their own jurisdiction and to give an interpretation to the instrument creating them, *a fortiori* must the same powers be regarded as vested in international arbitral courts.[3] Although they could rely in this matter on weighty precedents in the field of international arbitration and on an almost unanimous opinion of international lawyers,[4] they quoted extensively from private law cases and authorities.[5] The tribunal seems to have adopted the view advocated by the United States, although this part of the award is not so explicit as it might have been: 'The convention of July 4, 1868, concluded between the two States in litigation, had accorded to the mixed commission named by the two States, as well as to the umpire to be eventually designed, the right to pass upon their own jurisdiction.' It is not clear whether this is a conclusion reached on the ground of interpretation of the compromise of 1868,

[1] Cf. here the Advisory Opinion of the Permanent Court of International Justice in the case of the *Polish Postal Service* in Dantzig, Publications of the Court, Series B, No. 11, p. 30.

[2] Speech of M. Bernaert, p. 250.

[3] *Brief of the United States*, p. 27.

[4] *Brief, loc. cit.*, Speech of Mr. Ralston, pp. 111-116. See p. 208, *supra*.

[5] *Record of Proceedings*, pp. 96 ff.

or whether it is based on that part of the argument of the United States which was based on estoppel.

§ 112. *The Plea of Estoppel.*—For it was contended by the United States that Mexico was estopped by its conduct from denying the right of the Mixed Commission of 1868 to settle the entire question of the California Fund. They urged that throughout the whole dispute, both before and after the decision of the umpire, Mexico impliedly and by a uniform conduct conceded to that commission full powers of decision. This conduct consisted in the ratification, in 1872 and 1874, of the conventions providing for the extension of time within which the joint commission should settle the claims brought before it, and also in other acts of the agents of Mexico. The plea of estoppel was put forward in all its technical form: 'Her [Mexico's] course of conduct might have created against her what is known in English and American jurisprudence as an estoppel *in pais*. By such an estoppel she would be prevented from asserting that the court had no jurisdiction.'[1] The United States pointed out that Mexico, embarking, in 1868 and in the subsequent conventions, upon the litigation, took the risk of success or failure, and that she could not now, after having lost, question the jurisdiction of the tribunal. They disclaimed the intention of relying upon a mere technicality, but urged that if one party to the dispute contemplates the withdrawing of certain claims from arbitration, it is under the obligation to announce such intention in the beginning in order to enable the opposing party to make such claims the foundation of a separate convention.[2]

It seems also that estoppel was pleaded by the United States in another direction, although the doctrine was

[1] *Supplemental Brief*, pp. 47, 49.
[2] *Statement and Brief*, p. 30; see also *ibid.*, p. 43.

not here formally invoked. According to the terms of submission, the tribunal at the Hague had to answer two questions only : (*a*) is the case within the governing principle of *res iudicata* ? (*b*) if not, is the claim just ? It was now contended by the United States that, by virtue of these terms of submission, Mexico was precluded from raising such questions as, that the claimants ought to have resorted to local tribunals, that the award of Sir Edward Thornton was erroneous, and that the claim as such was barred by the Mexican statute of limitations.[1] This part of the argument, however, seems to have been somewhat strained, and it did not receive special attention on the part of the tribunal.

§ 113. *The Alleged Rejection of Prescription.*—The plea that the claims were barred by the statute of limitations was dealt with by the tribunal and expressly answered in the decision, which states that ' the rules of prescription, belonging exclusively to the domain of civil law, cannot be applied to the present dispute between the two States in litigation.'[2] It is frequently asserted that this decision is a clear instance of non-recognition of extinctive prescription in international law.[3] This, however, is most improbable if the following two facts are taken into consideration : (*a*) The question of extinctive prescription in international law did not form a contested issue in this arbitration. The relevant point was whether Article 1103 of the Mexican code, which provided that emphyteutic or annuity pensions, revenues, rents, etc., not collected when due, remain barred in five years, may be invoked in the case of the claims becoming the object of an international dispute. The decision of the tribunal, properly read, supplies the

[1] Speech of Mr. Penfield, p. 342.

[2] Scott, *Reports*, pp. 5-6 ; cf. here Wehberg, quoted below, p. 31.

[3] Cf., for instance, Wehberg, *The Problem of an International Court of Justice* (English translation, 1918), p. 30.

correct answer to this question.[1] (*b*) Even the United States were careful, in the course of the arbitration, not to oppose prescription as such. They distinguished between a municipal statute of limitations, which, they pointed out, is recognised in international law only so far as it may be agreed to exist for a particular case by a treaty, and prescription proper, which they did not oppose.[2] In the light of these considerations should be read the decision of the tribunal 'that the [*such*] rules of prescription, belonging [*as belong*] exclusively to the domain of civil law, cannot be applied to the present dispute between the two States in litigation.'[3]

II

THE VENEZUELAN PREFERENTIAL CLAIM

§ 114. *Roman Law as a Source of International Law.*—Of all international arbitrations the Venezuelan Preferential Claim case of 1903 is, perhaps, the most instructive instance of the invocation of Roman and private law by the contesting States. Ten States—Great Britain, Germany, Italy, on the one side, Belgium, France, Mexico, the Netherlands, Spain, Sweden, and Norway, on the other—were represented and pleaded before the tribunal,—a representative array of nations.[4]

[1] See Report of J. H. Ralston to the Secretary of State, p. 10 ('the controversy was eminently international in character, and . . . national rules of prescription could not be invoked to defeat such claims as ours, presented before an international body').

[2] Ralston, *Record of Proceedings*, p. 101; it is of interest to note that the chief agent of the United States in this case, when acting as the umpire in one of the Venezuelan arbitrations of 1903, devoted special attention, in an outspoken award, to the fact that the principle of prescription was not denied either by the United States or by the tribunal. See *Gentini* case, p. 274, *infra*.

[3] See here Scott, in Schücking, *op. cit.*, p. 189.

[4] For an analysis of this case, see Bar, in Schücking, quoted below, pp. 253-307; for a short summary, Scott, *Reports*, pp. 55, 56.

This is an additional reason for referring to this arbitration as to an authoritative illustration of the problem under discussion. A striking feature of the written and oral argument was the unanimity with which both parties turned to Roman law for guidance on nearly all contested questions. 'The three allied Powers naturally seek, as we do, to establish their contentions on the rules of civil and Roman law, the *ius gentium* "par excellence"'[1]—this passage from the Counter Case submitted by Spain adequately characterises the proceedings in this case. The same principle was accepted, with even greater emphasis, by the opposing party: 'The principle by which this matter should be governed in international law is laid down in the legal system exhibited by the "*ius*" and "*lex*" and the opinions of Roman jurisconsults. Rome has given a body of laws to all nations, called the law of nature. . . . By the general consent of nations the rules of Roman law were adopted, especially in the matter of contracts.'[2] However, it was not only Roman rules that were invoked in the course of the arbitration; the parties had recourse to modern systems of private law in so far as, in their opinion, they embodied a general rule of law.

§ 115. *Hypothecation, Lien.*—The Powers demanding preferential treatment appealed constantly to rules of private law. They contended, firstly, that the assignment in their favour of the thirty per cent. of the customs

[1] The *Counter Case* of Spain, p. 1094, printed in *The Venezuelan Arbitration before the Hague Tribunal, 1903, Proceedings of the Tribunal*, U.S. Sen. Doc., 58th Congress, 3rd Session, vol. vii.; see also the *Case* of Spain, pp. 916-918. ('Civil law is universally recognised to be the natural and necessary complement of international law. International persons make contracts and possess property exactly in the same way as real persons, and the rules set forth by civil law for the working of their rights and mutual juridical relations must necessarily find their counterpart in international law.')

[2] The *Case* of Italy, *op. cit.*, p. 860. The page references of the Cases, Counter Cases, and Arguments are to *Proceedings*, quoted in n. 1, above.

revenues of La Guaira and Puerto Cabello constituted a pledge or a real security governed by the Roman and private law of pledge and hypothecation, which recognises a title to preference for the creditor to whom the object is hypothecated.[1] A kind of international lien, it was asserted, has been created by the assignment of those revenues. The blockading powers demanded, secondly, preferential treatment as a reimbursement of the expenses incurred by them through the blockade as *negotiorum gestores* of the non-belligerent Powers, and to their profit.

§ 116. *Negotiorum Gestio.*—It was especially on this ground that their opponents were quite ready to meet them. They pointed to the constituent elements of *negotiorum gestio* in Roman law, namely, that another's business should have been the true object of the management by the claimant to compensation, and that the acts of the latter should have been performed with intention of managing the other party's affairs and as a means of obliging him, who must be ignorant of such procuration and not have expressly forbidden it,[2] and maintained that no one of these conditions was complied with in the action of the blockading Powers. It was even asserted that that action, far from having brought profit to the non-belligerent States, had injured their interests by diminishing the financial assets of the common debtor.[3] France was prepared to admit analogy to civil law only to the extent of granting preference to the blockading Powers proportionally to the expense incurred by them in the interest of other powers.[4]

[1] German *Argument*, p. 1197; *Case* of Italy, pp. 860-862, with ample references to Roman law. That the security granted to the blockading Powers constituted a kind of international lien is admitted by Bar, in Schücking, vol. i., pt. i., p. 283; see also Phillipson, *Studies in International Law*, 1908, p. 49.

[2] *Counter Case* of Spain, p. 1096.

[3] *Counter Case* of the Netherlands, Sweden, and Norway, p. 1110.

[4] *Case* of France, p. 883.

§ 117. *Bankruptcy of States.*—It was also on an analogy that the claim for equal treatment was founded. The non-belligerent Powers maintained that, the legal position of Venezuela being analogous to that of *cessio bonorum* or bankruptcy (or the German *Konkurs*), the principles of private law are to be applied, according to which the creditors of the debtor enjoy, as a rule, equal rights against his estate.[1] It was not difficult to show the inadequacy of this argument. It was pointed out that there is no uniform law of bankruptcy; that there is in international law no procedure in bankruptcy; that the seizure of the whole property of a State would be inconsistent with its continued existence as an independent community;[2] that in this case Venezuela was not compelled to distribute her assets amongst all her creditors;[3] that she was not insolvent; and, finally, that, although she had seldom paid her liabilities except under pressure, she could do so if her sources were properly administered. The blockading Powers invoked, in turn, civil law rules showing that that creditor is entitled to preference who first takes action in order to protect his rights—*vigilantibus non dormientibus subvenit lex*, or who first obtained possession of the creditor's goods—*prior in tempore, potior in iure.*[4]

§ 118. *The Argument of Estoppel.*—It seems, however, that the weightiest argument put forward by the blockading Powers was that of estoppel (preclusion in Roman law systems). In February 1903, separate protocols were signed between Venezuela on one side and Great Britain, Germany, and Italy on the other, in which the justice of the claims of these Powers was

[1] *Case* of France, p. 880.
[2] *Case* of Italy, pp. 857-858; *Counter Case*, pp. 1038-1039.
[3] P. 1043; Speech of Sir Robert Finlay, pp. 1248-1249; *Counter Case* of Great Britain, p. 976.
[4] *Case* of Italy, pp. 862-863.

admitted by Venezuela, and provision was made for the allocation of the customs revenues of two ports of Venezuela for the purpose of satisfying the claims of the blockading Powers.[1] These protocols were incorporated in the compromise of May 7, 1903, providing for an arbitration before the tribunal at the Hague. It was now argued by Great Britain [2] that the blockade was raised, and the Venezuelan vessels restored, in consideration of the Venezuelan admission contained in the protocols and incorporated in the compromise, and further, that, as the other Powers had acquiesced in the action of the blockading Powers, and as the latter had acted upon this acquiescence, it was now impossible for them 'to turn round and to say that the blockading Powers are to be deprived of the advantage which they have earned by taking the action in which the other Powers acquiesced.' [3] It is in the light of this plea that the relevant part of the award should be read:

'. . . Whereas the Government of Venezuela in the protocols of February 13, 1903 (Article 1), itself recognised "*in principle the justice of the claims*" presented to it by the

[1] *Op. cit.*, pp. 23-31.

[2] Speech of Mr. Cohen, p. 1254, and of Mr. Richards, pp. 1265-1266, *op. cit.*

[3] Reply by Sir Robert Finlay, pp. 1329, 1330; see also his Speech, pp. 1219, 1240. The following passage from Mr. Arthur Cohen's Speech may be quoted here in full: 'The protocol is itself recited in the *compromis* on the 7th of May—it is incorporated in it. Now, according to the first article of the protocol, the justice of the British claims is admitted, and it is from the *compromis* alone that the tribunal derives its jurisdiction. The *compromis* recites the protocol. It was in *consideration of the admission contained* in the protocol of the justice of the British claim that the blockade was raised and the Venezuelan vessels restored. It therefore would be . . . contrary to the most elementary and fundamental principles of jurisprudence to allow a person or a power which was a party to this *compromis* reciting the protocol, which itself contains the formal admission on the strength of which the *compromis* was signed . . . to deny . . . the truth of the formal admission so contained in the protocol.' He referred here to a similar case which arose in the course of the Pious Fund arbitration, and which established the principle that 'if a document contains an admission on the strength of which stipulations in the document are made, then the party signing the document is estopped from denying the truth of that admission.'

Governments of Germany, Great Britain, and Italy; . . . Whereas the Government of Venezuela, until the end of January 1903, in no way protested against the pretension of the blockading Powers to insist on special securities for the settlement of their claims; . . . Whereas the neutral Powers . . . did not protest against the pretensions of the blockading Powers to a preferential treatment . . .'[1, 2]

III

THE RUSSIAN INDEMNITY CASE

§ 119. *The State as a Debtor.* — In the Russian Indemnity case, decided in November 1912 by the Hague Court, the arbitrator relied almost entirely upon rules of private law. The question of interest had occupied many previous international tribunals, but this was the first time that such a claim formed the exclusive subject-matter of an international dispute. Russia claimed interest for the delayed payments of certain indemnity sums provided for by the Treaty of Constantinople of

[1] *Proceedings*, p. 95. The United States and Venezuela also availed themselves of the plea of estoppel. In the course of the negotiations preceding the raising of the blockade, the Venezuelan Government granted full powers to Mr. Bowen, the American representative, to effect a settlement with the representatives of the nations putting forward claims against Venezuela. As the blockading Powers accepted these powers and entered into negotiations in accordance with them, it was contended (see Speech of Mr. Penfield, p. 1279, and Mr. Bowen's *Protest* against the award, p. 141) that they were now precluded from disputing the legitimacy of these negotiations. See, however, the part of the award relating to the negotiations conducted by Mr. Bowen.

[2] In addition, other arguments based on analogy, besides those mentioned above, were put forward and discussed in the course of the arbitration; for instance, the rule *res inter alios acta aliis nec prodest nec nocet* (could the protocols of February 1903 curtail the equal rights of the neutral powers? *Case* of Spain, pp. 916-918); the application of the rule 'equality is equity' (Speech of Mr. Cohen, pp. 1259-1262. See for the application of the same rule the Cayuga Indians Claim before the British-American Claims Arbitral Tribunal, *A.J.*, xx. (1926) p. 594); the doctrine of *causa* and consideration (*Counter Case* of the Netherlands, Sweden, and Norway, p. 1110); the burden of proof (Does it rest upon those who claim a preferential treatment to the detriment of other Powers? This was the contention of the neutral Powers; see *Minutes*, p. 55. The blockading Powers contended, on the other hand, that the burden of proof rests upon the Powers asserting their right to intervene; see *Counter Case* of Great Britain, p. 975).

1879.[1] Turkey contended that the position of a State is not that of ordinary debtors under private law, that its responsibility is limited by the assets under its disposal, and that it decides itself the order and the manner of satisfying its creditors. Her counsel pointed out that while it is the first duty of a private person to pay his debts, it is the first duty of a State to defray the expenses of administration and defence. The creditors must know that the debtor State might be unable, for a time and from urgent reasons, to pay its debts. To compel a State to pay moratory interest and thus to become a debtor to a greater extent than it may have wished, is to expose it to the risk of compromising its finances and even its political existence.[2]

In other respects there was no hesitation on the part of Turkey to base her argument on private law. Article 1162 of the *Code Civil* was adduced in support of the contention that as the treaty contained no mention of moratory interest it cannot be demanded now. The *Code Civil* and the German Code were quoted in support of the plea of *vis maior*, which, it was alleged, had prevented Turkey from punctually fulfilling the obligation. On private law was based the contention that there was no formal demand on the part of Russia, that the gift character of the indemnities exempted them from the consequences of delay so far as moratory interest is concerned, and, finally, that Russia had waived, by an unconditional grant of extension of time, her right to demand moratory interest.[3] In the *Contre-réplique* the plea of *res iudicata* was added.[4]

[1] For summaries of this (and other) Hague cases, see Scott, *Reports*, p. 297. For a thorough analysis of this case, cf. Meurer, quoted below, pp. 251-342. See also Ruzé, in *R.I.*, 2nd ser., vol. xv. (1913) pp. 351-371; Strupp in *Z.V.*, vol. vi. (1912) pp. 533-566; Anzilotti, *Rivista*, vii. (1913) pp. 53-67.

[2] *Contre-mémoire* of Turkey, p. 33 (cited after Meurer, *der russisch-türkische Streitfall*, in Schücking, *Das Werk von Haag*, vol. i., pt. iii., p. 271.

[3] Meurer, *op. cit.*, pp. 270-274; *Contre-mémoire*, pp. 47 ff., 54 ff.

[4] Meurer, p. 279.

The Russian *Réplique* pointed out that the theory that States are not like ordinary debtors puts force and discretionary will in the place of law, and that, while dangerous even in the case of individuals being creditors of a State, it certainly has no application when the creditor is a State.[1]

§ 120. *Adoption of Analogy by the Tribunal. Interest, Moratory and Compensatory.*—The tribunal could not refuse to give a legal decision on the ground that positive international law was silent on the question at issue. It adopted private law rules governing analogous relations between individuals, and declared in the award that it was international *public* law that was being applied—a most important pronouncement showing that rules of private law, by the very nature of things and as a result of the legal similarity of relations forming the subject-matter of an international dispute, are deemed in such cases to form an integral part of international public law.

The tribunal refused to recognise the State's right to claim a privileged position in matters of money debts by pleading its character as a sovereign, and the political and financial consequences of a strict insistence on its obligations.[2] Turkey did not deny the general principles of State responsibility with regard to the fulfilment of pecuniary obligations, but, while invoking the Roman law distinctions of different kinds of default, and admitting her responsibility for compensatory interest should actual damage be proved by Russia, she denied such an obligation with regard to moratory interest. The tribunal, however, refused 'to perceive essential differences between various responsibilities.' It held that 'identical in their origin—culpability—they are the

[1] P. 276; for replies to other objections, see Meurer, *op. cit.*, pp. 267, 268, 275-277, and *Réplique*, pp. 20-27.

[2] See Award, Scott, *op. cit.*, p. 311.

same in their consequences—reparation in money,' and, applying a broad analogy, the arbitrator arrived at the conclusion 'that the general principle of the responsibility of States implies a special responsibility in the matter of delay of payment of a money debt, unless the existence of a contrary international custom is proven.' This Turkey was unable to prove. Russia, on the other hand, succeeded in reinforcing her position by invoking precedents in the field of international arbitration. Pursuing the path of analogy, the award defined in the following manner the form of that special responsibility :

'All the private legislation of the States forming the European concert admits, as did formerly the Roman law, the obligation to pay at least interest for delayed payments as legal indemnity when it is a question of the non-fulfilment of an obligation consisting in the payment of a sum of money fixed by convention, clear and exigible, such interest to be paid at least from the date of the demand made upon the debtor in due form of law.' [1]

§ 121. *The Formal Demand.*—Thus the tribunal adopted not only a private law form of responsibility (moratory interest), but also one of the formal conditions of such responsibility, namely, the express demand on the part of the creditor, the formal notice. The fact that most systems of private law, following the example of Roman law, require an express demand in due form, seemed to the tribunal sufficient to incorporate the rule in international law. It held that it would be contrary to equity to subject a debtor State to responsibility stricter than that of a private debtor. The divergencies of the different systems of private law with regard to the form of the demand,[2] and the special conditions of international

[1] *Ibid.*, p. 316.

[2] The *Code Civil* prescribes '*une demande judiciaire*' (Article 1154); no requirement of form is attached to the notice in German law (Article 284).

intercourse, gave occasion for the formulation of the rule that, diplomatic channels being the normal means of communication between States, a demand for payment made through them is regular and in due form. Accordingly, as the Russian Government had expressly, through its Embassy at Constantinople, demanded the payment both of the principal and of the interest, the tribunal held that Turkey was responsible for the interest for delayed payments from the date of the receipt of the demand.

The tribunal dealt shortly with the Turkish exceptions of *vis maior*, of *res iudicata*, and of the gift character of the indemnity on which interest was demanded. It rejected these exceptions not on the ground of a legal principle forbidding their recognition, but because it refused to admit that the indemnity had the character of a gift, that the judgments of the commission established at the Russian Embassy at Constantinople fell, for the purposes of arbitration, within the scope of *res iudicata*, or that Turkey had really been prevented by *vis maior* from fulfilling her obligations.

§ 122. *Waiver. Preclusion.*—There remained the last exception, a typically private law exception, *i.e.* that of presumptive and unrebuttable waiver, of 'preclusion.' The Ottoman Government maintained, and the accuracy of this assertion appeared clearly from the correspondence produced before the Court, that although the Russian Government demanded in 1891 the payment of both interest and principle, it did not subsequently reserve its rights to interest on the receipts given by the Embassy or in the notes granting extension of payment, and that the Embassy did not regard the received sums as interest. The award deals with admirable clearness with this exception, of which it approves and on which the final judgment of the Court is based :

'When the tribunal recognised that, according to the general principles and the custom of public international law, there was a similarity between the condition of a State and that of an individual, which are debtors for a clear and exigible conventional sum, it is equitable and juridical also to apply by analogy the principles of private law common to cases where the demand for payment must be considered as removed and the benefit to be derived therefrom as eliminated. In private law, the effects of demand for payment are eliminated when the creditor, after having made legal demand upon the debtor, grants one or more extensions for the payment of the principal obligation, without reserving the rights acquired by the legal demand.'[1]

The tribunal held accordingly that the Ottoman Government was not liable to pay interest-damages as demanded by Russia.[2]

§ 123. *Criticism of the Award.*—This judgment of the Court has been adversely criticised by positivist writers, notably by Strupp and Anzilotti.[3] They are of the opinion that both the rule regarding moratory interest and that relating to the implied renunciation of interest in case of an unconditional extension for the payment of a debt, are rules of private law solely and exclusively, and that no process of analogy justifies their incorporation in international law unless they have been adopted by international custom or treaty. But Meurer, in a detailed commentary on this arbitration, is clearly of the opinion that the award is just and well founded,

[1] *Ibid.*, p. 322.

[2] Can it be said that the opinion of the Court in this decisive part of the judgment amounts to an acceptance of the doctrine of estoppel? Has Turkey been induced, by a wilful misstatement on the part of Russia, to act to her own prejudice? It may be argued that Turkey would not have paid the rest of the indemnity but for the belief that she is thereby relieved from further demands; she might otherwise have made the claim a subject of separate diplomatic negotiations. If she had been misled, and if she had acted to her prejudice upon the strength of an expressed or implied waiver on the part of the Russian Embassy, then, clearly, the case is one of estoppel in its general formulation, although some of its technical requirements may be lacking.

[3] See pp. 144, 145, *supra*.

and that it is an important contribution to international jurisprudence.[1] The question of admissibility of interest is discussed elsewhere in this monograph[2] What may be added here is that the process of analogy adopted by the tribunal was not only in agreement with the methods adopted by States and tribunals in former arbitrations, but was also in essential accord with the necessities of international intercourse. States cannot refrain from entering into legal relations or from submitting them, in case of dispute, to a final decision, merely because international law, undeveloped as it is, does not specifically regulate the point in dispute. Having once submitted their dispute to a judicial decision, they must recognise that they are subject to a rule of law whose provisions, if not found in international custom and treaties, may be sought in the system of law which regulates the relations of other co-ordinated entities, *i.e.* in private law.[3]

[1] *Op. cit.*, pp. 300, 315-317.

[2] See pp. 143-146, *supra.*

[3] It may be asked whether the principle of moratory interest, as adopted by the tribunal, is a generally recognised rule. For it appears that English law is different in this regard. In an action for the non-payment of a debt, the measure of damages is the sum due, together with interest, if so stipulated by the parties; and nominal damages can only be claimed as moratory interest. And although interest may be allowed if a written demand for payment is made upon the debtor, giving him notice that interest will be claimed, the power to award it is in the discretion of the court or the jury (Halsbury, vol. xxi. p. 38, and note *r*). Interest, if any, so awarded is payable by way of damages. It may be doubted, however, whether the English exception affects the general rule. That it is no longer in accord with the trend of opinion is clearly shown, for instance, in the judgments of Lord Herschell, L.C., and Jessel, M.R., in the cases *London, Chatham, and Dover Railway Company* v. *South-Eastern Railway Company* (1893, A.C., p. 437) and *Wallis* v. *Smith* ([1882], 21 Ch.D., p. 243). 'It has always appeared to me,' says Jessel, M.R., in the latter case, 'that the doctrine of the English law as to non-payment of money—the general rule being that you cannot recover damages because it is not paid by a certain day—is not quite consistent with reason. A man may be utterly ruined by the non-payment of a sum of money on a given day, the damages may be enormous, and the other party may be wealthy. However, that is our law. If, however, it were not our law, the absurdity would be apparent' (p. 257). This remark relates only to interest as damages, but it is directed against the whole doctrine of moratory interest in English law. (In the same case Lord Watson and Lord Shand made reference to the law of Scotland as following the opposite principle in accord with Roman and continental law.) In addition, the exceptions

IV

OTHER HAGUE CASES [1]

§ 124. *The Japanese House Tax Case. The Juridical Nature of Leases and the Question of Interpretation.*—The Japanese House Tax case of May 1905 [2] is of interest with regard not so much to the questions decided by the tribunal as to those in which it refused to pronounce an opinion. The issue before the tribunal was *prima facie* one of interpretation. Article 18 of the revised Treaty of July 1894 between Japan and Great Britain provided that after the foreign quarters existing in Japan should have been incorporated in the individual communes, the existing leases in perpetuity under which their property was held should be confirmed, and no new conditions should be imposed upon the owner in respect of such property.[3] The Japanese Government contended before the tribunal that lands alone are exempted from the payment of imposts, taxes, and other charges, and not also the buildings constructed on such lands, as claimed by Germany, France, and Great Britain. Both parties based their argument on their own private law. The Japanese Government maintained that although the ownership of the land remained vested in the Government the ownership of the buildings belonged to the holders of

to this rule are so numerous (see Halsbury, *loc. cit.*) that they mitigate it considerably. It may therefore be accepted that the Hague award is, in this regard, in accordance with a general rule of law.

[1] Other cases decided by the Hague Court, except the North Atlantic Fisheries arbitration, which is discussed in the preceding chapter, did not, having regard to the subject-matter of these disputes, give rise to the application of private law. Nevertheless, in almost all of them the problem became relevant in this or the other form. See p. 265, n. 1. *infra.*

[2] For a short summary of the case, see Scott, *Reports*, p. 77. For an analysis of the case, see von Martitz, in Schücking, vol. i. pt. i. pp. 313-339; also *R.G.*, xii. (1905) pp. 492-516.

[3] The provisions of the treaties of 1896 with Germany and with France were virtually the same.

perpetual leases who have purchased or erected buildings at their own expense.[1] It stressed the fact that the Code of Japan, far from adhering to the civil and common law principle of accession in respect of buildings, preserved the ancient custom of dualism of land and buildings,[2] and it denied that the indivisibility of land and buildings constitutes a principle of natural as well as of general positive law.[3] The European Powers invoked their codes, the Pandects, and the general principles of law in support of the contention that accession is a mode of acquiring ownership, and that the building shares the legal position of the land on which it is erected.[4]

The question thus put before the tribunal, although *prima facie* one of private law, has, through the disputed term of private law having been incorporated in a treaty, become one of interest for international public law. The fact that the term in question defines private and not public rights is not decisive. Such rights, by becoming a part of a treaty and the subject-matter of an international dispute, cannot be ignored by international jurists. It is therefore to be regretted that the tribunal declined to enter into a discussion of private law, and based its decision exclusively on the interpretation of the intention of the parties.[5]

[1] *Reply of the Japanese Government to the Objections of the Governments of France, Germany, and Great Britain*, p. 23.

[2] *Statement of Objections of the Imperial Japanese Government to the Contre-mémoire and Conclusions of the Governments of Great Britain, France, and Germany*, p. 43.

[3] See p. 88, *loc. cit.* Articles 553 and 664 of the French Code Civil were adduced, as well as '*bail*' and '*covenant*,' in which the preservation of ownership of the land in the hands of the lessor co-exists with the ownership of the buildings by the lessee (p. 21, *op. cit.*).

[4] *Réponse présentée aux objections du Gouvernement Japonais*, pp. 21, 34, 36; *Contre-mémoire et Conclusions*, p. 17.

[5] Cf., on the other hand, p. 295, n. 4, *infra*.—The tribunal obviously disregarded the argument of the Japanese *Case* based on an assertion frequently encountered in international litigation, namely, that conventional provisions in derogation of the sovereignty of the State must be interpreted restrictively (Japanese *Statement of Objections*, pp. 11, 65, 68; see also pp. 178-180, *supra*).

§ 125. *The Grisbadarna Case. Prescription. Recourse to Roman Law. The Island of Timor Case.*—In the Grisbadarna case, decided by the Hague tribunal in October 1909, judgment was given on grounds amounting virtually to a recognition of the doctrine of prescription in international law, although the term itself was not mentioned by the tribunal.[1] It awarded to Sweden the Grisbadarna region in view of the fact that she had performed there various acts while under the conviction that the disputed regions were Swedish. The tribunal recognised that it is 'a settled principle of the law of nations that a state of things which actually exists and has existed for a long time should be changed as little as possible.' It is of interest to note how both States, especially Sweden, supported their claim by arguments drawn from private and especially from Roman law. This is the more characteristic since in both countries the influence of Roman law was and is very small so far as their municipal law is concerned. Sweden quoted Roman law writers of the sixteenth and seventeenth centuries,[2] and had recourse to such Roman law notions as *possessio nec vi, nec clam, nec precario.*

The second boundary dispute decided by the Hague tribunal had its origin in differences of opinion between the Dutch and Portuguese Governments as to the proper interpretation of certain conventions concerning the delimitation of their possessions in the island of Timor.[3] The award of the tribunal is noteworthy because of the complete adoption of the general rule of interpretation of treaties as propounded by Rivier, namely, that they should be interpreted in accordance with 'principles of common sense and experience already formulated by the Prudents of Rome.'[4] The arbitrator cited in full the provisions of the *Code Civil,* of the

[1] For summary and award, see Scott's *Reports*, pp. 121-133.

[2] See Strupp's analysis of this case in Schücking, vol. i. pt. ii. p. 128.

[3] Scott, *Reports*, pp. 354-386.

[4] Rivier, vol. ii. § 157.

German Civil Code, and of the Swiss Code of Obligations, all of them to the effect that the first object of the process of interpretation should be to ascertain the common intention of the parties, and added: 'It is useless to dwell on the entire coincidence of private and international law on this point.'[1]

[1] Other cases decided by the Court at Hague do not throw much light on the problem. It is impossible, in the absence of published reports of the proceedings, to say how far the parties availed themselves of private law rules and analogies. That they did it occasionally may be seen, for instance, from the German *Mémoire* in the *Casablanca* case, where the analogy of Roman law is invoked in support of the contention that he who takes the law in his own hands, without having called for assistance on the part of authorities, is precluded from invoking the law on which he bases his claim (see also French *Contre-mémoire*, p. 36), and from those parts of the argument and of the award which deal with the degrees of *culpa* of the officials in question (cf. Gidel in *R.G.*, xv. (1910) pp. 394-395). See also the *Orinoco Steamship Company* case (Scott, *Reports*, pp. 226-234) and the *Canevaro* case, (*ibid.*, pp. 284-296). The former case was concerned with the rules governing the revision of an arbitral award; the second is a typical case of international private law. See also French *Contre-mémoire*, p. 34, and *British Counter Case*, p. 25, in the *Savarkar* case with regard to *culpa in omittendo*, and p. 17 of the French *Mémoire* with regard to the burden of proof.

CHAPTER VIII

RECOURSE TO PRIVATE LAW IN INTERNATIONAL ARBITRATION

(*Miscellaneous Cases*)

§ 126. *The 'Rough Jurisprudence of Nations' and Judicial Settlement of International Disputes.*—There is an *obiter dictum* by Hall, hidden in an obscure footnote but frequently quoted with approval by writers, saying that 'there is no place for the refinements of courts in the rough jurisprudence of nations.'[1] It is not clear whether this was meant as a statement of an unavoidable fact inherent in the very nature of international relations, or as a piece of advice relating merely to the present undeveloped stage of international law. But be that as it may, it hardly applies to States as parties to a dispute before an international tribunal. The refinements of municipal courts are copied and surpassed in proceedings before these tribunals, and the importance of the subject-matter of the dispute and the love of argument, so dear to the hearts of lawyers, usually result here in numerous volumes of printed cases, counter-cases, and arguments, and weeks or months of oral pleading. International jurisprudence is rough when there is no forum, save the battlefield or political conferences and diplomatic negotiations, before which to fight out its problems. It is subtle and thorough and detailed when tested before or applied by an international judicial tribunal. That is perhaps one of the

[1] P. 395, n. 2.

reasons why neither States nor international tribunals share the current dislike and suspicion of private law. The arbitration cases discussed in the two preceding Chapters show that international tribunals apply private law whenever they deem it advisable; that States which are parties before an international tribunal have, as a rule, recourse to analogies of private law, especially when the subject-matter of the dispute would normally be governed by private law but for the fact that the parties to the dispute are sovereign States; and, finally, that this uniform practice remains, on the whole, unaffected by casual deviations, notably in cases where a State rejects a contention of the opponent by referring to an inadmissible analogy. It is intended, in the present chapter, to continue the illustration of these propositions by further references to miscellaneous cases of judicial settlement of international disputes beginning with minor arbitrations and ending with several decisions of the Permanent Court of International Justice. However, from the vast number of cases in which recourse was had, in this or some other form, to private law, reasons of space point to the selection, for the most part, of cases in which the tribunal or the parties expressly asserted the authority of individual rules of private law.

§ 127. *The Hamburg Judgments. Admission. Arrears of Interest. Recourse to Roman Law.*—Among the arbitral awards which, at the beginning of the second half of the nineteenth century, mark the advent of an era of more frequent recourse to arbitration, the awards given by the Senate of Hamburg occupy a prominent position so far as their juridical value is concerned. This relates especially to the *Croft* case and the *Yuille, Shortridge & Co.* case.

The *Croft* case was a dispute arising out of an alleged denial of justice to a British subject, to whom the Portuguese administrative authorities denied a patent of registration notwithstanding a judicial decision in his favour.[1] It was contended by Great Britain that the authorities acted illegally, and that the Portuguese Government was responsible for the consequences of the illegal proceedings. Both allegations were rejected by the arbitrator on grounds upon which it is not necessary to enter. What is of interest is that one of the main arguments on the part of Great Britain was that Portugal was estopped by her conduct from denying the truth of the British allegation. It appeared that the Portuguese Government, acting under strong representations on the part of Great Britain, issued in 1851 a decree in which the attitude of the administrative organs was described as a denial of justice, and the contested right was granted to Croft. The tribunal was prepared in principle to recognise the plea of admission (or estoppel)[2]—under certain conditions:

'If what was contained in the statement of the 17th November 1851 had been expressed in a note or other diplomatic communication, addressed to the British Government by the Portuguese Government as its view of the case, it might have been justly said, that the one Government had thereby of itself made an acknowledgment and an admission to the other by which the latter was now altogether exonerated from the task of proving that the case really stood as it was represented there.'

Should such an admission have taken place then, it was held, there could be no doubt that a perfectly valid

[1] For the award, see Moore, pp. 4979-4983; Lapradelle-Politis, vol. ii. pp. 1-37. For other cases of admission, see pp. 269, 278, 279, *infra*.

[2] It will be noted that the terms 'admission' and 'estoppel' are here used without sufficient regard being paid to the fact that they are not identical, and that it is only in certain cases that admission creates estoppel (see p. 260, *supra*). This method has been adopted in order to use, so far as possible, a terminology familiar also to the non-English reader.

title to satisfaction or indemnification would arise therefrom. The tribunal, however, was of the opinion that an act which was solely an address from the Government to the Council of State could not be regarded as an internationally binding declaration; only an international act, not an internal one, could be regarded as sufficient for the purpose of a plea of admission. This solution may not be altogether satisfactory, but it is important as the first instance of an exhaustive juridical treatment by an international tribunal of the effect of admission.[1]

The *Yuille, Shortridge & Co.* case furnishes an instructive instance of recourse to Roman law. The tribunal, after having arrived at a decision in favour of the British demand, was confronted with a claim for interest whose total amount largely exceeded the sum due as principal.[2] There exists in international law

[1] A similar point arose in the course of an arbitration between Great Britain and Argentine in 1870. (See Moore, pp. 4916-4925, and Lapradelle-Politis, vol. ii. pp. 637-667.) When engaged in a war with the Republic of Uruguay, the Government of Argentine prohibited vessels arriving from Montevideo from entering Argentine ports. Great Britain sought now to recover the losses of British subjects resulting from this measure. Argentine, however, pleaded that when, in November 1849, the two Governments signed a convention settling the claims arising out of the blockade, no mention had been made of any claims under this head. Evidence was further adduced by Argentine to the effect that British representatives repeatedly recognised the validity of the blockade. It was urged that the British claim could not, owing to these facts, be admitted. The arbitrator, however, rejected the claim on other grounds. He held that Argentine was not responsible, because a valid blockade of Montevideo had been officially proclaimed and it is a 'principle of universal jurisprudence that he who uses his right offends no one' (award, Moore, p. 4925). It is to be regretted that the tribunal did not answer the 'plea of preclusion.' The position here was a different one from that in the case of the *Canada*, in which Brazil was referring to the fact that the United States at one time offered to accept a reduced sum as a compromise for the claim. The obvious answer of the arbitrator was that after Brazil had declined this offer the United States could not be regarded as bound by it. (Cf. Lapradelle-Politis, vol. ii. p. 636, n. 4.) Similarly, in the case of the Hudson Bay Company Claims (cf. Moore, p. 254) an attempt was made to use as evidence various offers put forward in the course of abortive negotiations. See also the award in the Delagoa Railway arbitration (*infra*, p. 271; p. 165 of the award), where the tribunal held that the Portuguese Government was estopped from raising the question of the alleged defective construction of the railway, since, when the first section of line was opened, no official statement on the matter was issued.

[2] See award, in Lapradelle-Politis, vol. ii. p. 108; for a discussion of the case, see *ibid.*, pp. 79-118.

no statutory period of limitation for the recovery of arrears of interest, but the tribunal adopted simply the Roman law rule of *alterum tantum*. In fact, it held that Roman law is the only one applicable in such cases.[1, 2]

§ 128. *Damages for Loss of Prospective Profits. The Recourse to Civil Law. The Case of the 'Colonel Lloyd Aspinwall.' The Fabiani Case. The Delagoa Railway Arbitration. The Whaling and Sealing Claims.*—The proposition has been put forward in one of the preceding Chapters[3] that out of the practice of international tribunals alternately rejecting and recognising claims for loss of profits the rule gradually emerges that, although the remoteness of damage, when coupled with the fact that it is only 'prospective,' acts to defeat the claim,[4] in all other cases damages are as a rule awarded. This may be seen clearly in the case of the *Colonel Lloyd Aspinwall.*[5] The arbitrator felt here no hesitation in awarding damages for loss of prospective earnings. He did not regard governments as entitled to a privileged position; on the contrary, he thought, in a somewhat strained exaggeration, that 'a government more even than an individual should be held to make most liberal compensation for an unwarranted interference with legitimate business,' and he proceeded, on the ground of the distinction between *lucrum cessans* and *damnum emergens*, to define the amount of the sum to be awarded.

On the same Roman law distinction between actual and prospective damage, as well as on the distinction

[1] 'Comme d'après le droit commun, seul applicable ici, le cumul des intérêts arriérés s'arrête lorsqu'ils atteignent le principal (*Dig.*, *de cond. indeb.*, 12, 6), on a dû restreindre les intérêts de ce chef à £2589.'

[2] With regard to the measure of damages, the tribunal affirmed the principle *causa proxima non remota spectatur*. It did not, however, put a too limited construction on the 'directness' of the damage. An amount for prospective profits was included in the award (see Lapradelle-Politis, vol. ii. p. 117).

[3] See p. 147, *supra*.

[4] See p. 149, *supra*.

[5] See Moore, pp. 1007-1018; Lapradelle-Politis, vol. ii. pp. 668-675.

between the different degree of fault as adopted in private law, is based the outspoken decision of the President of the Swiss Confederation in the dispute between France and Venezuela in the *Fabiani* case in 1896.[1] The award, which resembles in some respects a dissertation on the private law of damages, is quite emphatic in awarding damages for prospective gains, although it defines them as indirect damages. The arbitrator took care to point out that the damages thus claimed are not of a merely speculative character.[2]

The same principle was reaffirmed in an equally thorough judgment rendered by a tribunal nominated by the Swiss Federal Council in the *Delagoa Railway* arbitration[3] between the United States and Great Britain on one hand, and Portugal on the other. The tribunal had to fix as it might deem most just the amount of compensation due from the Portuguese Government to the claimants in consequence of the rescission of the concession of the Lourenço Marques Railroad, and the taking possession of that railroad by the Portuguese Government.[4] The indemnity asked for was for the loss actually sustained and for lost profits, provided that the loss was the natural and direct consequence of the non-execution of the contract by the other party.[5] The tribunal called upon to award compensation such as 'it shall deem most just' rightly interpreted this clause as imposing upon it the obligation to give a legal decision. It based its award 'on the general principles of the common law of modern nations.'[6] After having found that Portugal was responsible for acting in contravention

[1] For the award, see Moore, pp. 4878-4915.

[2] For the apparent exceptions to this rule, for instance in the case of *The Canada*, see p. 150, *supra*.

[3] See *Sentence Finale du Tribunal Arbitral du Délagoa, du 29 mars, 1900, Berne*, 1900. For a concise statement of the history of the case, see Stowell and Munro, *International Cases*, 1916, vol. i. pp. 334 ff.

[4] Cf. Arbitration Treaty of June 13, 1891, Moore, p. 1874.

[5] See *Sentence Finale*, p. 155.

[6] See Stowell and Munro, *op. cit.*, vol. i. p. 343.

of the contract of concession, the tribunal ruled that there was but one principle of law applicable for the fixing of the compensation, namely, that of damages and interest, comprising, in accordance with rules universally admitted, *damnum emergens* and *lucrum cessans*.[1]

That the general principle of private law governing the measure of damages is equally applicable in international law is clearly stated in the award of Professor Asser in the arbitration concerning the 'Whaling and Sealing Claims' of the United States against Russia on account of arrest and seizure of the American vessels, *The Cape Horn Pigeon, The James Hamilton Lewis, The C. H. White*, and others.[2] The main point of the arbitration was that relating to the claim for indemnity for the loss of profit which the whalers, mistakenly suspected of illegal hunting and detained by Russian authorities, might have realised from the catch. Russia admitted that according to a generally recognised rule 'the indemnification for injury done to the property of others relates not only to the material damage (*damnum emergens*), but also to the loss of profit (*lucrum cessans*).'[3] She urged, however, that the latter must be understood in the sense of deprivation of a fixed revenue or of a certain profit, whereas the enterprise in question was fraught with risk and danger. She then referred to the *Alabama* arbitration tribunal, which established 'the general principle that claims for indemnification for indirect damages cannot be allowed.'[4] The *Argument* of the United States dealt at length with these objections.[5] It pointed out that the damages claimed were in no sense

[1] *Ibid.*

[2] See *U.S. For. Rel.*, 1902, House of Repres., 57th Congress, 2nd Session, Doc. No. 1, Appendix I. The award was given in November 1902.

[3] *Russian Counter Memorandum*, *op. cit.*, p. 288.

[4] *Loc. cit.* The same argument is repeated, with references to Roman law (*Fr.* 29 and *leg. Aquil.* 9, 2) in the *Surrejoinder* (*op. cit.*, p. 397), where the plea of *force majeure*, of legitimate defence, and of the principle *qui iure suo utitur neminem laedit*, was added.

[5] See pp. 220-224, *op. cit.*

indirect damages for loss of speculative profits, but that they represented actual loss. A large number of private law cases was quoted in support of the claim, as well as awards of international tribunals, beginning with the cases of *The Betsey* and *The Neptune* [1] and ending with the award in the *Costa Rica Packet* case.[2] Special stress was laid on the awards in the Behring Sea Commission, where the British claims for damages for loss of catch had been fully recognised.[3]

The arbitrator, who had to decide according to 'general principles of international law,' answered the questions at issue with admirable clearness. Firstly, he adopted 'the general principle of civil law, according to which the damages should include an indemnity not only for the loss suffered, but also for the profit of which one has been deprived,' which principle 'is equally applicable to international litigation.' Secondly, he rejected the contention that the loss must be exactly determined, and pointed out that it is sufficient to show that in the natural order of things one would be able to realise a profit of which one is deprived by the fact which gives rise to the claim. He also stressed the fact that damages for lost profits are not necessarily identical with indirect damages.[4]

§ 129. *Extinctive Prescription. The Williams Case. The Gentini Case.*—It would be a mistake to assume that the recourse had by international tribunals to rules of private law is a method uncritically adopted and simply following the line of least resistance. As a

[1] See p. 149, *supra.*
[2] See p. 149, *supra.*
[3] See pp. 223-224, *op. cit.*, especially the case of *The Triumph*, where the sole claim was for loss of catch.
[4] This arbitration is also instructive from the point of view of the award of interest; not only because the arbitrator awarded 6 per cent. interest from 1892 (the date of the injurious act) until payment in full, but also because the defendant party itself recognised as 'perfectly regular' the award of interest as from that date. See *Russian Counter Memorandum*, p. 290, *op. cit.*

matter of fact, it is frequently challenged by one of the parties on the ground that a certain rule is inapplicable as belonging exclusively to the domain of private law. This has been done especially in some cases where the question of extinctive prescription was under discussion. Thus in the arbitration between the United States and Chile regarding *The Macedonian* in 1863, the plea of prescription put forward by Chile was resisted by the United States as of doubtful application in international law.[1] Equally, in the dispute between Brazil and the United States regarding *The Canada*, the latter supported its position by referring to the maxim *nullum tempus occurrit regi*.[2] A challenge of this kind gave rise to a thorough exposition (covering fourteen pages) of the doctrine of prescription by Commissioner Little in the *Williams* case in the Claims Commission under the Convention of 1885 between the United States and Venezuela.[3] He said:

'On careful consideration of the authorities on the subject we are of the opinion that by their decided weight—we might say by very necessity—prescription has a place in the international system, and is to be regarded in these adjudications.'

Both private law and previous arbitral decisions were relied upon by the umpire in the *Gentini* case during the Venezuelan arbitrations of 1903.[4] In this case an Italian subject claimed damages for a series of injurious acts done to his person and property when resident in Venezuela in 1871. The proofs were taken the following year, and from that time no demand had been brought before the Venezuelan Government. Counsel for Venezuela, while recognising that national rules of prescription cannot be applied in this case,

[1] Moore, pp. 1449-1468.
[2] *Ibid.*, pp. 1733-1747.
[3] *Ibid.*, pp. 4181-4199.
[4] *The Venezuelan Arbitrations, Ralston's Report*, Government Printing Office, 1904, pp. 724-730.

invoked prescription *qua* international law. Italy, however, pleaded that prescription is not recognised in international law, and referred, amongst others, to the decision of the Hague Court in the Pious Fund case. The umpire, who had acted as the agent of the United States in the Pious Fund arbitration, rejected the Italian contention. He pointed out that the decision of the Hague tribunal referred not to the principle of prescription, but to the special rules of civil law governing that institute. After discussing the attitude of American and English courts of equity with relation to statutes of limitation and the law of *laches*, he reviewed a series of cases affirming the doctrine of prescription in international law,[1] as well as the possible exceptions to the general rule. The value of this decision is by no means impaired by the fact that several commissions acting under the same convention refused in individual cases to admit the plea of prescription. For, while recognising it in principle, they had to take into account special circumstances which rendered impossible its application.[2]

§ 130. *Prescription in Recent Boundary Arbitrations. The British Guiana Arbitration in 1904. The Chamizal and the Walfisch Arbitrations.*—With regard to acquisitive prescription, three modern boundary arbitrations may be mentioned. In the British Guiana arbitration of 1899 the question arose whether the term ‘ prescription ’ must, when used in a treaty, fulfil the same requirements as in private law, *i.e.* whether the element of time is sufficient, or whether the possession must also be peaceful, notorious, and continuous (*nec vi, nec clam, nec*

[1] *Loc. cit.*, p. 770.

[2] See, for instance, the cases: *Roberts*, p. 577, *op. cit.*, and *Stevenson*, p. 328, where the delay in the presentation of the demand was attributable to the defendant Government. Cf. also the case *Tagliaferro*, p. 764, and *Giacopini*, p. 766, *op. cit.* Cf. also p. 119, n. 1, *supra*. On the award of damages for prospective profits in these commissions, see p. 149, n. 1, *supra*.

precario).[1] A similar problem, although without reference to a term used in a treaty, arose in connection with the arbitration between Great Britain and Brazil concerning the boundaries of British Guiana. The award given in 1904 by the King of Italy[2] does not refer expressly to the doctrine of prescription; it states, however, that 'occupation cannot be held to be carried out except by effective, uninterrupted, and permanent possession, and that a simple affirmation of rights of sovereignty or a manifest intention to render the occupation effective cannot suffice.' It seems, on the other hand, that the arbitrator was prepared to admit that the exercise by Holland for a long time of acts of sovereignty over certain zones invested it with rights which passed afterwards to Great Britain. He obviously did not attach decisive importance to requirements of prescription other than time, and the award is therefore sharply criticised by writers who, as a rule, are not in favour of recourse to private law.[3] However, it is hardly possible to question the soundness of the arbitrator's attitude if we consider that the private law requirements of prescription can only be applied with great difficulty to conditions in which precariousness and force are the characteristic features of the situation.

That these requirements hold good under modern and, consequently, more orderly conditions, may be seen clearly from the award in the Chamizal Arbitration between the United States and Mexico, of June 15, 1911.[4] The United States advanced here the contention that, apart from its title under treaty provisions, it had acquired by prescription a good title over the territory

[1] See *supra*, p. 229.

[2] Hertslet's *Treaties*, vol. xxiv. p. 173.

[3] See Lapradelle and Politis, *L'arbitrage anglo-brésilien de* 1904, *Revue du droit public et de la science politique*, 1905, pp. 340-343.

[4] The award is printed in *A.J.*, v. (1911) pp. 785-812.

in dispute. But the tribunal examined closely whether the possession was 'undisturbed, uninterrupted, and peaceable'—and it did not find any of these requirements fulfilled. The evidence showed especially that the possession was not peaceable, and that it was thus lacking in another characteristic 'serving as a foundation of prescription.'[1] Accordingly, the tribunal had no hesitation in dismissing this part of the United States argument.

Finally, in the dispute of 1911 between Great Britain and Germany in the matter of the southern boundary of the territory of Walfisch Bay,[2] the arbitrator took the fact of unchallenged and continued possession on the part of Great Britain as 'evidence of a wish to acquire and of an effective occupation by which in any case British sovereignty could have been established over the zone in dispute."[3]

§ 131. *The British-American Claims Arbitral Tribunal under the Convention of 1910. Admission.*—To give an exhaustive account of recourse to private law in individual arbitration cases would mean, as mentioned above, to cover almost the entire field of international arbitration—a task which cannot be attempted in this monograph. What is intended is no more than to draw attention to cases most illustrative of the question under discussion. A considerable number of such cases are to be found in the decisions of the British-American Claims Arbitral Tribunal constituted under the Convention of 1910.[4] In the terms of submission two private law questions were settled in advance by the agreement of the parties. One relates to the effect to be given to admissions by a party: 'The arbitral tribunal shall

[1] See the award, p. 806, *loc. cit.*

[2] For the award, see Hertslet's *Treaties*, vol. xxvi. pp. 187-250.

[3] P. 249, *ibid.*

[4] Treaty Series, 1912, No. 11 (Cmd. 6201); also Martens, *N.R.G.*, 3rd ser., vol. vi. p. 361.

take into account as one of the equities of the claim, to such extent as it shall consider just in allowing or disallowing a claim, any admission of liability by the Government against whom a claim is put forward.' The tribunal was thus provided with a clear rule for dealing with the questions of admission and, partly, of estoppel. We shall see that the parties made frequent use of this provision. The other deals with the award of interest.[1]

In the case of *The Lindisfarne*[2] the tribunal took as one of the grounds of its decision an implied admission of liability on the part of the United States. The fact that the Congress had defrayed the cost of the repairs of the ship damaged in the collision was regarded

[1] 'The arbitral tribunal, if it considers equitable, may include in its award in respect of any claim interest at a rate not exceeding 4 per cent. per annum for the whole or any part of the period between the date when the claim was first brought to the notice of the party and that of the confirmation of the Schedule in which it is included.' The question of interest has thus been disposed of, and the tribunal used its discretion in awarding or disallowing it. The provision itself seems to be strongly influenced by the common law rule governing the award of interest, and little can be said in favour of the determination of the *dies ad quem* as provided by the terms of submission.

Notwithstanding the clear provision of the arbitration agreement, attempts were made to apply the rule of municipal public law which liberates States from paying interest. The United States invoked, for instance, in the case of *The King Robert* (Claim No. 4; see especially *Memorandum to the Oral Argument of the U.S.*), federal statutes according to which no interest should be allowed on any claim against the United States up to the time of the judgment, unless upon a contract expressly stipulating for the payment of interest. The argument shows how slowly counsel become familiar with the fact that a claim, after having become an international one, is no longer governed by the public law of one State. The privileged position of a State in relation to individuals cannot be maintained in relation to another State. This line of argument seems to have been influenced by some decisions of the Supreme Court of the United States in which it had been held that States are not liable for interest (cf. Scott, *Judicial Settlement of Controversies between States of the American Union*, 1918: *United States* v. *State of North Carolina*, vol. ii. p. 1063—Analysis, p. 253; *United States* v. *State of New York*, vol. ii. p. 1157—Analysis, p. 313).

[2] Claim No. 1.—This was a claim by Great Britain for one day's demurrage for the steamship *Lindisfarne*, injured in a collision with a United States army transport vessel. On the day following the collision the necessary repairs to the injured vessel were made by order of the army transport officials. The cost of the repairs was subsequently defrayed by an appropriation of the Congress. No action was, however, taken by the Congress in order to satisfy the claim of the shipowners for demurrage.

as sufficient to establish admission.[1] The difficulty which frequently confronted the tribunal in this and similar cases was: May the acts of every State official or every State organ be treated as an admission of this kind, or should only such admissions preclude a Government from denying liability as had been duly authorised by it and transmitted to the other Government?[2] It seems that the terms of submission referring to admissions as to the 'equities of the claim' influenced the tribunal to take a middle course.

In the case of *The Newchwang* it was contended by Great Britain that a letter addressed by the Secretary of the Navy to the Chairman of the Committee on Claims of the House of Representatives, and containing a recommendation in favour of the claim, contains an admission of liability by which the United States are estopped from denying responsibility. The tribunal, however, held that the letter was merely a personal or private recommendation and had never been officially published, and that it could not therefore be regarded as an admission of liability on the part of the United States.[3] On the other hand, in the case of *The Eastry* the award is based, *inter alia*, on an admission on the part of the United States: 'The course adopted by the United States authorities, both at the time the injuries occurred, and in making the preliminary repairs, is wholly inconsistent with the contention now made that the United States were not responsible for the damage inflicted.'[4]

[1] See Award, p. 5. The awards given by this tribunal are printed in *American and British Claims Arbitration, Report* of Fred K. Nielsen, Washington, Government Printing Office, 1926. Nearly all are printed in the different volumes of the *American Journal of International Law*. However, the pages of the awards in this and the following footnotes refer to awards as originally printed on separate leaflets.

[2] Cf. here the *Oral Argument* in the case of *William Hardman*, pp. 63-68 and 71, and the *Croft* case, p. 268, *supra*.

[3] Claim No. 21; award, p. 7.

[4] Claim No. 4; award, p. 4.

§ 132. *The Plea of Estoppel. The Yukon Lumber Case. Damages for Prospective Profits.*—In the *Yukon Lumber* case both the argument of the United States and the award were based mainly on estoppel.[1] This was a claim on the part of Great Britain for the value of some timber cut in trespass upon Canadian territory, sold subsequently to the Government of the United States, and used by it in the construction of certain military bridges in Alaska. The United States contended in reply that Great Britain, by the course taken by her officials, was estopped from denying that a full and complete title to the timber had legally vested in the United States, that the Canadian land and timber agent stood by silently and watched the American Government acquire this timber *bona fide* and continue for six months to pay the instalments due in respect of it, and that, accordingly, Great Britain could not now be heard in a demand that the United States should pay for the timber which it was permitted to acquire under false representations.[2] This plea, in support of which a vast number of English and American cases on estoppel was cited, was fully adopted by the tribunal.[3, 4]

A number of cases decided by this tribunal are of importance owing to the clear decisions of the arbitrator on the question of the measure of damages. They are, on the whole, in accord with the tendency to award damages for prospective profits. Thus in the case of *The Favourite*, Great Britain demanded damages based upon 'a reasonable estimate of the sums which the owners would have received as the proceeds of the voyage, if it had been completed.' The United States availed

[1] Claim No. 5.

[2] See United States *Memorandum on the Oral Argument*, pp. 10-22, and *Reply of the United States*, p. 15.

[3] Award, pp. 5-6.

[4] The plea of estoppel was also put forward by Great Britain in the cases of *The Favourite* (Claim No. 12) and *The Wanderer* (Claim No. 13).

themselves this time of the argument that international law does not allow damages of this nature.[1] The tribunal, however, taking as a basis the number of the seals caught by the vessel in the 24 days preceding the seizure, considered that although it is not certain that *The Favourite* would have continued to take skins at the daily average of the first 24 days, the loss of the prospective catch should be compensated.[2] Similar are the decisions of the tribunal in *The Horace B. Parker*,[3] *The Wanderer*, and in *The Kate*,[4] in the latter case the actual catch of another steamer forming the basis of computation.[5]

The decisions in the *Fiji Land Claims* show, on the other hand, that if the prospective gains are merely speculative they will be excluded.[6] Neither are damages awarded which are only indirectly consequent upon the injurious act. 'It is a well-known principle of the law of damages that *causa proxima non remota inspicitur*,' says the arbitrator while fixing the amount of compensation in the case of *The Newchwang*.[7, 8]

§ 133. *The Union Bridge Company Case. Conversion, Trespass, Other Instances of Analogy.*—Several cases

[1] *Answer of the United States*, p. 19.

[2] Award, p. 5.

[3] Claim No. 76.

[4] Claim No. 23. See, however, *Answer of the United States*, p. 10, and *Memorandum to the Oral Argument of the United States*, pp. 18-30.

[5] Award, p. 7.

[6] See, for instance, the case of *G. R. Burt* (Claim No. 44), or of *Isaac M. Brower*, award, p. 6: 'Passing to the question of damages, it is plain that the island forming the subject-matter of the claim had only a speculative and precarious value. . . . In these circumstances we consider that notwithstanding our conclusion on the principle of liability, the United States must be content with an award of nominal damage.'

[7] Claim No. 21.

[8] In this and similar cases the tribunal did not go further than to allow compensation in accordance with the ordinary rule of demurrage. Where it refused to allow compensation for prospective profits, it explained its decision by the absence of sufficient proof of actual loss or of reasonable proof of the amount claimed. See, for instance, the cases of *The Tattler*, Claim No. 19; *The Canadienne*, Claim No. 16: *The Jessie, The Thomas F. Bayard, The Pescawha*, Claims Nos. 24, 25, and 26 respectively: *The Sidra*, Claim No. 23 (cf. here *Comments upon the Memorandum to the Oral Argument of the United States*, pp. 9-14, containing ample references to the practice of international tribunals).

decided by the tribunal show how frequently—and sometimes how indiscriminately—the parties resort to the use of analogies. In the Union Bridge Company case the United States claimed damages arising out of a wrongful interference, after the annexation of the Orange Free State, with certain bridge material belonging to the Union Bridge Company, an American firm. It was argued by the United States that the seizure of this material by the British authorities, with intent to appropriate the same to their own use, 'was such an exercise of dominion over them as to constitute a conversion' for which Great Britain should respond in damages. The case was conducted by both parties as if it were an action before a municipal tribunal of Great Britain or the United States. Numerous English and American cases and authorities were quoted in support of the contention that conversion really took place;[1] that it is not necessary for this purpose that the defendants should have acquired actual property in the thing converted; and that it is immaterial that the conversion was the result of a mistake. The oral argument was devoted to a large extent to the discussion of this aspect of the case. The difference between an action of trover and an action of conversion was discussed in detail.[2] The tribunal, however, seems to have preferred a construction based on a principle of international law. It held that the action of the British authorities constituted 'an international tort committed in respect of neutral property, and falls to be decided not by reference to nice distinctions between trover, trespass, and action of the case, but by reference to that broad and well-recognised principle of international law which gives what, in all the circumstances, is fair

[1] *Memorandum to the Oral Argument of the United States*, pp. 1-36.

[2] See *Oral Argument*, pp. 35-41.

compensation of the wrong suffered by the neutral owner.' [1]

In the case of *Yukon Lumber* the argument of Great Britain showing that the United States could not acquire property in the timber cut in trespass, was based on private law rules of accession and trespass.[2] The cases of *The Newchwang*,[3] of *Robert E. Brown*,[4] and of *William*

[1] Award, p. 7.

[2] See *List of Authorities in support of the Claim*, pp. 1-20, and the *Memorial of Great Britain*, p. 3.

[3] In this case Great Britain claimed, on behalf of a private company, damages for a loss resulting from a collision, in 1902, between the steamship *Newchwang* and a United States naval collier. In July of the same year the United States brought an action against the company in the British Supreme Court of China and Corea in Admiralty. The Court, however, dismissed the claim on its merits. It was now argued by Great Britain that the United States, after having voluntarily withdrawn its appeal to the Privy Council, was now, in virtue of *res iudicata*, estopped from denying that the naval collier alone was at fault (see *Memorandum of Authorities* quoted by Great Britain, pp. 11-13). The United States, in reply, pleaded: (*a*) that the findings of a municipal tribunal are not binding upon the arbitration tribunal; (*b*) that 'the principle of *res iudicata* as applied by the municipal courts has no application here' (see *Memorandum to the Oral Argument*, pp. 1-5). It does not seem that the tribunal agreed with this part of the argument of the United States. Although it declined to discuss the value of *res iudicata* before an international tribunal, it proceeded to inquire whether the contention of Great Britain conforms with the requirements of *res iudicata*. It found that it does not, for 'it is a well-established rule of law that the doctrine of *res iudicata* applies only where there is identity of the parties and of the question at issue.' The matter before the two courts was, however, not identical: in 1902 the company owning the *Newchwang* was the defendant party, whereas before the Claims Tribunal the British Government, acting on behalf of the company, appeared as the claimant party. Thus the tribunal rejected the plea of *res iudicata* on its merits. Although the case does not relate to the binding force of a judgment of an international tribunal, the award is nevertheless instructive owing to the application by the tribunal of the rules governing *res iudicata* in municipal law.

[4] In this case the question of succession of an annexing State in obligations arising out of a tortious act of its predecessor was discussed by the parties and dealt with by the tribunal (Claim No. 30; see award, pp. 17-22, and Sir Cecil Hurst in the *B. Y.* (1924), pp. 163-168). The United States claimed here for £330,000, with interest, on account of the alleged denial of property rights acquired in 1895 by Robert E. Brown in the territory of the South African Republic, which was annexed by Great Britain in 1900. The case is of interest because of the concordant opinion of both parties and of the tribunal to the effect that there is no liability in international law for the torts of a defunct State. The United States, who originally relied on succession, subsequently withdrew this part of the argument, and based their claim on certain acts of British authorities after the annexation, and on the relation of suzerainty between the British Government and the South African Republic. This contention the tribunal refused to accept, and dismissed the claim. Although the plea of succession had been withdrawn in the course of the proceedings, it nevertheless occupied a prominent

Hardman,[1] respectively, are of interest with regard to the questions of *res iudicata*, of State succession, and of sources of decision resorted to by international tribunals.

§ 134. *The Cayuga Indians Claim Case. Meaning of Equity. The Corporate Entity. Prescription and Laches.* —The Cayuga Indians Claim case is, of all cases decided by this tribunal, perhaps the most instructive one from the point of view of the subject under discussion.[2] This was a claim of Great Britain, on behalf of the Cayuga Indians in Canada, against the United States, by virtue of the Treaty of Ghent of 1814, and of certain treaties previously concluded between the Cayuga nation and the State of New York. In the latter treaties, the

place in the written argument. It is of interest to note how the current 'will theories' of succession were incorporated in the *Answer of H.B.M. Government*: 'conquest and annexation is merely an act of appropriation by force; the title of the conqueror is founded on might; his title to the property of the former Government upon the fact of physical control and his expressed intention to maintain it' (p. 17). The opposing theory was described as pernicious, because 'it would enable a small and backward State to withstand all pressure from a better-governed neighbour, and to render itself secure from intervention and absorption, by perpetuating anarchy and misrule within its borders' (*ibid.*, p. 18). It does not seem that this argument (see p. 131, *infra*) was absolutely necessary for the purpose. The British *Answer* itself contains numerous references to the practice of States (pp. 6-15), and to rules of Roman and private law—both fully supporting the contention that there is no succession in obligations arising out of tort. In fact, in the Hawaiian Claims case before the same tribunal (Claim No. 84) the arbitrator, while stating that the analogy to private law succession is a contested one, pointed out that it would nevertheless be quite sufficient to defeat a claim based on succession in torts.

[1] This case contains, *inter alia*, instructive references to the question of the law to be applied by international tribunals. The question was discussed in detail by counsel for the United States in an able argument dealing with the scope and meaning of the phrase contained in the arbitration agreement to the effect that the tribunal has to decide 'in accordance with treaty rights and with the principles of international law and equity' (see *Proceedings*, pp. 56, 68. The Argument, delivered by Mr. J. Reuben Clark, jun., is printed in *A.J.*, vii. (1913) pp. 687-707). In the absence of a rule of strict international law, was the opinion of the United States counsel, it is the duty of the tribunal to apply international private law and the principles of maritime law; in the absence of rules from this source, the tribunal should apply 'the fundamental principles of jurisprudence of the various systems of law, particularly the common law . . . and the principles of civil law. Whatever is fundamental to those two main systems of law is properly applicable by this tribunal to guide its decisions.'

[2] The award is printed in *A.J.*, xx. (1926) pp. 574-594.

Cayuga Indians, both those residing in the United States and those who had previously removed to Canada, ceded to the State of New York the territories formerly occupied by the tribe, in consideration of an annuity to be paid to the tribe as a whole. Since 1811, in consequence of measures adopted by the State of New York, no payments reached the Canadian Cayugas, who constituted the majority of the tribe; nor were payments resumed as a result of the Treaty of Ghent, which stipulated for the restoration of the rights of Indians as existing before the war. The United States put forward before the tribunal two exceptions barring the claim of Great Britain: (*a*) that the 'Cayuga nation' not being an international person, the New York State was competent to decide who constituted the 'nation' and what was the legal unit to which payments should be made, and that in strict law the State of New York was entitled to regard the American Cayugas as the Cayuga nation: (*b*) that the claim was barred by prescription and laches on the part of Great Britain.[1]

It seems that the tribunal, quite apart from legal considerations, adopted the view that according to universally recognised principles of justice the Canadian Cayugas, who had been penalised for their participation in the war of 1811 on the side of Great Britain, who constituted the majority of the tribe, and who, since 1816, protested continuously against the wrong done to them, were entitled to their share of the annuity. Accordingly, it was not prepared to let their just claims be defeated by technicalities. Basing itself on the terms of submission, which instructed the arbitrator to decide in accordance with treaty rights and with the principles of international law and equity, the tribunal devoted seven pages of the weighty judgment to an

[1] Cf. here *Answer of the United States*, pp. 9, 102-104, and *Reply of His Britannic Majesty's Government in support of the Claim*, p. 30.

analysis of nearly fifty arbitration conventions, in support of the proposition that in anomalous cases it is the duty of the arbitral tribunal 'to find the grounds of the decision . . . in general considerations of justice, equity, and right dealing, guided by legal analogies and by the spirit and received principles of international law.'[1] Starting from this interpretation of the term 'equity,' the tribunal adopted the analogy of cases in which English and American courts look behind the 'corporate fiction,' and, citing the well-known case of *Daimler Co. Ltd.* v. *Continental Tyre and Rubber Co. Ltd.*,[2] arrived at the conclusion that the Cayuga Indians, as forming a part of the real substance of the corporate entity, are entitled to the proportionate share of the annuity. As to the plea of prescription and laches, the tribunal agreed that the exception is in principle well founded, but it pointed to the rules of civil and common law according to which prescription and statutes of limitation do not run against persons who are unable to act, and that laches cannot be imputed to such persons. It found that these rules of private law embody those principles of justice which it was bound to apply according to the terms of submission, and held that the Cayuga Indians being under guardianship and having no *locus standi* in international law must be regarded as persons under disability. It will be observed how strikingly this judgment illustrates one of the main propositions of this monograph, namely, that rules of equity are identical with legal rules proper, and that, in turn, these legal rules are in practice co-extensive with rules of private law.[3]

[1] *Ibid.*, p. 581.

[2] [1916] 2 A.C. 307.

[3] The student will be indebted to the arbitrators for this clear pronouncement on the judicial character of international arbitration, the more so as the learned exposition of this point was not essential for the decision. As the award points out, the provisions of the Treaty of Ghent provided a sufficient basis for an award in favour of the claimants.

§ 135. *The Central American Court of Justice. The Question of Due Diligence.*—Two decisions rendered by the Central American Court of Justice are of interest for the subject discussed in this monograph.[1] Soon after its inauguration, the Court was called upon to give a decision in a dispute between Honduras on one side, and Guatemala and Salvador on the other. The two States were charged by Honduras with fostering revolution within its borders and with tolerating within their territories unlawful acts calculated to endanger its safety and independence. The award of the Court [2] shows, as has been said, 'the complete analogy between public and private law.' [3] This complete analogy is to be sought primarily in the way in which the Court attempted to determine the international responsibility of Guatemala and Salvador on the basis of the private law conception of fault. For this purpose the 'Three Rules of Washington,' the resolution of the Institute of International Law of 1875, and the XIII. Hague Convention were invoked. The main rule formulated by the tribunal runs as follows: 'The mere fact of a hostile act having been committed on neutral territory is not sufficient to render the State responsible. In order to charge it with a violation of its duties it is necessary to prove either a hostile intention (*dolus*) or patent negligence (*culpa*).' [4] The tribunal found that no such culpable lack of diligence could in this case be attributed to the defendant States.

[1] The Court was established by a Convention between the five Central American States in December 1907 (see *A.J.*, Suppl., ii. (1908) p. 231) for a period of ten years, subject to a subsequent renewal. It is now defunct. In its place a new International Central American tribunal, with a somewhat limited jurisdiction, has been created by the Central American Conference of 1921. See *A.J.*, xvii. (1923) p. 316. On the work of the Court, see Politis, *La Justice Internationale*, 1924, pp. 139-155.

[2] It is printed *in toto* in Martens, *N.R.G.*, 3rd ser., vol. v. pp. 325-359. The final conclusions and the decision are given in *A.J.*, iii. (1909) pp. 729-736. See also *A.J.*, ii. (1908) p. 835.

[3] *A.J.*, iii. (1909) p. 436.

[4] Martens, *loc. cit.*, p. 347.

§ 136. *The same. Co-ownership and Quasi-contracts.*—Even more instructive is the judgment rendered by the Court in the dispute between Salvador and Nicaragua.[1] This action arose out of the so-called Bryan-Chamorro treaty concluded in 1914 between the United States and Nicaragua, and providing for a grant for the term of 99 years (renewable for a further term of the same duration) of a naval base in the Gulf of Fonseca.[2] Costa Rica complained that this treaty violated her rights under previous treaties and arbitral awards.[3] Almost every passage of the bulky award shows that the Court was determined to treat the dispute as one between neighbouring landowners. It held that the Bryan-Chamorro treaty related to 'property located in Central America,' and that the action may therefore be called a real one;[4] that the Gulf of Fonseca was the common and exclusive property of Salvador, Honduras, and Nicaragua in virtue of 'secular or immemorial possession accompanied by *animo domini* both peaceful and continuous and by acquiescence on the part of other nations';[5] that this property constituted a community or co-ownership, and that 'although community is not common in relations among nations, it is not an inconceivable or an isolated fact.'[6] The Court then proceeded to quote in full passages from Heffter on quasi-contracts and on accidental community (*communio rei vel iuris*) in relation to cases where 'a country belongs at once to various States or sovereignties, or in the event of an acquisition of a thing in common over which the dispositions of the civil laws of a single country are not applicable.'

[1] For the award, see *A.J.*, xi. (1917) pp. 674-730.

[2] See Martens, *N.R.G.*, 3rd ser., ix. p. 350.

[3] Cf. P. M. Brown in *A.J.*, xi. (1917) pp. 156-160.

[4] Award, *loc. cit.*, p. 699.

[5] *Ibid.*, p. 705. (The author has been unable to obtain a copy of the judgment in the Spanish language, and this and the following quotations are taken from the translation which appeared in the *American Journal of International Law*. The translation does not appear to be satisfactory.)

[6] *Ibid.*, p. 712.

After referring to historical instances of such ownership and to the civil codes of several countries,[1] the Court held that Nicaragua had no right to make dispositions, independently of other co-tenants, of the gulf in question,

'in view of the status of community in which the Gulf has been and is held, thanks to the universal principle handed down by Roman law and faithfully observed in modern law, that coparceners may not perform any act disposing of a thing possessed in common except jointly or with the consent of all. The absence of that *joint will* is equivalent to the omission of an empowering formality, since the Government of Nicaragua lacks the legal capacity to alter by itself the *status jure* existing in the Gulf, and hence is born the right of the high party complainant to hold that the Bryan-Chamorro treaty violates its rights.' [2]

Similar was the attitude of the Court in the action brought against Nicaragua by Costa Rica,[3] who claimed that her rights of free navigation on the San Juan River had been violated by the above-mentioned treaty between the United States and Nicaragua, and that 'the present case before the Court is one of pure Civil Law.' [4] The Court seems to have agreed with this contention, because it proceeded to examine whether by the Bryan-Chamorro treaty a simple option is conveyed or a sale consummated. It felt no hesitation in coming to the conclusion that there was in that treaty 'a full manifestation of the will to divest with complete renunciation of all the incidents and elements that define and constitute ownership,' [5] and that Costa Rica's contention was, accordingly, well founded.[6]

[1] Award, *loc. cit.*, p. 713.
[2] *Ibid.*, p. 728.
[3] For the award, see *A.J.*, xi. (1917) pp. 181-229.
[4] *Ibid.*, p. 200.
[5] *Ibid.*, p. 217.
[6] However, in both cases the Court held that it is not competent to declare the Bryan-Chamorro treaty null and void.

§ 137. *The Tacna-Arica Arbitration. Treaties under Condition. Specific Performance.*—What may be called a typical private law question constituted the central issue of the recent Tacna-Arica dispute between Chile and Peru.[1] Article 3 of the Treaty of Ancon of 1883, which put an end to the state of war between the two countries, provided that the occupied territory of Tacna-Arica 'shall continue in the possession of Chile subject to Chilean laws and authority during a period of ten years,' and that 'after the expiration of that term a plebiscite will decide by popular vote whether the territory of the above-mentioned provinces is to remain definitely under the dominion and sovereignty of Chile or is to continue to constitute a part of Peru.' The negotiations conducted between the two countries before and after 1893 failed to produce an agreement putting into effect the provisions of the treaty relating to the holding of the plebiscite. After an unsuccessful attempt on the part of Peru to refer the question to the League of Nations under Article 19 of the Covenant, the parties agreed to submit the dispute to an arbitral decision by the President of the United States. The main task of the arbitrator was to decide whether the plebiscite should or should not be held, and, in case of an affirmative answer to this question, to determine the conditions under which the plebiscite should be held.

Peru, who contended for the immediate restoration of Tacna-Arica without a plebiscite, based her claim on a purely private law construction of the treaty and of the legal position arising out of the failure to carry through the plebiscite. 'Between States, international law endeavours to apply that which most nearly approximates civil law';[2] on this formal basis was grounded

[1] For the award, given on March 4, 1925, see *A.J.*, xix. (1925) pp. 393-432. For a short account of the dispute, see Wright, in *R.I.*, 3rd ser., vol. vi. (1925) pp. 295-302.

[2] See the *Opinion* of Sir Thomas Barclay, *Appendix to the Counter Case of Peru*, p. 10, and the *Counter Case of Peru*, p. 211.

the legal argument of Peru. She maintained that, with regard to Chile, the plebiscite and its successful outcome in her favour were a condition precedent to the inception of Chilean sovereignty in Tacna-Arica, whereas they constituted a resolutive condition so far as her own sovereignty was concerned. The failure of Chile to hold the plebiscite, and the fact that, as maintained by Peru, she prevented the performance of the only condition upon which her sovereignty could rest, was adduced in support of the contention that Chilean sovereignty has never begun and Peruvian sovereignty never terminated.[1] Roman law, a large number of modern codes, leading English and American cases, as well as publicists, from Pothier to Laurent, were quoted to the effect that a condition was to be regarded as fulfilled or performed whenever its realisation had been intentionally prevented by the party interested in its non-fulfilment or non-performance.[2] This rule Peru regarded as a universal principle of the municipal law of contracts, which 'may properly be applied in international law to determine the legal relations arising out of the breach or failure of performance of a condition in that treaty.'[3] The possession of Tacna-Arica by Chile, so ran the argument of Peru, was a temporary one and comparable with a ten-year leasehold with an option to purchase.[4] The option in this case was that of permanent acquisition subject to the consent of the population, and the failure on the part of Chile to carry out the plebiscite operated, it was alleged, as a waiver of the right conferred by the option. Since 1894 Chile has been no more than a trespasser upon foreign territory.[5, 6] The case was

[1] *Case of Peru*, pp. 231, 250-252.
[2] *Ibid.*, pp. 232-239.
[3] *Ibid.*, p. 232. The authors of the *Case* expressed here the opinion that 'it is in this way that international law has grown,' and that 'a universal principle cannot be denied application in international law.'
[4] *Counter Case of Peru*, pp. 50-56.
[5] *Ibid.*, p. 66.
[6] This last contention was pressed with great vigour in order to show the inadmissibility of Chile's demand

therefore, in the opinion of Peru, as simple as 'if it were one between private parties presented to a Chancellor in a suit for specific performance of a contract.'[1] Specific performance demanded that the territory, a plebiscite over which would now, owing to the existing conditions, be unjust and unfair, should be handed over to Peru without a plebiscite.

As to the argument propounded by Chile, it is sufficient to say that she regarded the condition imposed by the Treaty of Ancon as a resolutive one, and that she in no way accepted the blame for the frustration of its fulfilment.[2] It was left to the arbitrator to deal with the private law aspect of the case as represented by Peru. He did not reject Peru's argument as one based upon an inadmissible analogy. Neither did he hesitate to declare that should he have found in the action of Chile an intent to frustrate the plebiscite, or bad faith, he would have stated it expressly and held 'the party guilty thereof to the consequences of its action.'[3] But he urged that such an intent or bad faith should not be lightly imputed, and that, although circumstantial evidence is also here admissible, the *onus probandi* 'should not be lighter where the honor of a nation is involved than in a case where the reputation of a private individual is concerned.'[4] Only the existence of clear proof to this effect could justify Peru in claiming to be discharged from performance. The fact of particular negotiations having failed, or of particular protocols not having been ratified, was not regarded by the arbitrator as sufficient to establish bad faith on the part of Chile.[5] He accordingly answered

to be reimbursed for any expenditure made on behalf of the contested territories in case of their being handed back to Peru.

[1] *Counter Case of Peru*, p. 213.

[2] See pp. 100-105 of the *Counter Case of Chile*, where the similar case of Article 34 of the Treaty of Versailles concerning the conditional cession of Eupen and Malmédy to Belgium is discussed. See here also the *Chilean Notes on the Peruvian Case* and *Appendix*, p. 169.—See also, for a plea of estoppel, the *Case of Chile*, p. 62.

[3] Award, *loc. cit.*, p. 399.

[4] *Ibid.*

[5] *Ibid.*, p. 403.

in the affirmative the question whether the plebiscite should be held.[1, 2]

§ 138. *The Permanent Court of International Justice. The Question of Succession and other Private Law Questions.*—Finally, some cases decided by the Permanent Court of International Justice may be mentioned as showing that the problem of the application of private law is likely to occupy also this tribunal. Thus a most instructive instance both of interpretation of certain terms of private law defining private rights, and of a typical problem of analogy to private law, is offered by the case of the *German Settlers in Poland.* Here the Court's opinion was sought on the question of the obligation of the Polish Government to recognise contracts of leases of a certain type (*Rentengutsverträge*) concluded between the German Colonisation Commission and individual German settlers who had now become Polish nationals.[3] The contracts in question were of such a character as to supply a test case for the application of the theory of succession in international law. They did not create a distinct right *in rem*, but they were

[1] Award, *loc. cit.*, p. 415.—The question as to the nature of the condition imposed by the obligation to hold a plebiscite was also of importance for the purpose of determining the character of Chile's authority over the disputed territory and of the administrative acts performed by her in the course of over thirty years. Here, however, the arbitrator adhered to a strict interpretation of Article 3 of the Treaty, which provided, without further qualifications, that the territory has to be 'subject to Chilean laws and authority.'

[2] No expression of opinion is here intended on the merits of the decision of the arbitrator. It would, however, be difficult to deny that there was some force in that part of the Peruvian argument which dealt with the 'specific performance' character of the plebiscite, and that the failure of the arbitrator to recognise this, and his insistence on the literal interpretation of the provision that the plebiscite should be held *after* the expiration of ten years, were liable to render the decision defective both juridically and practically. In a matter like plebiscite, time is of the essence of the agreement, especially when the territory in question is administered by an interested party. It is hardly surprising, therefore, that the award proved impossible of execution. (See *A.J.*, xx. (1926) p. 624.)

[3] See Advisory Opinion, No. 6, Publications of the Permanent Court of International Justice, Series B, pp. 6, 7, 29-37.

nevertheless more than merely personal contracts; the settlers acquired a *ius ad rem*, which, however, did not assume the character of a *ius in rem* before the final transfer of property, the so-called *Auflassung*, had taken place. Now, the *Auflassung* had been prevented by the occurrences of the war and the cession to Poland of that part of Germany where the leases were situated, and a much-disputed point in the theory of State succession was thus brought before the Court.[1] For, in consequence of the fact that the chief purpose of the colonisation scheme had been a political one, the leases were of a mixed—public and private—character, and thus the somewhat theoretical distinction between 'continuation' and 'substitution' presented itself as a question of practical importance.[2] If, as alleged, State succession means substitution as opposed to continuation of the personality of the State, and if substitution is tantamount to a clear breach with the past, a breach which makes the recognition of private rights of public character or origin entirely dependent upon the discretion and policy of the successor State, then there was, with regard to this kind of leases, no obligation on the part of the Polish Government to recognise the *Rentengutsverträge*.[3]

The Court held that the Polish Government, in refusing to recognise the contracts in question, acted in contravention of its international obligations. It based its decision mainly on the Minority Treaties concluded by Poland, but its opinion is at the same time an important contribution to the theory of State succession. Poland's contention that the contracts in question being of a

[1] It will be observed that some authors, while recognising succession in obligations with regard to rights *in rem*, deny them with regard to purely contractual rights (see p. 132, *supra*).

[2] See *Acts and Documents* relating to this case, Series C, No. 3, vol. iii., 3rd Session; especially *German Case*, pp. 1012-1023.

[3] See especially *Oral Argument*, Speech of Sir Ernest Pollock on behalf of the Polish Government, *ibid.*, vol. i. pp. 536-540, 575-578.

purely personal nature need not be recognised by the successor State, was answered by the Court to the effect that although they do not constitute rights *in rem* proper, they nevertheless create rights *ad rem* similar to those enjoyed by the usufructuary, and as such are entitled to recognition.[1] The Court accepted it as a well-established proposition that private rights are to be protected by the new territorial sovereign, and that no treaty provision is required for their preservation. But it is of special importance that it did not restrict the meaning of the term 'private right' to complete title of property, and that it extended it not only to all rights to land, complete and inchoate, but also to other rights. Thus the judgment, after quoting the Annex to Section V. of Part X. of the Versailles Treaty to the effect that, amongst others, leases, contracts of mortgage, concessions concerning mines, quarries, and deposits, and, generally, contracts between individuals or companies and States, provinces, or other similar juridical persons charged with administrative functions, and concessions granted by them, are to be maintained, puts forward the general proposition that if in case of cession between enemies such contracts are maintained, it is impossible to assume that a treaty should have countenanced the annulment of contracts between a State and its newly acquired national.[2] As to the mixed public and private character of the contracts, the Court held that the political motive originally connected with them does not deprive them of their character as contracts under private law.[3] The judgment of the Court marks an important step in the direction of recognition of the principle of succession.[4]

Of other cases, in which questions of private law were

[1] Advisory Opinion, p. 33.

[2] *Ibid.*, p. 39.

[3] *Ibid.*

[4] On the other hand, the thorough manner in which the Court answered the question as to the legal nature of the leases contrasts favourably with the curt refusal of the Hague Court in 1905 to answer a similar question in the Japanese House Tax case (see p. 263, *supra*).

discussed before or by the Court, may be mentioned the case of *The Wimbledon*, in which counsel for Germany and the German national judge construed the provision of the Treaty of Versailles concerning the Kiel Canal as an international servitude.[1] The Court, however, contented itself with stating that that doctrine is of a very controversial character.[2] In the same case the question of damages for loss of profits was argued by the parties. The Court rejected here, as quite unconnected with the action of the defendant State, the claim for repayment of the share of the vessel in the general expenses of the owning company. That the theory of the privileged position of States in the matter of damages dies hard is shown by the fact that the written and oral arguments of Germany were, in this respect, based on the assertion that international law does not recognise damages for loss of profits.[3] The same question occupied the Court in the *Mavrommatis Palestine Concessions* case, where this part of the claim was rejected on the ground that no loss had been proved.[4] Finally, the case of the *Polish Postal Service in Dantzig* may be mentioned, in which the question as to the scope of *res iudicata* was argued before and answered by the Court,[5] as well as those numerous judgments and advisory opinions in which the much-abused rule as to the restrictive interpretation of treaties imposing limitations of sovereignty was reduced by the Court to its true proportions.[6]

[1] See Publications of the Court, Series A, No. 1, pp. 43, 44.

[2] *Ibid.*, p. 24.

[3] See *Contre-mémoire présenté au nom du gouvernement allemand*, Acts and Documents, p. 53; but see *Réplique* of the claimant party, *ibid.*, pp. 104, 151, and Speech of Prof. Basdevant, pp. 242-246.

[4] See the *British Counter Case*, Acts and Documents, No. 7 (ii.), p. 223, where it is pointed out that compensation for lost profits cannot be claimed under the Lausanne Protocol. In addition, the Counter Case declares that Great Britain is prepared to prove that neither the Electricity Concessions nor the Water Concessions would, if put into operation, yield any profit to the *concessionnaire*. No attempt was made to invoke the alleged principle of the inadmissibility, in international law, of awarding compensation for lost profits.

[5] See Publications of the Court, Series B, No. 11, p. 30.

[6] See pp. 179, 180, *supra*.

CHAPTER IX

CONCLUSIONS

THE conclusions reached in the preceding Chapters of this book may now be summarised as follows :—

The question of the authority of Roman and private law in the law of nations occupied a prominent place in the writings of publicists before, during, and after the classical period. It has been answered by them in the affirmative not only, as is commonly assumed, as a result of the patrimonial ideas then prevalent, or of the necessity of filling the gaps in a newly created branch of jurisprudence, but also in consequence of their conception of the law of nations as addressing its commands to moral entities, individual and corporate, and of the conviction that international law is the realisation, as between States, of the law of nature, whose precepts have, to a large extent, been embodied in the general rules of Roman and other private law.

In modern international law the application of private law is, as a rule, rejected by positivist publicists as threatening the independence and the scientific character of international law, and as introducing by a side wind the discarded law of nature. An uncritical iconoclasm in relation to private law is indeed one of the characteristic features of modern international law, in spite of the fact that the rejected analogy reappears in the writings of modern positivists under the form of conceptions of general jurisprudence, of the reason of the thing, and of logical deductions.

The modern British - American international jurisprudence constitutes an exception to the general rule in so far as, having never completely discarded the historical connection of international law and the law of nature, it regards Roman law as a subsidiary source of international law.

The origin of the repudiation of private law may be traced to the two predominant aspects of the doctrine of sovereignty, namely: (*a*) to a rigidly conceived positivism which rejects any wide use of juristic analogy as implying an extensive interpretation of State obligations and as subjecting sovereign States to rules not expressly recognised by them; (*b*) to the widely accepted notion of the absolute value of the State as the exclusive subject of international law, and of the absolute character of the interests protected by it. However, an examination of leading treatises shows that modern positivism as it appears in its current formulation does not supply a basis upon which a coherent system of international law could be built, and that positivist writers themselves are unable to give effect to it in their exposition of international law. In addition, the necessity of grounding international law, especially conventional international law, on objectively binding rules independent of the will of States, is beginning to be realised also by leading positivists. And the practice of States as expressed in arbitration treaties determining the sources of law to be applied by international judges shows that, rules of international law stipulated by custom and treaty being regarded as incomplete and insufficient, other sources of decision are being formulated and incorporated into the common stock of international law. There exists a customary rule of international law to the effect that 'general principles of law,' 'justice,' and 'equity' should, in addition to and apart from custom and treaties, be treated as binding upon international tribunals. These sources, which are shown by the practice of international tribunals to connote legal rules proper and not precepts *ex aequo et bono*, are, for the most part, identical with generally recognised rules of private law.

On the other hand, the repudiation of private law, in so far as it results from the notion that the subjects of and the interests protected by international law are absolutely different from and weightier in the scale of values than those of private law, is no longer warranted. The notion of the fundamental difference of the two spheres of law in respect of their subjects is now being gradually abandoned, as also is its inevitable corollary, namely, the artificial personification of the metaphysical State.

A study of instances of analogy to private law apart from treaties reveals that the constant recourse to private law is more than a lingering echo of the patrimonial conception of State or an expression of an imperfect development of international law. Thus the analogy to private law with regard to the nature, acquisition, and loss of territorial sovereignty is the outcome of both the legal similarity of relations and of the practice of States. In the science of international law, the 'object theory,' which regards the relation of the State to its territory as identical with or as analogous to the private law right of property, is successfully holding the field as against rival theories. It is corroborated by the modern practice of governments showing, through instances of exchange, purchase, pledge, and lease of territory, that, now as in the past, they regard the territory as an object of the State's right. The private law principle of effective possession, apart from having proved in the past centuries a regulative principle of paramount value in relation to acquisition of territory, was the main legal argument in the development of the conception of the freedom of the sea and of the law of territorial waters, and it is likely to play an ever-growing part in the discussions centring round the problem of the sovereignty of the air. Prescription, both acquisitive and extinctive, so frequently rejected on account of its private law origin, is now generally recognised as forming a part of international law. Although the indiscriminate application of the doctrine of servitudes to nearly all restrictions of territorial sovereignty has largely contributed to bringing into disrepute this particular conception, it is still being retained by the great majority of writers, and can hardly be discarded in cases where there is no doubt that a permanent restriction of territorial sovereignty was contemplated. In the theory of State succession the analogy to private law is being vindicated not only by the practice of States and the majority of publicists, but, ultimately, even by those positivist writers who regard the will of the successor State as the exclusive source of the law relating to changes of sovereignty. With regard to the problem of State responsibility, the current rejection of private law, coupled with the refutation of the requirement of culpability as a condition of liability of States for international delinquencies, may now be regarded as an exploded theory. In the matter of allowance of interest on State debts or on sums awarded against States, the practice of States and of international tribunals clearly discards the notion that the special character of States liberates them from paying interest unless expressly stipulated. Similar is the fate of the attempts to introduce into international law a special measure of damages which reduces the liability of States to losses actually sustained, to the exclusion of damages for the loss of prospective profits.

Equally great is the influence of private law on the subject of treaties. Treaties and contracts being in strict law identical notions, both classical and modern writers have no hesitation in treating them as identical, or at least as analogous, conceptions. The disregard of the vitiating influence of duress and the recognition of the *clausula rebus sic stantibus*, although constituting exceptions which seem to break the analogy to contracts in its most essential points, are less expressive of an essential difference between treaties and contracts than of the defective legal development of the international community. Here lies the reason why, independently of the prevalent doctrine, there is a strong current of international opinion, from Grotius and Vattel to recent publicists, to the effect that treaties concluded under duress have legal effect only so far as compulsion has been used in order to enforce a rule of international law. On the other hand, the *clausula rebus sic stantibus*, whose legal and beneficial element has been rendered inapplicable owing to the absence of appropriate juridical organs within the international society, has never become a rule of international law so far as it is expressive of the view that sovereign States stand above their stipulations. But in the same way as the new international order embodied in the Covenant of the League of Nations supplies, as a result of the virtual abolition of conquest, the missing links of analogy with regard to acquisition of territorial sovereignty, so it also works in the direction of rendering the free will of the parties an essential element of an international contract, and of creating remedies calculated to mould the *clausula rebus sic stantibus* into a true institute of law.

Although the current repudiation of private law has led many publicists to deny recognition even to those international enactments in which the contracting parties avail themselves *expressis verbis* of a conception of private law, an analysis of two typical instances, *i.e.* international leases and mandates, has shown that such a course is neither sound in law nor in accordance with facts. As the science of international law is not called upon to give a political interpretation of international conventions, but to elucidate the juridical meaning of the declared common intention of the parties, the accepted juridical meaning of the term used in a treaty cannot be ignored. Whenever in a treaty a generally accepted term of private law is being used, the interpretation and construction of the treaty must, unless the contrary is stipulated in the treaty itself, follow the principles generally recognised as implied in this particular term. The acceptance of the view that a conception of private law when used in a treaty loses its usual meaning, would deprive international law of an important source of development and of a working rule of interpretation.

That those principles of private law which are generally accepted, and which embody a rule of justice and common sense, are recognised as principles applicable in international law, even when of a technical and formal character, is illustrated by the fact that the notions of admission and estoppel play an important part in international arbitration. The same applies to the principle of *res iudicata* and to many private law rules of evidence and procedure. Further, private law is being freely invoked with regard to the right of an arbitral court to determine its jurisdiction and to the question of the finality of an arbitral award.

Finally, it has been shown in the three Chapters dealing with international arbitration how frequent is the recourse to private law in the settlement of international disputes. International tribunals, in appropriate cases, either state expressly that a particular rule of private law is applicable to the case in question, or give a decision which, although identical with the corresponding provisions of private law, is described as a general principle of law or as a rule of universal jurisprudence. Even more frequent is the use made of private law by States appearing as parties before international tribunals.

The object of this monograph, if to the above summary of conclusions a few observations may be added, is to draw attention to the following facts :—

Firstly, that in the great majority of cases the measure of approach to standards or to analogy of private law is co-extensive with the strengthening of the element of law, as against the absence of law, within the body of rules governing the conduct of States. Secondly, that the approximation to corresponding general principles of private law is, as a rule, tantamount to the realisation of a principle of justice and equity hitherto obscured by the part which force plays in international relations. Thirdly, that such a reception of private law by the practice of States and by international tribunals has taken place to an extent much larger than the current positivist attitude made it appear, and that, this being so, the uncritical rejection of private law created an artificial and unnecessary obstacle in grasping the legal relations of international life, past and present. Finally, that the work of international tribunals would be greatly facilitated by an impartial study of this problem, especially in view of their having to apply 'generally recognised principles of law' supplementing international law proper.

The importance of these general conclusions need not be overestimated. In particular, they do not purport to convey the suggestion that all parts of international law should be framed after the private law pattern. But when the relation is one *prima facie* analogous to that obtaining between individuals, when States enter into relations which must remain ineffective but for the application of a generally recognised principle of private law, when they expressly avail themselves of conceptions of private law, or when, in cases where the similarity of relations is patent, we are seeking a test of the reasonableness of existing rules or a standard according to which new rules could be framed, then the work of construction and interpretation should not be hampered by the force of habit inculcated by a dogmatic positivism.

No doubt, the facts of international life may have modified or rendered impossible the application of many a principle of private law. And although it is a mistake to attribute to such modifications the character of a legal rule in all those cases in which they are due to the absence of law within the international community, they must not be disregarded when they owe their origin to the altogether special character of international relations. Caution, however, must not be pushed too far.

In especial, a vigilant attitude of criticism must be maintained with regard to the argument that the structure—psychological, economic, and sociological—of the international legal community is so different from that on which private law is based within the State, that every analogy must needs be superficial. There is certainly much force in this contention. But the sociological conception of international law, instead of being a source of adjustment and development, threatens to become a disorganising and disruptive element, if we forget that it was just this conception of the 'special character' of the international society which most obstructed the path of its progress towards an international community under the reign of law. Law must be based on facts—sociological, historical, and others—and it must take facts into account. But it can never be a mere reflection of them.

As there is in law a perpetual conflict between the element of stability and the element of change, between the traditional form of law and the substance of social life, so there is also in every legal community, and especially in the international community, a constant conflict between the idea of right and justice and the immediate powerful interests shaping the law. There were, and are, many factors which combined in order to create, to maintain, and to develop in international law those elements of stability, of the generally accepted conception of law, and of the ideals of right and justice as against the crude reality of an unorganised community where every change, however lawless and discretionary, tends to become a legal rule, where every aspect of international life, however wanton and repugnant, claims to set a legal standard, and where every predominant interest asserts itself as law. This monograph shows that private law was and is one of these factors. Its aim was to examine the practice of States and of international tribunals in order to show that it is precisely that empirical and sociological treatment of the foundations of the international society and of its needs which leads to the adoption of analogy to private law in the most essential parts of the law of nations. The book was certainly not written *pro maiore iuris privati gloria* or as a plea for private law in the legal *curriculum* of international lawyers. Its object is to point out that there is no need or justification for divorcing international law, a still undeveloped law of co-ordinated entities, from a system of law, equally governing relations of co-ordinated entities, in which the ideals of legal justice and of the sovereignty of law are admittedly realised in a very high degree. An ever-growing body of international legal opinion —from Westlake and Lorimer to Krabbe, Kelsen, and

Duguit—has been engaged during the past half-century in impressing upon the mind of the student and the statesman what the author believes to be a true and beneficent notion, namely, that behind the personified institutions called States there are in every case individual human beings to whom the precepts of international law are addressed. Thus interpreted, the exalted conception of the father of international law and of other publicists of the classical period which regarded nations as moral individuals *respectu totius generis humani*, is still an ideal worthy of pursuance.

BIBLIOGRAPHY

THE following is a bibliography of treatises, monographs and articles dealing with the general problem of application of private law in international public law, or, in some cases, with the question of analogy of States and private persons. The works of authors whose discussion of the problem appears to be of special importance are printed in larger type.

As to the application of conceptions of private law to particular questions of international law—for instance, to State servitudes, State responsibility, State succession, etc.—the reader is referred to the authors quoted in the footnotes to the respective sections, and, with regard to international arbitration, to the *Table of Cases*.

For other literature referred to in this monograph, see *Index of Authors Cited* (pp. 313-15, *infra*).

Anzilotti, *La teoria generale della responsibilità dello Stato nel diritto internazionale*, 1902, pp. 143-152, 154, 179, 180.

Sugli effetti dell' inadempienza di obbligazioni internazionali aventi per oggetto una somma di danaro, in *Rivista*, vii. (1913) pp. 60-68.

[A lucid and much-quoted statement of the positivist point of view.]

Corso di diritto internazionale, 1923, pp. 62-64.

[A general discussion of the problem of analogy. An important modification of the somewhat rigid attitude maintained in the previous writings.]

Bergbohm, *Staatsverträge und Gesetze als Quellen des Völkerrechts*, 1877, pp. 79-81.

Bulmerincq, *Praxis, Theorie und Codification des Völkerrechts*, 1874, p. 130.

Die Systematik des Völkerrechts, 1858, *passim*, and especially p. 65.

[The first-mentioned monograph contains an impressive exposition of the dangers of the recourse to analogy of

Bulmerincq (*continued*), private law. In the second, written in a similar vein, we find (at p. 65) the following significant passage adequately characterising the intricacies of the problem: 'It is in the similarity to private law that the element of law contained in international law comes to light, whereas it is in its deviations from private law that the special character of international law expresses itself.']

Bütemeister, *De usu juris Romani aliorumque privatorum jurium in decidendis controversiis liberarum gentium*, 1692.
[Referred to by Triepel, quoted below. I was unable to consult this book.]

Bynkershoek, *De Dominio Maris*, 1702, ch. ix.
De Foro Legatorum, 1721, chs. ii., vi.
[See this monograph, pp. 15, 16, *supra.*]

Cavaglieri, *La dottrina della Successione di Stato a Stato e il suo valore giuridico*, 1910, pp. 18 *et seq.*
Corso di diritto internazionale (parte generale), 1925, pp. 100, 101.
[A valuable discussion of the question of analogies.]

Creasy, *First Platform on International Law*, 1876, pp. 83-85.

Donati, *Stato e territorio*, 1924, pp. 2-15.

Fricker, *Vom Staatsgebiet*, 1867, p. 6.

Gentilis, *De Jure Belli*, 1598, bk. i. chs. iii., v., xx.; bk. ii. ch. xviii.
Hispanicae advocationis libri duo, 1613, bk. i. ch. xxi.
[See this monograph, pp. 10-12, *supra.*]

Gerber, *Öffentliche Rechte*, 1852, p. 40.

Gierke, *Deutsches Genossenschaftsrecht*, 1868, vol. i. p. 843.

Grotius, *De Jure Belli ac Pacis*, 1625.
[See this monograph, pp. 12-15, *supra.*]

Halleck, *International Law*, 4th ed. by Baker, 1908, p. 61.

Hatschek, *Völkerrecht, etc.*, 1923, p. 28.

Hedemann, in *Blätter für Rechtspflege in Thüringen und Anhalt*, 1915, pp. 97 *et seq.*
[Referred to by Liszt, p. 79. I was unable to consult it.]

Heffter, *Das europäische Völkerrecht der Gegenwart*, 8th ed. by Geffcken, 1888.
[Heffter's treatise—perhaps the most influential textbook of international law in the last hundred years—is in itself, both in respect of its classification and its contents, a classical instance of a thorough application of analogy to private law. See also the significant statement at p. 219, n. 1.]

Heilborn, *System des Völkerrechts*, 1896, p. 413.

Grundbegriffe des Völkerrechts (in Stier-Somlo's *Handbuch des Völkerrechts*), 1912, pp. 103-107.

Heimburger, *Der Erwerb der Gebietshoheit*, 1888, pp. 41-43.

Heineccius, *Elementa Juris Naturae et Gentium*, 1737. Preface.

Hofer, *Der Schadenersatz im Landkriegsrecht*, 1913, pp. 16-23.

[A separate chapter entitled 'The Influence of Private Law on International Law.']

Holland, *Studies in International Law and Diplomacy*, 1898, p. 152.

Jurisprudence, 12th ed., 1916, pp. 393, 394.

Holtzendorff, *Handbuch des Völkerrechts*, 1885, vol. i. p. 72.

Huber, *Ein Beitrag zur Lehre von der Gebietshoheit an Grenzflüssen*, in *Z.V.*, i. (1907) pp. 160, 161.

Jellinek, **Die rechtliche Natur der Staatenverträge**, 1880, pp. 50, 51.

Die staats- und völkerrechtliche Stellung Kiautschous, in *Deutsche Juristenzeitung*, iii. (1898) p. 253. (Reprinted in Jellinek's *Ausgewählte Schriften und Reden*, 1911, vol. ii. pp. 501, 502.)

[Although the two above-mentioned essays deal with the application of private law to special questions, *i.e.* to treaties and leases respectively, they contain illuminating remarks on the general problem of private law analogies.]

Kosters, *Les Fondements du droit des gens*, *Bibliotheca Visseriana*, iv. (1925) pp. 111-114.

[An exposition of the influence of Roman law on international law in the post-Grotian period.]

Lammasch, *Die Lehre von der Schiedsgerichtsbarkeit in ihrem ganzen Umfange* (in Stier-Somlo's *Handbuch des Völkerrechts*), 1914, pp. 175-181.

[Although not relating directly to the question of application of private law, this section is of importance on account of the lucid statement of the problem of gaps and analogy in international arbitration.]

Liszt, *Völkerrecht*, 12th ed., 1925, p. 79, and especially note 2 at the same page, added by Fleischmann.

Lorimer, **Studies, National and International**, 1890, pp. 158, 159.

[Here, as in many other cases, Lorimer discusses the problem with his characteristic independence of judgment.]

M'Nair, *So-called State Servitudes*, in *The British Year Book of International Law*, 1925, pp. 121, 122.

Maine, *International Law*, 1894, 2nd ed., pp. 20, 21, 26-29.

Ancient Law, 10th ed., 1910, pp. 100-106.

Manning, *Commentaries on the Law of Nations*, 1839, p. vi.

Meier, *Über den Abschluss von Staatsverträgen*, 1874, pp. 36-39.

Moser, *Teutsches Staatsrecht*, 1738, pt. ii., bk. i., p. 214.

Neumeyer, **Ein Beitrag zum internationalen Wasserrecht**, in *Festschrift für Georg Cohn*, 1915, pp. 17-21.

[A stimulating and useful contribution to the problem.]

Neyron, *Essai historique et politique sur les Garanties*, 1777, pp. 70, 76.

[See this monograph, p. 17, *supra*.]

Nippold, **Der völkerrechtliche Vertrag**, etc., 1894, pp. 80-91.

[A separate section entitled 'The Relation of International Law to Private Law.' The treatment of the question is a typical one. It starts with the usual warnings against the use of private law, and ends with the adoption of 'conceptions of universal jurisprudence' as the necessary complement of international law.]

Oppenheim, H. B., **System des Völkerrechts**, 2nd ed., 1866, pp. 8, 80.

[A clear and much-quoted statement of the two main arguments usually resorted to in this connection, namely, the difference of subjects, and the 'eternal and inalienable' character of the rights protected by the State.]

Phillimore, **Commentaries upon International Law**, 3rd ed., 1879, vol. i. pp. 34-36.

[A detailed discussion of the function of Roman law as a source of international law.]

Phillipson, *Albericus Gentilis*, in *Journal of Comparative Legislation and International Law*, New Series, vol. xii. (1912) p. 58.

Richard Zouch, *ibid.*, vol. ix. (1908) pp. 285, 286.

Pollock, *A First Book of Jurisprudence*, 3rd ed., 1911, p. 81.

Pound, **Philosophical Theory and International Law,** in *Bibliotheca Visseriana*, vol. i. (1923) pp. 79 *et seq.*

[See this monograph, p. 73, n. 1, *supra.*]

Ralston, **The Law and Procedure of International Tribunals,** revised edition, 1926, Preface, pp. xxxi-xxxiv, especially p. xxxiv.

Rivier, **Principes du droit des gens,** 1896, vol. i. pp. 34; vol. ii. pp. 123, 175.

Ruegger, **Privatrechtliche Begriffe im Völkerrecht,** in *N.Z.*, xxviii. (1919-1920) pp. 426-502.

[The title is more comprehensive than the actual contents of this otherwise scholarly and exhaustive article seem to warrant. It deals almost exclusively with the interpretation of such conceptions of private law used in treaties as define private rights or merely economic interests; it is not concerned with the application of private law to international public law proper.]

Die völkerrechtliche Verantwortung des Staates für die auf seinem Gebiete begangenen Verbrechen, 1925, p. 7.

Schön, **Die völkerrechtliche Haftung der Staaten aus unerlaubten Handlungen,** 1917, pp. 58, 126-128.

Schönborn, *Staatensukzessionen* (in Stier-Somlo's *Handbuch des Völkerrechts*), 1913, p. 4, n. 4, and p. 9.

Selden, *Mare clausum sive de Dominio Maris*, 1635, bk. i., ch. xxiv. (pp. 152-156 of Nedham's translation in 1652).

[As might be expected from the purpose of Selden's argument, he challenges the authority of Roman law in matters of international law.]

Spiropulos, *Haftung der Staaten für indirekten Schaden*, in *N.Z.*, xxxv. (1925-1926) pp. 178-179.

Strupp, *Das völkerrechtliche Delikt* (in Stier-Somlo's *Handbuch des Völkerrechts*), 1920, p. 57 and n. 1, *ibid.*

Taylor, *A Treatise on International Public Law*, 1901, pp. 20-21.

Triepel, **Völkerrecht und Landesrecht,** 1899, pp. 211-226 (translated in 1920 into French, in Bibliothèque internationale de Droit des Gens).

[A separate chapter entitled 'The Reception of Municipal Law into International Law.' The argument there propounded serves to illustrate and to support the author's

Triepel (*continued*), dualistic conception of the relation between international and municipal law. Nevertheless, the chapter is by far the most searching and influential discussion of the problem of private law analogies.]

in *Recueil des Cours, Académie de Droit International*, 1923, pp. 99-103.

[A recapitulation of the view set forth in *Völkerrecht und Landesrecht.*]

Vinogradoff, *Historical Types of International Law*, in *Bibliotheca Visseriana*, vol. i. (1923) pp. 54-57.

Westlake, *International Law*, 2nd ed., 1910, vol. i. pp. 15-16.

[Roman law, in addition to custom and reason, recognised as a source of international law.]

Wildman, *Institutes of International Law*, 1849, pp. 22-24.

Williams, *Sovereignty, Seisin and the League*, in *The British Year Book of International Law*, 1926, pp. 31-41.

[The author of the article deals mainly with the question of conquest, and the resulting lack of analogy to private law. But his general remarks on the problem of analogies merit attention.]

Wiseman, *The Excellency of the Civil Law*, 1656.

[See p. 25 of this monograph.]

Yntema, *The Treaties with Germany and Compensation for War Damages*, in *Columbia Law Review*, xxiv. (1924) pp. 140-141.

INDEX OF AUTHORS CITED

TABLE OF CASES

(Cases decided by municipal courts are enclosed in brackets)

INDEX

Printed in Great Britain by T. and A. Constable Ltd
at the University Press, Edinburgh

www.ingramcontent.com/pod-product-compliance
Lightning Source LLC
Jackson TN
JSHW081945150125
77143JS00002B/43
9781584771845